HUGO'S SIMPLIFIED SYSTEM.

SPANISH
SIMPLIFIED.

COMPLETE—CONSISTING OF

I.—A SIMPLE BUT COMPLETE GRAMMAR.

Containing all the Rules necessary for Speaking and Writing
Spanish correctly.

(The Pronunciation of Every Word Exactly Imitated.)

II.—SPANISH READING MADE EASY.

Consisting of Anecdotes and Short Stories, with about *Sixty foot-
notes on each Page*, so that Reading becomes a pleasant Recreation,
even to beginners.

III.—SPANISH CONVERSATION.

Practical and Colloquial Sentences, introducing all the important Idioms.

IV.—A KEY to the EXERCISES in the GRAMMAR.

Published by HUGO'S
Institute for Teaching Foreign Languages,
33 Gracechurch Street, London, E.C. ; and Branches.

PREFACE.

Hugo's 3/6 'Simplified' language manuals are intended to meet the frequently expressed demand for the System strongly bound in one volume, for school use. Of the original editions, published in separate parts for convenience of carrying, millions have been sold.

The ever-increasing demand, and the flattering Testimonials constantly being received from teachers, travellers, tourists, couriers, and others who can testify to the practical value of a system, prove that Hugo's is by far the easiest and quickest way of learning Foreign Languages, and is beyond doubt the system of the future. Those interested are invited to call and inspect these Testimonials, none of which have been asked for, and which come from all classes of society, in all parts of the world.

—————:o:—————

The following are the chief distinctive features
of Hugo's System :—

I.—Hugo's books quickly teach the Student to speak and write correctly in simple language, which is sufficient for all practical purposes.

Most systems, being written to enable students to pass technical examinations, are intelligible to none but the expert grammarian, and aim at teaching the foreigner more of the Grammar than the average educated native knows. This being an impossible task, the result is usually a complete failure.

II.—Hugo's Grammars contain everything necessary for correct writing and speaking, in one-fourth of the usual compass.

This is secured by omitting rules which are the same in English, and unimportant exceptions which rarely occur in practice. Long tables of Conjugations and Declensions, the mere sight of which disheartens the learner, are avoided. The Conjugations and Declensions, etc., are acquired, not by this tedious method, but by a few simple rules which show clearly how one tense can be formed from another.

III.—Hugo's Rules are always concise and clear, so that they are a help, not an impediment, even to the student unacquainted with grammatical terms.

In the larger Grammars, matter of no practical importance frequently occupies more space than important rules, the student being left to pick out the essential points for himself, and acquire the language as he best can.

IV.—Hugo's books, in contrast to these unwieldy Grammars, tell the student what to learn, and how to learn it ; and are complete, notwithstanding their small size The contents do not correspond with the early lessons only in the larger text-books sold at a far higher price. Hugo's books contain the GIST OF THE WHOLE, the careful way in which the matter is condensed and simplified being their chief beauty. In the bulky works referred to, useless padding, which seriously hinders the student, is inserted, simply because 5s. or 6s. could not be asked for a small grammar, however complete. HUGO'S GRAMMARS are concise and simple, but they contain every rule that is worth learning.

V.—Hugo's Reading Lessons are one of the most important time-saving features of the System. Every word is translated in a foot-note until it has occurred several times, so that an extensive Vocabulary is easily and insensibly acquired, and Reading becomes a pleasant recreation instead of a laborious task. To learn to read by any other method, the student must spend HUNDREDS OF HOURS in consulting Dictionaries. It is therefore no exaggeration to say that **French, German, Spanish, Italian**, etc., can be thoroughly mastered by HUGO'S SYSTEM in about HALF THE TIME OTHERWISE WASTED IN REFERRING TO DICTIONARIES.

VI.—The Imitated Pronunciation, which so greatly assists those learning without a master, is a feature which no other grammar contains.

VII.—The Exercises in Hugo's Grammars are eminently practical, and contain nothing but natural sentences which occur in ordinary every-day conversation.

Such phrases as "The fat ugly friar was afraid in the large formidable castle," "Hast thou the magic mirrors ?" "Fear the avenging thunderbolt," "The nose of the friend is long," etc.,* find no place therein.

---

*These are genuine extracts from modern Grammars.

CONTENTS.

INSTRUCTIONS TO STUDENTS.

After acquiring a general idea of the Pronunciation, learn five or six lessons in the Grammar. This can best be done by reading carefully several times through each rule, pronouncing the new words aloud, and writing out the translation to the Exercise on that rule. Then compare your work carefully with the Key, marking all errors, and afterwards reading again through the Examples to the rule forgotten. If necessary, translate the Exercise a second or third time, and on no account attempt the Collective Exercise until you can do the short Exercises correctly.

(Students who experience any difficulty in translating the Collective Exercises may first translate them from the Key into English.)

After having mastered five or six lessons in this way, a page or two of the Reading matter may be advantageously translated with each lesson. This will relieve the monotony of learning so many rules, and greatly enlarge the number of words at the student's command, if each page is gone through two or three times. No attempt need be made to learn the words in the reading pages by heart; they will be acquired gradually and without effort.

Advanced Students will derive great benefit from writing out the Literal translation of these pages in English, afterwards re-translating without reference to the original.

The conversation pages will well repay the trouble of careful study; but 12 or 14 lessons should be learned before this section is attempted.

SPANISH

SIMPLIFIED.

AN EASY & RAPID SELF-INSTRUCTOR.

GRAMMAR,

EXERCISES AND VOCABULARIES,

WITH THE

PRONUNCIATION EXACTLY IMITATED.

"STANDARD" EDITION,

ENLARGED AND REVISED.

All rights reserved.

PUBLISHED BY

Hugo's Institute for Teaching Foreign Languages,

33 GRACECHURCH STREET, LONDON, E.C. ; and Branches.

PREFACE.

All Hugo's Grammars are contained in about a fourth of the usual compass, because rules which are the same in English are omitted ; but everything necessary for practical purposes is fully given, and clearly explained. It is not assumed that the student is an expert in English grammar, a mistake which most grammarians make, with the result that their rules are quite incomprehensible to the average man.

Our rules are given in the order best tending to rapid progress, and in such a way that the student can at once make practical use of what he has learnt. This departure from custom will be found of special advantage with the Verbs, which are given in the way that shows how each Tense can be most naturally formed from another previously learnt.

After the Regular Verbs have been fully treated, the Irregular ones follow, in order of importance.

As no one should attempt a systematic study of the Irregular Verbs until he has thoroughly mastered the Regular ones, we have saved space, and simplified the student's work, by only giving the Tenses that need be learnt. All other Tenses are regular, or formed according to our rules on the Irregular Verbs. But for reference purposes, not for study, **every Tense of every Irregular Verb is given in our Spanish Verbs Simplified, a work which purchasers of our Grammar and Key can obtain from us at the reduced price of 1/-,—see notice at the beginning of the Key.**

The Familiar Form, which is quite useless to foreigners, is dealt with in a manner which still further simplifies the Verb. In the conjugation of each Tense, this form merely appears as a note, so that the student has only three or four endings to learn instead of six.

The Subjunctive Mood, a grammatical nicety which few natives understand properly, was dealt with in the original edition for reference purposes only. We have now added a simple explanation of all the important rules on the use of this Mood, together with practical exercises.

The Pronunciation is given in the first twelve lessons ; but as every Spanish word is pronounced according to the few simple rules on pages 5 to 9, the student cannot fail to pronounce any new word correctly, long before he has reached Lesson 12.

Special attention is called to the remarks on varying pronunciations on page 9. The Spanish Academy says that B, D, and V should be pronounced in Spanish as in French and English, and there is no reason whatever for foreigners to depart from this rule, although they will often hear educated natives do so.

The Augmentative and Diminutive terminations were needlessly introduced in his grammar by a pedant more than a century ago ; and his idea was copied by all succeeding grammarians, until we had the courage to ignore precedent, and relegate this utterly trivial matter to the Appendix. These terminations have in the past made many a student discontinue the study of Spanish in despair. Yet a knowledge of them is absolutely useless, because no foreigner can possibly know to which words they may be added. A dictionary will always tell him this ; it is the grammarian's province to teach what CANNOT be found in dictionaries.

Hugo's Spanish Grammar, originally published in 1888, was the first attempt ever made to simplify that language. All previous grammars dealt with the ten parts of speech in the old-fashioned stereotyped order, without any attempt at simplification, condensation, or—what is most important of all—separation of trivial detail from matters of fundamental importance. An enormous number of the original edition have been sold, and the numerous highly flattering testimonials received from all parts of the world testify to its clearness, conciseness, and simplicity.

The principle on which the work is written was copied almost immediately in various quarters, often without acknowledgment. In one case, a well-known firm of London publishers brought out a Spanish Grammar which calmly appropriated, not only the wording and order of our original rules, but even our exercises and vocabulary, with hardly a word altered.*

As our original edition applied for the first time the principles of Hugo's ' French Simplified ' to Spanish, it speedily became the standard text-book on the subject ; but it bore many traces of the haste with which it was written, to meet the sudden demand occasioned by the Argentine Republic boom of some twenty years ago. Since then, we have used the book for teaching thousands of students, and consequently learnt its weak points. Guided by this extended experience, we have re-written the work with the utmost care, correcting errors, improving the rules, and adding many additional explanations ; while every word of the Spanish has been revised and re-revised by competent educated natives.

The work therefore now takes a permanent stereotyped form ; and we shall watch that this present improved and revised edition is not copied.

*Teachers and students are hereby warned that any other book purporting to be Hugo's Spanish System is nothing of the sort, but merely an imitation of the first edition, with just enough alterations to spoil the arrangement, and make the exercises laughable.**

---

*We may mention a very amusing instance of this. Not to copy our exercises exactly, the plagiarist altered one of our sentences, ' Is your brother smoking ? ' to ' Is your sister smoking ? ' thus avoiding the charge of copying word for word, but making himself ridiculous in the process.

CONTENTS.

SPECIAL NOTE. — These five preliminary pages need not be learnt at first. They merely contain the Rules of Pronunciation ; and as the pronunciation of each new word is given as it occurs in the Rules or Exercises, THE STUDENT SHOULD AT ONCE COMMENCE AT THE FIRST LESSON (page 10). Pages 5 to 9 can best be mastered gradually, by occasional perusal.

In studying the Lessons, first read each Rule carefully, comparing with the Examples underneath. Then translate and re-translate (preferably in writing) the Exercise which follows, until you can translate every sentence correctly and readily.

THE SPANISH ALPHABET (for reference only);

with the names of the 29 letters.

(K and W only occur in words taken from other languages)

A	B	C	CH	D	E	F	G	H	I
ah*	bay	thay*	chay	day	ay	eff-ay*	_H_ay*	ah-chay	ee

J	K	L	LL	M	N	Ñ	O	P	Q
_H_o-tah*	kah	ell-ay	ell-yay	emm-ay	enn-ay	enn-yay	o*	pay	koo

R	S	T	U	V	W	X	Y	Z
airr-ay	es-ay*	tay	oo	vay	do-blay-vay	ay-kis*	ee gre'ay-gah	thay-tah

Pron.:

---

*If our Imitated Pronunciation is pronounced as if each syllable were part of an English word, it will always be understood ; but the exact sound will be still more nearly obtained if the following instructions are borne in mind :

th must be pronounced like TH in 'thin,' never like TH in 'they.'

_H_ is to be pronounced gutturally.

s is always to be pronounced like the **ss** in 'missing,' never like the s in 'easy.'

a The Spanish a is pronounced like 'ah,' but shorter than in 'harm,' 'part,' 'cast.' We imitate it by 'ah,' because the sound is never like a in 'hat'; but the 'ah' must be pronounced short and sharp.

o The Spanish o resembles the sound of o in 'not,' and even slightly approaches the aw in 'law.' It is not so long as in the o in go.'

PRONUNCIATION OF THE VOWELS.

The VOWELS in Spanish are a, e, i, o, u, y. The remaining letters are CONSONANTS.

			EXAMPLES.	PRONOUNCED :
A	is pronounced like	ah	AL, LA, AMAN	ahl, lah, ah-mahn*
E	„	ay	ME, DE, LE	may, day, lay
I or Y	„	ee	MI, PRIMA, Y	mee, pree-mah, ee
O	„	o	LO, NO, SIDO	lo, no, see-do
U	„	oo	TU, SU, UNO	too, soo, oo-no

*The syllable that takes the stress is printed throughout in **thick type.**

REMARKS.—Each vowel has only one sound in Spanish, which sound is not quite so long and broad as the English equivalent given above. The pronunciation of the vowels is also shortened, as in other languages, when they occur in an unstressed word or syllable, or precede a consonant.

EMPHASIS OR STRESS IN PRONUNCIATION.

Words ending in a Consonant stress the last syllable ; words ending in a Vowel stress the last syllable but one, thus :

papel	bastón	tomar	edad	pluma	rico	golpe
paper	stick	to take	age	pen	rich	blow
pah-**pel**	bah-**ston**	to-**mar**	ay-**dahd**†	**ploo**-mah	**rree**-ko	**goll**-pay

But the Consonants (always n or s) which are merely added to form the Plural do not then affect the stress, which is always the same in the Plural as in the Singular, thus :

la	otra	pluma,	las	otras	plumas
the	other	pen	the	other	pens
lah†	**o**-trah	**ploo**-mah	lahs†	**o**-trahs	**ploo**-mahs

mi	primo	lee	una	hermosa	novela
my	cousin	reads	a	nice	novel
me	**pree**-mo	**lay**-ay	**oo**-nah	air-**mo**-sah	no-**vay**-lah

mis	primos	leen	unas	hermosas	novelas
my	cousins	read	some	nice	novels
mis	**pree**-mos	**lay**-en	**oo**-nahs	air-**mo**-sahs	no-**vay**-lahs

† ' ah ' always to be pronounced short,—see previous page.

PRONUNCIATION OF THE CONSONANTS.

Z is pronounced like **th** in MONTH or THICK, thus :

voz	luz	paz	zapato	capaz	vez
voice	light	peace	shoe	capacious	time
voth	looth	pahth	thah-**pah**-to	kah-**pahth**	veth (*or* vayth)

J is pronounced like the German guttural **ch** (as in AUCH), or as in the Scotch word LOCH, thus :

ojo	jugar	juzgar	jefe	bajo	caja
eye	to play	to judge	chief	under	box
o-*H*o	*H*oo-**gar**	*H*ooth-**gar**	*H*ay-fay	bah-*H*o	kah-*H*ah

This sound is merely the English **h**, pronounced in the throat ; and students who experience any difficulty with the Spanish guttural are advised to pronounce it like an aspirated **h**.

Z and **J** are the only two consonants pronounced quite unlike the English way ; but the following points should be noted.

C before **e** or **i** is pronounced like the Spanish **z** ; and

G   ”   ”   ”   ”   **j**, thus :

cena	cinco	once	general	gigante	coger
supper	five	eleven	general	giant	to seize
thay-nah	thin-ko	on-thay	*H*ay-nay-rahl	*H*e-**gahn**-tay	ko-*H*air

G   before any other letter is like **g** in GO ;

GU before **e** or **i** is pronounced like the **g** in GO ; before any other vowel like **gw** or **goo** ;

H   is not pronounced at all, thus :

gato	guerra	guía	hablar	ha	hijo	herir	humo
cat	war	guide	to speak	has	son	to wound	smoke
gah-to	gairr-rah	ghee-ah	ah-**blar**	ah	ee-*H*o	ay-reer	oo-mo

(**gh** as in GHOST)

LL is pronounced nearly like **ll** in MILLION ;

Ñ   ”   ”   ”   **ni** in COMPANION, thus :

calle	silla	llamar	niño	señor	cuña
street	chair	to call	child	sir	wedge
kah-l'yay	see-l'yah	l'yah-mar	nee-n'yo	say-n'yor	koo-n'yah

QU is pronounced like **k** ;

CH   ,,   as in the English CHEAP or MUCH ;

R   is rolled (on the tip of the tongue) more than in English, especially at the beginning of a word or syllable ;

S   is always pronounced sharp, as in SEE or LAST ; never like Z, as in EASY, MISER, thus :

que	quince	muchacha	raro	casa	mesa
that	fifteen	girl	rare	house	table
kay	kin-thay	moo-chah-chah	rrah-ro	kah-sah	may-sah

DIVISION OF WORDS INTO SYLLABLES.

As already shown, words ending in a consonant stress the last syllable, while words ending in a vowel stress the last syllable but one. The following rules are therefore important.

RULE.

When two vowels come together, they are pronounced separately, and form DISTINCT SYLLABLES ; as,

deseo, desire ;   teatro, theatre (PRON. day-say-o, tay-ah-tro).

EXCEPTION.

If, however, one of the vowels is **i** or **u**, the other vowel takes the stress, and the **i** or **u** is lightly pronounced in the SAME SYLLABLE (i.e., with the same emission of the voice) ; as,

cuando, when ; jaula, cage ; aire, air ; viaje, voyage.
(PRON. koo'ahn-do, Hah'oo-lah, ah'e-ray, ve'ah-Hay)

When **i** and **u** occur together, the stress is on the vowel which comes last ; as, viuda, widow ; cuita, grief (ve'oo-dah, koo'ee-tah)

When the stress is not in accordance with rule, an acute accent is always placed in Spanish* over the emphasized vowel ; as,

allí, there ; hábil, clever (PRON. ah-l'yee, ah-bil).

---

*Until the latter half of the nineteenth century, the stress was not marked in words ending in **n** or **s**, thus : nacion, jamas. But as **n** and **s** are the two consonants added when forming the plural in Spanish, it is now customary to add the accent (nación, jamás, bastón, después, etc.), to show that the **n** or **s** is not merely a plural termination.

Similarly, it is no longer customary to mark the accent in words ending in **n** or **s** when the stress is not on the last syllable, thus : antes, joven (pronounced ahn-tace, Ho-ven), and formerly written ántes, jóven.

VARYING PRONUNCIATIONS.

The lisping pronunciation of z, and of c before e or i (ce=ze, ci=zi), is usual in Castile ; and as Castilian is considered the best Spanish, we advise Englishmen to adopt this pronunciation in preference, thus : luz (LIGHT), 'looth'; cinco (FIVE), 'thin-ko'; once (ELEVEN), on-thay, and so on. But in South and Central America, and in some parts of Spain, it is usual to pronounce z, and c before e or i, like the English s.

Many Spaniards pronounce the final d like th in the English THIN, MYTH ; and some pronounce d in the middle of a word something like th in the English 'THEN.' Thus, edad (AGE)=ay-dahth ; madre (MOTHER) =mah-thray.

It is also not unusual for Spaniards to confuse the sound of b with that of v. But foreigners should pronounce the Spanish d, b, v, exactly as they are pronounced in English, not making the final d too sharp and distinct.

ACCENTS, SIGNS OF PUNCTUATION, ETC.

The ACUTE ACCENT (´) is the only accent used in Spanish. It indicates that the STRESS or EMPHASIS is to be laid on the vowel over which it is placed ; as, médico, physician (PRON. may-de-ko). It is also used to distinguish between words similarly spelt, but of different meaning: te, thee ; té, tea (PRON. of both, tay). It never alters the pronunciation of a letter.

The accent is also used in such words as cuando (WHEN), donde (WHERE), when they actually ask a question, thus : When does the boat arrive ? ¿ Cuándo llega el buque ? but : Does he know when the boat arrives ? Sabe él cuando llega el buque ?

(Literally, when arrives the boat ?   knows he when arrives the boat ? pronounced : sah-bay el kwahn-do l'yay-gah el boo-kay).

The NOTES OF INTERROGATION and EXCLAMATION are placed at both ends of the phrase, the first one being inverted ; as,
¿ qué tiene él ? what has he ?—¡ gracias á Dios ! thank God !

The DIARESIS (¨) is placed over u (ü) preceded by g, to indicate that the u must be pronounced ; as, agüero, omen (PRON.: ah-goo'ay-ro).

The TILDE (~) is placed over n, when that letter is to be pronounced like ni in union ; as, niño, child (PRON.: nee-n'yo).

FIRST LESSON.

1.

	SINGULAR.		PLURAL.
1st Person I	yo	*1st Person* we	nosotros*
2nd „ thou	tú	*2nd* „ you	vosotros*
3rd „ he, él ; she,	ella	*3rd* „ they	ellos*

* When these words are FEMININE, the ending os is changed to as.

PRON. yo, too, ell, ell-yah, nos-o-tros, vos-o-tros, ell-yos, etc.

THE SECOND PERSON is only used in addressing near relations, very intimate friends, children, and animals. The ordinary polite form of address is usted (SINGULAR), commonly written V. or Vd., and ustedes (PLURAL), written Vs. VV. or Vds. PRON. oos-ted, oos-tay-dace.

Usted is a contraction of vuestra merced (your honor), and the Verb of which it is the subject must therefore be in the THIRD PERSON :

you have (SING.)=your honor has   Vd. tiene

„   „ (PLUR.)=your honors have   Vds. tienen

have you (SING.)=has your honor ?   ¿ tiene Vd. ? etc.

The Second Person (i.e., the familiar form) is given throughout this book for Reference only, as foreigners must always use the polite form when addressing any adult. The employment of the Familiar Form will be explained later on.

---

2.   PRESENT TENSE *of* to have, **tener.**

I have **yo tengo**	we (M.) have	**nosotros**	} tenemos
you „ **Vd.** }	we (F.) „	**nosotras**	
he has **él** } tiene	you „	**Vds.**	
she „ **ella** }	they (M.) „	**ellos**	} tienen
	they (F.) „	**ellas**	

PRON. ten-go, te-ay-nay, tay-nay-mos, te-ay-nen.

Familiar Form : thou hast, **tú tienes** ; you have, **vosotros tenéis.**

---

3. NOT is translated by **no**, which is placed BEFORE THE VERB ; as, I have not, **yo no tengo** ; has he not ? ¿ **no tiene él ?**

EXERCISE I.

1. ellos tienen ;   2. ¿ tengo yo ?   3. ¿ no tengo yo ?   4. ella no tiene ;   5. ¿ tenemos nosotros ?   6. Vd. no tiene ;   7. ¿ no tienen ellas ?   8. ¿ tienen Vds.?   9. nosotros no tenemos.

10. she has ;   11. have they not ?   12. have you (SING.) ? 13. I have not ;   14. you (PLUR.) have not ;   15. have I not ? 16. we have ;   17. have you (PLUR.) not ?   18. she has not.

THE PLURAL OF NOUNS.

4. The PLURAL is formed by adding

> s to Nouns ending in a VOWEL ;
> es to Nouns ending in a CONSONANT or y.

boy, **muchacho** ; boys, **muchachoS** ; train, **tren** ; trains, **trenES** ; pen, **pluma** ; pens, plumaS ; king, **rey** ; kings, reyES.

If the SINGULAR ends in z, the PLURAL is formed by changing the z into ces ; as voice, **voz** ; voices, **voces.**

PRONUNCIATION: moo-chah-cho, moo-chah-chos ; trane, **tray-nace** ; **ploo**-mah, **ploo**-mahs ; ray'e, ray-yace ; voth, **vo**-thace.

THE GENDER OF NOUNS.

(Names of living beings have the same Gender as in English.)

5. Nouns ending in a, ion, d, z, are FEMININE.   All others are MASCULINE.

The Gender of Nouns will only be given in the Vocabularies when not in accordance with the foregoing rule.

EXERCISE II.

Form the Plural of :—1. **padre**, father ; 2. **libro**, book ; 3. **nuez**, nut ; 4. **señor**, gentleman ; 5. **lápiz** (MASC.), pencil ; 6. **pluma**, pen ; 7. **ciudad**, town ; 8. **hombre**, man ; 9. **luz**, light ; 10. **tía**, aunt ; 11. **iglesia**, church ; 12. **ley** (FEM.), law ; 13. **sombrero**, hat.

PRON.: 1 pah-dray ; 2 lee-bro ; 3 noo'aith ; 4 say-n'yor ; 5 lah-pith ; 6 **ploo-mah** ; 7 the'oo-**dahd** ; 8 **om**-bray ; 9 looth ; 10 tee-ah ; 11 **e-glay**-se-ah ; 12 **lay**-e ; 13 som-**bray**-ro.

---

6.   THE   ARTICLES.

SINGULAR.   PLURAL.

a, an **un** (M.), **una** (F.) | some, any **unos** (M.), **unas** (F.) the **el** (M.), **la** (F.) | the **los** (M.), **las** (F.)

PRON.: oonn ; oo-nah ; el ; lah ('ah' always pronounced short) ; oo-nos ; oo-nahs ; los ; lahs.

Articles take the GENDER and NUMBER of the following NOUN ; as,

> a man, **un hombre** ;   an aunt, **una tía** ;
> the man, **el hombre** ;   the aunt, **la tía** ;
> some men, **unos hombres** ; some aunts, **unas tías** ;
> **the men, los hombres** ;   the aunts, **las tías.**

7. The MASCULINE ARTICLE is used before a FEMININE SINGULAR NOUN commencing with **a** or **ha**, if the **a** or **ha** takes the stress ; as,

the wing, **el ala** (fem.) ; a beech, **un haya** (fem.) ;
  but : the flour, **la harina** ; a spider, **una araña.**

REMARK.—The Neuter Article **lo**, which has no plural, is only used before other Parts of Speech used as Nouns, thus : **lo difícil**, the difficult.

PRON.: **ah**-lah ; **ah**-yah ; ah-**ree**-nah ; ah-**rah**-n'yah ; de-**fee**-thill.

EXERCISE III.

1. a brother[1] ;   2. a sister[2] ;   3. some brothers[1] ;   4. some sisters[2] ;   5. the brother ;   6. the brothers ;   7. the sister ; 8. the sisters ;   9. the houses[3] ;   10. the water[4] ;   11. a wing[5] ; 12. the beautiful[6] ;   13. a father ;   14. the books ;   15. a pen ; 16. the pencil ;   17. the ink[7] ;   18. some pencils ;   19. a village[8].

---

1 hermano ; 2 hermana ; 3 casa ; 4 agua ; 5 ala ; 6 hermoso ; 7 tinta; 8 aldea.   PRON. 1 air-**mah**-no ;   2 air-**mah**-nah ;   3 **kah**-sah ;   4 ah-gwah *or* ah-**goo**'ah ;   5 **ah**-lah ;   6 air-**mo**-so ;   7 **tin**-tah ;   8 ahl-**day**-ah.

EXERCISE IV.

TRANSLATE :—1. Yo no tengo un libro.   2. ¿ Tiene él las plumas ?   3. Nosotros tenemos una casa.   4. Vds. tienen unas plumas ; nosotros tenemos unos libros.

5. You have a brother.   6. The bird[1] has two[2] wings. 7. You (PLURAL) have not the books.   8. Has he not the ink ?   9. The mother[3] has two[2] houses.   10. I have not a pen, but[4] my[5] friend[6] has some pens.   11. Has he the letter[7] ?

---

1 pájaro ; 2 dos ; 3 madre ; 4 pero ; 5 mi ; 6 amigo ; 7 carta.
  PRON. 1 pah-*H*ah-ro ;   2 dos ;   3 **mah**-dray ;   4 **pay**-ro ;   5 me ; 6 ah-**mee**-go ; 7 **kar**-tah.

READING AND PRONUNCIATION EXERCISE.

¿Sabe   Vd.   los   números   españoles ?   Sí ;   son los
Know   you   the   numbers   Spanish ?   Yes ; (they) are the
sah-bay oos-**ted** los **noo**-may-ros es-pah-n'**yo**-lace   see   son los

siguientes :   uno, dos, tres,   cuatro,   cinco,   seis,   siete,   ocho,
following :   one, two, three,   four,   five,   six,   seven,   eight,
se-ghe-**en**-tace oo-no dos trace koo'**ah**-tro **thin**-ko say-is se-**ay**-tay o-cho

nueve,   diez,   once,   doce,   trece,   catorce,   quince.
nine,   ten,   eleven,   twelve,   thirteen,   fourteen,   fifteen.
noo'**ay**-vay de-**eth on**-thay **do**-thay **tray**-thay kah-**tor**-thay **kin**-thay

SECOND LESSON.

8. OF or FROM is translated by **de** (PRON. day);

TO or AT is translated by **á** (PRON. ah).

> **de el** is contracted to **del,** and **á el** to **al ; as,**
>> of the man, **del hombre** ; to the father, **al padre**

de and **á** are NOT contracted with any word but **el,** thus ;
> of the houses, **de las casas** ; to the men, **á los hombres ;**
> of a pen, **de una pluma** ;   to a father, **á un padre.**

9. There is NO POSSESSIVE CASE in Spanish. The construction must therefore be changed as in the following examples.

my friend's houses=the houses of my friend, **las casas de mi amigo** ;
the man's hat   =the hat of the man, **el sombrero del hombre** ;
the boys' books =the books of the boys, **los libros de los muchachos.**

EXERCISE I.

1. of the man[1] ; 2. to a man[1] ; 3. from the church[2] ; 4. of the water of the pond[3] ; 5. to a book ; 6. of the mothers ; 7. to the stones[4] ; 8. of some letters ; 9. from the wings of a bird ; 10. to some books ; 11. of some birds ; 12. to a house; 13. to the book ; 14. of the ink ; 15. of the brothers ; 16. of the wings of the birds ; 17. the boy's[5] book ; 18. a soldier's[6] horse[7] ; 19. the soldier's horses.

---

1 hombre ; 2 iglesia ; 3 pantano ; 4 piedra ; 5 muchacho ; 6 soldado ; 7 caballo. PRON. 1 om-bray ; 2 e-glay-se-ah ; 3 pahn-tah-no ; 4 pe-ay-drah ; 5 moo-chah-cho ; 6 sol-dah-do ; 7 kah-bah-l'yo.

---

10. The Pronoun which is the SUBJECT of a Spanish Verb is generally omitted, if the meaning is clear without it ; as,

I have a pen, **tengo una pluma** or **yo tengo una pluma** ;
have I a pen? ¿ **tengo una pluma** ? or ¿ **tengo yo una pluma** ?

It is, however, never wrong to insert the Pronoun ; and it cannot be omitted when emphasized, thus :

SHE has two books, and WE have three, **ella tiene dos libros, y nosotros tenemos tres.**

Usted cannot be omitted, as it stands for **vuestra merced** (your honor), and is therefore really a Noun.

11.   PRESENT TENSE *of* to have, **haber.**

I have	**yo he**	we (M.) have	**nosotros** } **hemos**
		we (F.) „	**nosotras** }
you „	**Vd.** } **ha**	you „	**Vds.** } **han**
he has	**él** }	they (M.) „	**ellos** }
she „	**ella** }	they (F.) „	**ellas** }

PRON.: ay, ah, ay-mos, ahn.

Familiar Form : thou hast, **tú has** ; you have, **vosotros habéis.**

12.   There are two Spanish Verbs meaning ' to have.' **Tener** is used as a principal Verb, meaning to hold, to possess.

   Haber is only used as an AUXILIARY ; i.e., to form the COMPOUND TENSES of other Verbs. It must therefore precede a Past Participle.

   If ' possess ' can be substituted for ' have,' **tener** must be employed. Thus, in the Collective Exercise below, sentences 3 and 4 might be worded : ' Do we not possess the hats ?' ' Does the church possess an altar ?' Therefore, **tener** is the verb to employ.

   But in sentences 1 and 2, ' we possess written,' ' you possess not seen,' makes no sense whatever. **Haber** must therefore be used.

   The Student should carefully compare the following examples :

I have a house	I have seen a house
(Yo) tengo una casa	**(Yo) he visto una casa**
They have the letter	They have written the letter
(Ellos) tienen la carta	**(Ellos) han escrito la carta**
You have a book	You have taken a book
Vd. tiene un libro	**Vd. ha tomado un libro**

13.   (A) In Compound Tenses, **no** precedes the AUXILIARY ; as, He has not written the letter, (él) **no ha escrito la carta.**

   (B) In Compound Tenses formed with the Present Tense of **haber,** the Subject in questions is usually placed AFTER the Past Participle, this construction being considered more elegant ; as,

Have you seen the house ?	¿ **Ha visto Vd. la casa ?**
Has he not taken the nuts ?	¿ **No ha tomado él las nueces ?**
Have the men written ?	¿ **Han escrito los hombres ?**

COLLECTIVE EXERCISE.

1. We have written[1] some letters.   2. You have not seen[2] the houses.   3. Have we not the hats[3] ?   4. Has the church an altar[4] ?   5. I have seen[2] the altar[4] of the church.   6. The kings have the horses.   7. Who[5] has taken[6] the ink ?

8. The man has an axe.[7] 9. The vessel[8] has an anchor.[9]
10. Has the servant[11] given[10] a chair[12] to the gentleman[13] ?
11. I have not an envelope,[14] but my[15] brother has some
envelopes. 12. What[16] have you (PLUR.) done[17] ? 13. Have
you seen the king's gardens[18] ? 14. The men have some
horses. 15. Why[19] have you not written[1] the letters ?
16. A man has spoken[20] with[21] the servant.[11] 17. Have we
not a book for[22] the woman[23] ? 18. Yes,[24] we have a book
and two pens. 19. We have not seen the man's house.
20. The girls[25] have not taken[6] the pens. 21. You have
some letters. 22. You have not the books. 23. The girl's[25]
brother has not written a letter to the gentleman.[13]

---

1 escrito ; 2 visto ; 3 sombrero ; 4 altar ; 5 quién ? 6 tomado ;
7 hacha ; 8 buque ; 9 ancla ; 10 dado ; 11 criado ; 12 silla ; 13 caballero ; 14 sobre ; 15 mi ; 16 qué ? 17 hecho ; 18 jardín ; 19 por qué ?
20 hablado ; 21 con ; 22 para ; 23 mujer ; 24 sí ; 25 muchacha.

PRON.: 1 es-**kree**-to ; 2 **vis**-to ; 3 som-**bray**-ro ; 4 ahl-**tar** ;
5 ke-**en** ; 6 to-**mah**-do ; 7 **ah**-chah ; 8 **boo**-kay ; 9 **ahn**-klah ;
10 **dah**-do ; 11 kre-**ah**-do ; 12 **see**-l'yah ; 13 kah-bah-l'**yay**-ro ;
14 **so**-bray ; 15 me ; 16 kay ; 17 **ay**-cho ; 18 *Har*-**deen** ; 19 por **kay** ;
20 ah-**blah**-do ; 21 kon ; 22 **pah**-rah ; 23 moo-*Hair* ; 24 see ;
25 moo-**chah**-chah.

READING AND PRONUNCIATION EXERCISE.

Los otros números son : dieciseis *or* diez y seis, diecisiete,
The other numbers are : sixteen, seventeen,
los o-tros **noo**-may-ros son de-eth-e-**say**-is, de-eth-e-se-**ay**-tay

dieciocho, diecinueve, veinte, etc.
eighteen, nineteen, twenty, etc.
de-eth-e-o-cho de-eth-e-noo'**ay**-vay **vay**-in-tay et-thay-tay-rah

¿ Cómo está Vd. ? Muy bien, gracias. La llave
How are you ? Very well, thanks. key
ko-mo es-**tah** oos-**ted** **moo**'e be-**en** **grah**-the-ahs lah l'**yah**-vay

de la puerta no está aquí. ¿ Quién está hablando
door is here. Who is speaking
day lah poo'**air**-tah no es-**tah** ah-**kee** ke-**en** es-**tah** ah-**blahn**-do

en la calle ? La cerveza no es buena.
in street ? beer is good.
en lah **kah**-l'yay lah **thair**-vay-thah no ess boo'**ay**-nah

THIRD LESSON.

14.   POSSESSIVE ADJECTIVES.

	SINGULAR.			PLURAL.	
1st Person	my	**mi**	our	**nuestro***
2nd „	thy	**tu**	your	**vuestro***
3rd „	his, her, its	**su**	their	**su**

* When the following Noun is FEMININE, the final **o** is changed to **a** ;
thus :—**nuestrA, vuestrA.**

mi, tu, su, are ALIKE in Masculine and Feminine.

PRON. me, too, soo, noo'es-tro, noo'es-trah, etc.

15. The PLURAL of these words is formed by adding **s** to the
Singular, thus :   **miS, nuestroS, nuestraS, suS.**

Possessive Adjectives always take the GENDER and NUMBER of the
following NOUN, thus :

my house, **mi casa** ;	my houses, **mis casas** ;
his, her *or* their pencil, **su lápiz** ;	his, her *or* their pencils, **sus lápices** ;
our book, **nuestro libro** ;	our books, **nuestros libros** ;
our church, **nuestra iglesia** ;	our churches, **nuestras iglesias** ;
my brother, **mi hermano** ;	my sisters, **mis hermanas** ;
his, her *or* their aunt, **su tía** ;	his, her *or* their aunts, **sus tías.**

---

16. YOUR (polite form), **su** (singular), **sus** (plural).

Foreigners cannot employ **tu** (thy) or **vuestro** (your), any more than
tú (thou) or **vosotros** (you). As all adults must be addressed as **Usted**
(=your honor), phrases like ' have you lost your hat ?' become ' has your
honor lost HIS hat ?' (¿ **Ha perdido Vd. su sombrero** ?) and so on.

Consequently, **su** is used, not only for HIS, HER, THEIR, but also for YOUR,
the context usually showing which is meant. In conversation, **su** usually
means YOUR, unless another person has just been mentioned.   When it is
desired to make a distinction, ' the hat of you,' ' the books of her,' ' the
mother of them,' etc., must be employed, thus : **el sombrero de Vd., los
libros de ella, la madre de ellos** (or **ellas**).

[After a Preposition, HIM is **él**, HER **ella**, and THEM **ellos, ellas**,—
see paragraph 65.]

The construction **su sombrero de Vd., sus libros de ella, su
madre de ellos**, is also occasionally used.

Exercise I.

1. my garden ; 2. his ink ; 3. her ink ; 4. their ink ;
5. our glass[1] ; 6. our village ; 7. my aunt[2] ; 8. my aunts[2] ;
9. their cat[3] ; 10. their cats[3] ; 11. our gloves[4] ; 12. his shoes[5];
13. his sisters ; 14. her sisters ; 15. their money[6] ; 16. my
servant ; 17. our hands[7] ; 18. his eyes[8] ; 19. her wish[9] ;
20. his wish[9] ; 21. their names[10] ; 22. your pen ; 23. your
book ; 24. your (PLUR.) house ; 25. your (SING.) hands[7] ;
26. your (PLUR.) hands ; 27. He has not broken[11] his pipe[12] ;
28. Have the children[13] taken your gloves[4] ? 29. Have you
taken your money[6] ?

---

1 vaso ; 2 tía ; 3 gato ; 4 guante ; 5 zapato ; 6 dinero ; 7 mano (FEM.);
8 ojo ; 9 deseo ; 10 nombre ; 11 roto ; 12 pipa ; 13 niño.

PRON. 1 vah-so ; 2 tee-ah ; 3 gah-to ; 4 goo'ahn-tay ; 5 thah-
pah-to ; 6 de-nay-ro ; 7 mah-no ; 8 o-Ho ; 9 day-say-o ; 10 nom-bray ;
11 rro-to ; 12 pee-pah ; 13 nee-n'yo.

---

17.   Present Tenses *of* to be, **estar** *and* **ser.**

	estar	ser		estar	ser
I am	estoy	soy	we are	estamos	somos
you are you are he *or* she is	} está	es	you „ they„	} están	son

PRON. es-to'e, es-tah, es-tah-mos, es-tahn ; so'e, ess, so-mos, son.

Familiar Form of **estar** : estás (sing.), estáis (plur.) ;
   „   „   of **ser** : eres (sing.), sois (plur.).

The full conjugation is as follows :

	estar	ser		estar	ser
I am	yo estoy	yo soy	we are	nosotros estamos	nosotros somos
thou art	tú estás	tú eres	you are	vosotros estáis	vosotros sois
he is	él está	él es	they are	ellos están	ellos son
she is	ella está	ella es	„ (F.)	ellas están	ellas son

Exercise II. (on **ser**).

1. somos ; 2. no son ; 3. ¿soy yo ? 4. ella no es ; 5. ¿ no
somos nosotros ? 6. no soy ; 7. ¿ es Vd.? 8. Vds. no son.

9. is she ? 10. he is not ; 11. are they (FEM.) not ? 12. you
(PLUR.) are ; 13. are you not ? 14. are we ? 15. am I not ?
16. I am ; 17. she is not ; 18. I am not.

H.S.S. 2.

EXERCISE III. (on estar).

1. no estoy ; 2. ¿ está él ? 3. ¿ no estamos nosotros ?
4. Vd. no está ; 5. ¿ están ellos ? 6. ¿ está Vd. ? 7. Vds. están.

8. we are ; 9. are you not ? 10. they (F.) are not ; 11. am
I ? 12. you (PLUR.) are ; 13. is he not ? 14. she is not ;
15. are we ? 16. you are not ; 17. I am not ; 18. are you ?

---

18. **Estar** is used in speaking of any TEMPORARY condition or
  action, or of the place in which a person or thing is, thus :
  he is at the door, **está á la puerta*** ; I am here, **estoy aquí**
  we are speaking, **estamos hablando** ;
  they are not busy, **no están ocupados**

Ser is used in speaking of a PERMANENT state or condition,
  a profession or calling, or a natural characteristic.
  am I tall ? ¿ **soy yo alto** ?   he is not English, **no es inglés** ;
  they are soldiers,   **son soldados** ;
  the paper is white,   **el papel es blanco** ;
  he is the manager of the firm, **es el gerente* de la casa.**

SPECIAL REMARKS.

Estar is of course used before any Present Participle, as the phrase
then expresses WHAT ONE IS DOING at the time only.

I am smoking   estoy fumando

PLACE is always expressed by **estar,** no matter how long the person
or thing has been in the place referred to. **Estar** is really almost equivalent to ' stand,' thus :
  Madrid is (=stands) in Castile, **Madrid está en Castilla***
    the Bank of England is in London,
    el Banco de Inglaterra* está en Londres*

☞ **Ser** should always be employed, unless the action or condition spoken of must necessarily by its nature be temporary.

Property in (i.e. possession of) anything is always expressed by **ser,**
thus : this book is mine, **este libro es mío.**

The Passive Voice is always expressed by **ser** : he is loved, **es amado**

*PRONOUNCED : poo'**air**-tah, *H*ay-**ren**-tay, kah-**stee**-l'yah,
    in-glah-**tairr**-rah, lon-dress.

EXERCISE IV. (on ser and estar).

1. We are not workmen.[1] 2. Are you ready[2] ? 3. They
(FEM.) are here.[3] 4. Are you [a] soldier ? 5. I am not listening.[4] 6. Who is in the street[5] ? 7. He is very[6] indus-

trious.[7] 8. I am [an*] Englishwoman.[8] 9. I am not [an]
Italian.[9] 10. We are speaking[10] with his cousin.[11] 11. Are
they not princes[12]? 12. We are sailors.[13] 13. He is not
writing.[14] 14. He is [a] postman.[15] 15. We are not smoking.[16]
16. Are you [a] Spaniard[17]? 17. They are my uncles.[18] 18.
My aunt is not here.[3] 19. She is not at[19] home.[19] 20. We
are waiting.[20] 21. He is [a] professor.[21]

1 obrero ; 2 listo ; 3 aquí ; 4 escuchando ; 5 calle (FEM.) ; 6 muy ; 7
laborioso ; 8 inglesa ; 9 italiano ; 10 hablando ; 11 primo (M.), prima (F.) ;
12 príncipe ; 13 marinero ; 14 escribiendo ; 15 cartero ; 16 fumando ; 17
español ; 18 tío ; 19 en casa ; 20 aguardando ; 21 profesor.

PRON. 1 o-**bray**-ro ; 2 lis-to ; 3 ah-**kee** ; 4 es-koo-**chahn**-do ;
5 **kah**-l'yay ; 6 **moo**'e ; 7 lah-bo-re-o-so ; 8 in-**glay**-sah ; 9 e-tah-le-**ah**-
no ; 10 ah-**blahn**-do ; 11 **pree**-mo ; 12 **prin**-the-pay ; 13 mah-re-**nay**-
ro ; 14 es-kree-be-**en**-do ; 15 kar-**tay**-ro ; 16 foo-**mahn**-do ; 17 es-pah-
n'**yol** ; 18 **tee**-o ; 19 enn **kah**-sah ; 20 ah-goo'ar-**dahn**-do ; 21 pro-fess-**or**.

COLLECTIVE EXERCISE.

1. Our friends[1] are in[2] the garden, looking[3] for[3] their dogs.[4]
2. Are you my friend's uncle? 3. No,[5] sir,[6] I am not his
uncle, I am his father. 4. My friend is in[2] the street,
smoking a cigar.[7] 5. Who is there[8]? 6. What are you
(PLUR.) looking[3] for[3]? 7. I am writing a letter to your
father. 8. Your children[9] are growing[10] very[11] fast.[11] 9. My
friend's brother is not industrious.[12] 10. Have you a servant?
11. Our sister is clever.[13] 12. Your mother is in the garden.
13. My shoes are on[2] the floor,[14] near[15] the chair. 14. You
are not soldiers. 15. My book is in the drawer.[16] 16. Is
your[b] brother[b] smoking[a]? 17. To whom[17] have you written a
letter? 18. We are not studying[18] our lessons.[19]

1 amigo (M.), amiga (F.) ; 2 en ; 3 buscando ; 4 perro ; 5 no ; 6
señor ; 7 cigarro ; 8 allí ; 9 hijo (son); 10 creciendo ; 11 mucho (much) ;
12 laborioso ; 13 hábil ; 14 suelo ; 15 cerca de ; 16 cajón ; 17 quién ; 18
estudiando ; 19 lección.

PRON. 1 ah-**me**-go ; 2 enn ; 3 booss-**kahn**-do ; 4 **pairr**-ro ; 5 no ;
6 say-n'**yor** ; 7 the-**gahrr**-ro ; 8 ah-l'**yee** ; 9 ee-*H*o ; 10 kray-the-**en**-
do ; 11 **moo**-cho ; 12 lah-bo-re-o-so ; 13 ah-bil ; 14 soo'**ay**-lo ; 15 **thair**-
kah day ; 16 kah-*H*on ; 17 ke-en ; 18 es-too-de-**ahn**-do ; 19 lek-the-**on**.

*In the Exercises, words not to be translated are placed between square
brackets [   ], and words which are required in Spanish, but not in English, between parentheses (   ).

FOURTH LESSON.

QUALIFYING ADJECTIVES.

19. Adjectives agree in Gender and Number with the **Noun** they qualify ; and generally FOLLOW that Noun. Thus :

a cheap watch, **un reloj barato** ;   cheap watches, **relojes baratos**
a cheap chain, **una cadena barata** ; cheap chains, **cadenas baratas**
an English newspaper, **un periódico inglés**
English newspapers, **periódicos ingleses**
French literature, **la literatura francesa**
Spanish grammars, **gramáticas españolas**

REMARK.—Adjectives generally PRECEDE the Noun they qualify if they are shorter than the Noun, or are used figuratively ; as,

a poor(=in poverty) writer   **un escritor pobre**
a poor(=unfortunate) writer   **un pobre escritor**

PRON. ray-lo*H*, bah-rah-to, kah-**day**-nah, pay-re-o-de-ko, in-**gless**, le-tay-rah-**too**-rah frahn-**thay**-sah, grah-**mah**-te-kahs es-pah-n'**yo**-lahs, es-kre-**tor**, po-bray.

Bueno (good) and **malo** (bad) usually precede the Noun. They are then contracted to **buen** and **mal,** but in the MASCULINE SINGULAR ONLY,— see Paragraph 94.

PRON. boo'**ay**-no, **mah**-lo, boo'**en,** mahl.

An Adjective is sometimes put before the Noun for EMPHASIS :
a magnificent day, **un magnifico día** ; a splendid day, **un espléndido día**

PRON. mahg-**nee**-fe-ko, es-**plen**-de-do, dee-ah.

The position of the Adjective before or after the Noun which it qualifies is largely a matter of taste and euphony, respecting which no exact rules can be given.

A few Adjectives nearly always precede the Noun,—see pars. **94, 95.**

THE FEMININE OF ADJECTIVES.

20. If the MASCULINE ends in **o**, the FEMININE is formed by changing the **o** into **a** ; as,

industrious, **laborioso** (masc.), **laboriosA** (fem.)
Russian, **ruso** (masc.), **rusA** (fem.)

21. If the Adjective denotes NATIONALITY,* and ends in a consonant, the Feminine is formed by adding **a** to the Masculine ; as,

Spanish, **español** (m.), **española** (f.); English, **inglés** (m.), **inglesa** (f.)

REMARK I.—Adjectives denoting NATIONALITY can also be used as Nouns : an Englishman, **un Inglés** ; an Englishwoman, **una Inglesa**.

REMARK II.—Most other Adjectives which can be used as Nouns denoting a person add **a** in the FEMININE, whether used as Nouns or Adjectives. These generally end in **n** or **or**. Thus :

an idle servant, **un criado holgazán** (m.), **una criada holgazanA** (f.)
an idler, **un holgazán** (m.), **una holgazanA** (f.)

22. Adjectives not included in the foregoing Rules DO NOT CHANGE in the Feminine ; as,

an easy book, **un libro fácil** ; easy books, **libros fáciles**
an easy lesson, **una lección fácil** ; easy lessons, **lecciones fáciles**
PRON. ol-gah-**thahn**, fah-thil, leck-the-**on**.

THE PLURAL OF ADJECTIVES.

23. The Plural of Adjectives is formed in the same way as the Plural of Nouns† (see paragraph 4) ; as,

a skilful workman, **un obrero hábil** ; skilful workmen, **obreros hábiles**
a happy girl, **una muchacha feliz** ; happy girls, **muchachas felices**
a sick child, **un niño enfermo** ; sick children, **niños enfermos**
an English manuscript, **una escritura inglesa**
English manuscripts, **escrituras inglesas**
PRON. fay-**leeth** or fay-lith, en-fair-mo, es-kre-**too**-rah.

EXERCISE I.

Form the Feminine Singular, and the Masculine and Feminine Plural, of the following Adjectives :

1. good, **bueno** ; 2. dear, **caro** ; 3. capacious, **capaz** ;
4. diligent, **aplicado, laborioso** ; 5. French, **francés** ;
6. easy, **fácil** ; 7. cheap, **barato** ; 8. dry, **seco** ; 9. brave,

---

* These Adjectives do not commence with a capital letter in Spanish.
† The Plural is of course formed from the Singular of the SAME GENDER.

valiente; 10. cold, **frío**; 11. hot, **cálido**; 12. German, **alemán**; 13. difficult, **difícil**; 14. English, **inglés**; 15. heavy, **pesado**; 16. Persian, **persa**.

17. a good horse; 18. good horses; 19. a bad pen; 20. bad pens; 21. a difficult lesson; 22. difficult lessons.

PRON. 1 boo'ay-no; 2 kah-ro; 3 kah-pahth; 4 ah-ple-kah-do; 5 frahn-thess; 6 fah-thil; 7 bah-rah-to; 8 say-ko; 9 vah-le-enn-tay; 10 free-o; 11 kah-le-do; 12 ah-lay-mahn; 13 de-fee-thil; 14 ingless; 15 pay-sah-do; 16 pair-sah.

COLLECTIVE EXERCISE.

1. His friends are not brave. 2. The French milliner[1] has sold[2] a cheap hat. 3. Our lessons[3] are very easy. 4. Have you a good servant? 5. No, sir, my servants are not good [ones]. 6. I have seen (to)* a brave soldier. 7. I have [some] cold meat.[4] 8. We are English sailors. 9. Why are you (PLUR.) not studying[5] your lessons? 10. The German girls are happy[6]. 11. To whom[7] have you given your books? 12. I have given my Spanish books to my friend's cousin. 13. Our lesson is very difficult. 14. How[8] are you? 15. Very well,[9] thank[10] you[10]; but I have been[11] ill.[12] 16. Your sister is not ill.[12] 17. Your (PLUR.) aunts are very clever. 18. Her brothers are ill. 19. Your friend (FEM.) is [an] Italian. 20. She is not Italian, she is Spanish. 21. What have you done with my book? 22. It is on the table.[13]

1 modista; 2 vendido; 3 lección; 4 carne (FEM.); 5 estudiando; 6. feliz; 7 quién? 8 cómo? 9 bien; 10 gracias (*thanks*); 11 estado; 12 enfermo; 13 mesa.   * see paragraph 37.

PRON. 1 mo-dis-tah; 2 ven-dee-do; 3 lek-the-on; 4 kar-nay; 5 es-too-de-ahn-do; 6 fay-leeth; 7 ke-en; 8 ko-mo; 9 be-en; 10 grah-the-ahs; 11 es-tah-do; 12 en-fair-mo; 13 may-sah.

SPECIAL REMARK.—It must be constantly borne in mind that the English and Spanish vowel sounds do not correspond exactly, and that the Spanish sounds are not so long as those given in our Imitated Pronunciation. THEY SHOULD ALL BE PRONOUNCED SHORT (especially 'ah' and 'ay'). To remind students of this, we give such words as trenes, feliz, indifferently as trenn-ess or trane-ace, fay-leeth, fay-lith, or fell-ith.

FIFTH LESSON.

REGULAR VERBS.

The INFINITIVE of every Spanish Verb ends in **ar, er,** or **ir.** The part PRECEDING these terminations is called the STEM.

Thus : INFINITIVE :—to speak hablAR   STEM :—habl...
  „   to owe debER   „   deb...
  „   to live vivIR   „   viv...

PRESENT INDICATIVE OF REGULAR VERBS.

24. The Present Indicative of Verbs ending in **ar** is formed by adding to the STEM the following terminations :

SING.—1st Pers. 2nd Pers. 3rd Pers.   PLUR.—1st Pers. 2nd Pers. 3rd Pers.

| O | as | A | AMOS | áis | AN |

The full Conjugation of the Present Indicative is therefore as follows :

I speak	(yo) hablO	we speak (nosotros) hablAMOS
you speak	Vd. } hablA	you „ Vds. } hablAN
he speaks	(él)	they „ (ellos)

PRON. ah-blo, ah-blah, ah-blah-mos, ah-blahn.

Familiar Form : thou speakest, (tú) hablas ; you speak, (vosotros) habláis.

NOTE.—Except in the FIRST PERSON SINGULAR, these terminations are the same as those of **estar** (see Paragraph 17) ; but in Regular Verbs the STRESS IS REGULAR (see page 6).

EXERCISE I.

1. I buy[1] ;   2. you buy ;   3. he buys ;   4. we buy ;   5. you (PLUR.) buy ;   6. they buy ;   7. he takes[2] ;   8. we find[3] ; 9. I find ;   10. they (F.) take ;   11. you find ;   12. you (PLUR.) take ;   13. he smokes[4] ;   14. they smoke ;   15. you carry[5] ; 16. I carry ;   17. we send[6] ;   18. you (PLUR.) send.

---

1 comprar ; 2 tomar ; 3 hallar ; 4 fumar ; 5 llevar ; 6 enviar.
PRON. 1 kom-prar ; 2 to-mar ; 3 ah-l'yar ; 4 foo-mar ; 5 l'yay-var ; 6 en-ve-ar.

---

25. The Present Indicative of Verbs ending in **er** is formed like that of Verbs ending in **ar,** except that **E** is substituted for **A** in the terminations.

The full Conjugation of the Present Indicative is as follows:

I owe (yo) debO	we owe (nosotros) debEMOS
you owe Vd. } debE	you „ Vds. } debEN
he owes (él)	they „ (ellos)

PRON. day-bo, day-bay, day-bay-mos, day-ben.

Familiar Form : thou owest, (tú) debes ; you owe, (vosotros) debéis.

EXERCISE II.

1. I drink[1] ; 2. you drink ; 3. he drinks ; 4. we drink ; 5. you (PLUR.) drink ; 6. they drink ; 7. he believes[2] ; 8. we believe ; 9. they eat[3] ; 10. I eat ; 11. you learn[4] ; 12. you (P.) believe ; 13. he learns ; 14. I possess[5] ; 15. they possess.

---

1 beber ; 2 creer ; 3 comer ; 4 aprender ; 5 poseer. PRON. 1 bay-bair ; 2 kray-air ; 3 ko-mair ; 4 ah-pren-dair ; 5 po-say-air.

---

26. In the Present Indicative of Verbs ending in **ir**, **IMOS** is added to the Stem to form the 1ST PERSON PLURAL, and **IS** to form the 2ND PERSON PLURAL.

☞ The terminations of the **er** and **ir** Verbs are otherwise EXACTLY ALIKE, in every other Mood and Tense.*

The full Conjugation of the Present Indicative is as follows :

I live (yo) vivO	we live (nosotros) vivIMOS
you live Vd. } vivE	you „ Vds. } vivEN
he lives (él)	they „ (ellos)

PRON. vee-vo, vee-vay, ve-vee–mos, vee-ven.

Fam. Form : thou livest, (tú) vives ; you live, (vosotros) vivís (ve-veess)

EXERCISE III.

1. I receive[1] ; 2. you receive ; 3. he receives ; 4. we receive; 5. you (PLUR.) receive ; 6. they receive ; 7. he writes[2] ; 8. we write ; 9. you supply[3] ; 10. I supply ; 11. he divides[4] ; 12. we divide ; 13. you (PLUR.) write ; 14. we supply.

---

1 recibir ; 2 escribir ; 3 surtir ; 4 dividir.
PRON. 1 rray-the-beer ; 2 es-kre-beer ; 3 soor-teer ; 4 de-ve-deer.

* The only other exception is the Plural Familiar Form of the Imperative (see par. 57). It is therefore the simplest plan for foreigners, who should never use the Familiar Form, to consider the ir Verbs as conjugated exactly like the er Verbs throughout, except that the former take IMOS instead of EMOS in the First Person Plural of the Present Indicative.

Note.—All Regular Verbs ending in **AR** are conjugated like **hablar**, all in **ER** like **deber**, and all in **IR** like **vivir**.

Tener, haber, ser and estar are irregular.

27. Questions are formed by putting the Verb before the Subject ; do, does, did, are not translated. Thus :

does he speak ?=speaks he ?   ¿ habla él ?

does his friend smoke ?=smokes his friend ? ¿ fuma su amigo ?

do you owe ?=owe you ?   ¿ debe Vd. ?

do the men write ?=write the men ? ¿ escriben los hombres ?

28. Negations are formed by putting **no** before the Verb or Auxiliary (see paragraph 13) ; do, does, did, are not translated. Thus :

you do not buy=you buy not   **Vd. no compra**

do you not buy ?=buy you not ?   ¿ no compra Vd. ?

the boy does not learn=the boy learns not   el muchacho no aprende

does not the boy learn ?=learns the boy not ? ¿ no aprende el muchacho ?

does the train start ?=starts the train ?   ¿ sale el tren ?

does not the boat arrive=arrives not the boat ? ¿ no llega el buque ?

Exercise IV.

1. you find, you do not find ;   2. do you find ? do you not find ?   3. the men drink, the men do not drink ;   4. do the men drink ? do the men not drink ?   5. we discover, we do not discover ;   6. do we discover ? do we not discover ;   7. I receive, I do not receive ;   8. do I receive ? do I not receive ?   9. the girl owes, the girl does not owe ;   10. does the girl owe ? does the girl not owe ?   1. descubrir.

COLLECTIVE EXERCISE.

1. Do you owe [any] money to my friend ?   2. I do not owe [any] money to your friend.   3. The Spanish servant calls[1] to his dog.   4. We do not smoke cigars.   5. The industrious pupil[2] learns his[b] lessons[b] * easily.[3a]   6. What does your mother want[4] ?   7. Do they (FEM.) not work[5] well ?

---

*Words and phrases marked A precede in Spanish those marked B.

8. Who lives in your aunt's house ?   9. My cousins live there, but my uncle is in Madrid.[6] 10. The officer[7] drinks a delicious[8] wine.[9]   11. We receive letters from your uncles every[10] day.[11]   12. I do not want[4] a stick[12], because[13] I have an umbrella.[14] 13. We believe that[15] his samples[16] are in the shop.[17] 14. How[18] much[18] money do we owe ? 15. I believe that we owe four[19] shillings[20] to the shopkeeper,[21] and three[22] shillings to the servant.   16. Perhaps[23] he does not smoke. 17. Who lends[24] money to my friend ?   18. I often[25b] lend[a] money to your friend.   19. At what time[26] does the train[27] for London[28] leave[29] ?   20. My train[27] does not start[29] yet.[30] 21. I do not fear[31] the punishment[32] ; it is not very great.[33] 22. The boys do not throw[34] stones. 23. You do not drink beer.[35] 24. Do you not understand[36] the lesson ? 25. I understand[36] the lessons very well. 26. Do they understand your explanation[37] ? 27. Where[38] do your cousins live ? 28. My cousin (FEM.) lives in Madrid, and I live in London.[28]

---

1 llamar ; 2 discípulo (M.), discípula (F.) ; 3. fácilmente ; 4. desear ; 5 trabajar ; 6 Madrid ; 7 oficial ; 8 delicioso ; 9 vino ; 10 cada (*each*) ; 11 día (MASC.) ; 12 bastón ; 13. porque ; 14 paraguas (SING. and PLUR. the same) ; 15 que ; 16 muestra ; 17 tienda ; 18 cuánto ? 19 cuatro ; 20 chelín ; 21 tendero ; 22 tres ; 23 tal vez ; 24 prestar ; 25 amenudo ; 26 hora ; 27 tren ; 28 Londres ; 29 salir (par. 148) ; 30 todavía ; 31 temer ; 32 castigo ; 33 grande ; 34 tirar ; 35 cerveza ; 36 comprender ; 37 explicación ; 38 dónde ?

PRON.* 1 l'yah-**mar** ; 2 dis-**thee**-poo-lo ; 3 **fah**-thil-**men**-tay ; 4 day-say-**ar** ; 5 trah-bah-*Har* ; 6 mah-**drid** ; 7 o-fee-the-**ahl** ; 8. day-lee-the-o-so ; 9 **vee**-no ; 10 **kah**-dah ; 11 **dee**-ah ; 12 bahs-ton ; 13 **por**-kay ; 14 pah-**rah**-goo'ahs ; 15 kay ; 16 moo'**ess**-trah ; 17 te-**en**-dah ; 18 koo'**ahn**-to ; 19 koo'**ah**-tro ; 20 chay-**leen** ; 21 ten-**day**-ro ; 22 tress ; 23 tahl veth ; 24 pres-**tar** ; 25 ah-may-**noo**-do ; 26 o-rah ; 27 tren ; 28 lon-dress ; 29 sah-leer ; 30 to-dah-**vee**-ah ; 31 tay-**mair** ; 32 kahs-tee-go ; 33 **grahn**-day ; 34 te-**rar** ; 35 thair-**vay**-thah ; 36 kom-pren-**dair** ; 37 ex-ple-kah-the-**on** ; 38 **don**-day.

* Respecting the Imitated Pronunciation, note once more that TH must always be pronounced as in ' month,' and S SHARP, like SS in ' hiss.' The vowel sounds must not be made too long ; **peseta** (franc), for example, which we give as ' pay-**say**-tah,' might almost as well be imitated thus : ' pess-ett-ah.'

SIXTH LESSON.

DEMONSTRATIVE ADJECTIVES & PRONOUNS.*

	MASC.	FEM.			MASC.	FEM.
this	este	esta	these		estos	estas
(this) that	ese	esa	(these) those		esos	esas
that	aquel	aquella	those		aquellos	aquellas

29.

PRON. es-tay, ay-say, ah-kel ; es-tah, ay-sah, ah-kell-yah; es-tos, etc.

Note that the Feminine Plural is formed by adding s to the Singular, and that the Masculine Plural only differs from the Feminine in the vowel of the termination.   Examples :

this man, este hombre   these men, estos hombres
that pencil, ese or aquel lápiz ;   those pencils, esos or aquellos lápices
this letter, esta carta   these letters, estas cartas
that house, esa or aquella casa ; those houses, esas or aquellas casas

Este usually indicates something near the speaker, ese something near the person addressed, and aquel something near neither.   Thus : these chairs (close to me), estas sillas ;   those chairs (close to you), esas sillas ; those chairs (close to neither), aquellas sillas.

30. The Neuter forms for THIS (esto) and THAT (eso, aquello) differ in the same way as the above.   They have no plural, and neither precede nor replace a Noun, thus :

Who has done this ?   ¿ Quién ha hecho esto ?
I have not heard that.   No he oído eso.

aquello is seldom used unless three things are referred to ; as,

I take this, my friend takes that, and his brother takes that
yo tomo esto, mi amigo toma eso, y su hermano toma aquello

EXERCISE I.

1. that boy ; 2. these women ; 3. those envelopes ; 4. this table ; 5. that church ; 6. those streets : 7. these horses ; 8. this ink ; 9. this cat ; 10. those pictures[1] ; 11. that bread[2]; 12. this town ; 13. these numbers[3] ; 14. that lady[4] ; 15. we are not sure[5] of that ; 16. I do not believe this.

---

1 cuadro ; 2 pan ; 3 número ; 4. señora ; 5. seguro.   PRON. 1 koo'ah-dro ; 2 pahn ; 3 noo-may-ro ; 4 say-n'yo-rah ; 5 say-goo-ro.

*ADJECTIVES are always followed by a Noun, and take the Gender and Number of that Noun.   PRONOUNS are used instead of a Noun, and take the Gender and Number of that Noun.

PRESENT AND PAST PARTICIPLES.

31. The Participles are formed by adding to the STEM the following terminations :

	PRESENT PARTICIPLE.	PAST PARTICIPLE.
Verbs ending in **ar**	...**ANDO**	...**ADO**
„ „ **er** or **ir**	..**IENDO**	...**IDO**

EXAMPLES.

1 speaking, **hablando** ;	spoken, **hablado** ;
2 owing, **debiendo** ;	owed, **debido** ;
3 living, **viviendo** ;	lived, **vivido** ;
4 sending, **enviando** ;	sent, **enviado** ;
5 receiving, **recibiendo** ;	received, **recibido** ;
6 believing, **creyendo*** ;	believed, **creído**.

An unaccented **i** between two vowels is always changed to **y**.

The Stress in Past Participles is invariably on the first vowel of the termination.

PRON. 1 ah-**blahn**-do, ah-**blah**-do ; 2 day-be-**en**-do, day-**be**-do ; 3. vee-ve-**en**-do, ve-**vee**-do ; 4 en-ve-**ahn**-do, en-ve-**ah**-do ; 5 rray-thee-be-**en**-do, rray-the-**bee**-do ; 6 kray-**yen**-do, kray-ee-do.*

The Participles of **tener, haber, ser,** and **estar** are regular, thus :

1 having, **teniendo, habiendo** ;	2 had, **tenido, habido** ;
3 being, **siendo, estando** ;	4 been, **sido, estado**

PRON. 1 tay-ne-**en**-do, ah-be-**en**-do ; 2 tay-**nee**-do, ah-**bee**-do ; 3 se-**en**-do, es-**tahn**-do ; 4 see-do, es-**tah**-do.

---

32. When the Subject in questions is a Noun, it is sometimes put last ; as,

Is the girl industrious ?	¿ **Es aplicada la muchacha ?**
Is my servant waiting ?	¿ **Está aguardando mi criado ?**
Are not the men drinking ?	¿ **No están bebiendo los hombres ?**
Is that wine good ?	¿ **Es bueno ese vino ?**

(see also Paragraph 13)

This is optional, the English construction being preferable when the meaning would otherwise be doubtful. Thus : Is the boy ill-treating the dog ? ¿ **Está el muchacho maltratando el perro ?** The other construction might mean "Is the dog ill-treating the boy ?"

Exercise II.

1. smoking, smoked ;   2. owing, owed ;   3. living, lived ;
4. asking,[1] asked ;   5. reading[2], read ;   6. have you not had ?
7. I am not having ;   8. being soldiers;   9. being in the room[3] ;
10. not having written the letter ;   11. Have you been in
Spain[4] ?   12. We have not been sailors.   13. She is not
reading.   14. What is he drinking ?   15. Where has the man
been ?   16. Are not the English soldiers brave ?   17. Is not
this lady speaking ?   18. My uncle has not arrived.[5]

1 preguntar ; 2 leer ; 3 cuarto *or* habitación ; 4 España ; 5 llegar.

PRON. 1 pray-goonn-**tar** ; 2 lay-**air** ; 3 koo'**ar**-to, ah-be-tah-the-**on** ;
4 ess-**pahn**-n'yah ; 5 l'yay-**gar**.

COLLECTIVE EXERCISE.

1. Have you not read that letter ?   2. Why is that boy not
studying his lessons ?   3. Those servants have drunk a bottle[1]
of good wine, and five[2] bottles of German beer.   4. Are
they smoking cigars ?   5. Having read the book, I[3] shall send
it[3] to my brother.   6. When[4] does the boat[5] start ?   7. How
much money has the merchant[6] sent to his banker[7] ?   8.
Have not the pupils learned these lessons ?   9. These white[8]
envelopes are my uncle's [translate : of my uncle].   10.
Those ladies are my nieces.[9]   11. The Spanish professor is
speaking now.[10] 12. I am reading a French newspaper.[11] 13.
We have been in the country.[12]   14. These bottles[1] are not
full.[13] 15. I have been [a] carpenter.[14]   16. Have you had
time[15] to[16] read[16] this letter ?   17. Have you forgotten[17] this ?
18. Are those ladies looking for a cab[18] ?   19. Do you believe
that ?   20. I do not understand this.   21. Not being satisfied[19]
with the book, I[20] shall sell it.[20]   22. Is not that dog ugly[21] ?

1 botella ; 2 cinco ; 3 lo enviaré (see pars. 43 and 67) ; 4 cuándo ?
5 buque ; 6 comerciante ; 7 banquero ; 8 blanco ; 9 sobrina ; 10 ahora ;
11 periódico ; 12 campo ; 13 lleno ; 14 carpintero ; 15 tiempo ; 16 para
leer ; 17 olvidar ; 18 coche ; 19 satisfecho ; 20 lo venderé ; 21 feo.

PRON. 1 bo-**tell**-yah ; 2 **thin**-ko ; 3 lo en-ve-ah-**ray** ; 4 koo'**ahn**-do ;
5 **boo**-kay ; 6 ko-**mair**-the-ahn-tay ; 7 bahn-**kay**-ro ; 8 **blahn**-ko ; 9 so-
bree-nah ; 10 ah-o-rah ; 11 pay-re-o-de-ko ; 12 **kahm**-po ; 13 l'**yay**-no ;
14 kar-pin-**tay**-ro ; 15 te-em-po ; 17 ol-ve-**dar** ; 18 **ko**-chay ; 19 sah-tis-
fay-cho ; 20 lo ven-day-**ray** ; 21 **fay**-o.

SEVENTH LESSON.

INTERROGATIVE ADJECTIVES AND PRONOUNS.

33. who? whom? quién? (SING.) quiénes? (PLUR.)

WHOSE? ¿de quién? literally: of whom?

Who is upstairs?	¿ Quién está arriba ?
To whom are you speaking?	¿ A quién está Vd. hablando ?
Whose are these pens?	¿ De quién son estas plumas ?
Whose hat is this?	¿ De quién es este sombrero ?

34. which *or* which one? cuál? which *or* which ones? cuáles?
what? qué? (SING. & PLUR.)

which brother? ¿cuál hermano?	which house? ¿cuál casa?
which men? ¿cuáles hombres?	which chairs? ¿cuáles sillas?
what dog? ¿qué perro?	what village? ¿qué aldea?
what churches? ¿qué iglesias?	which churches! ¿cuáles iglesias?
what is that? ¿qué es eso?	

WHAT? is translated by cuál? cuáles? if preceding part of ser
followed by a Noun.

What is your opinion?	¿ Cuál es su opinión (de Vd.) ?
What are his intentions?	¿ Cuáles son sus intenciones ?

35. qué is also used for WHAT A! in exclamations; as,

what a misfortune! ¡qué desgracia!	what a hat! ¡qué sombrero!
what pictures! ¡qué cuadros!	what a mistake! ¡qué error!

NOTE.—If an Adjective occurs in such exclamations, tan (so) is generally
inserted for emphasis; as,

what an ugly dog!	¡qué perro tan feo (=so ugly)!
what beautiful horses!	¡qué caballos tan hermosos!

EXERCISE I.

1. which gentleman? 2. which gentlemen? 3. which
chair? 4. which streets? 5. what name? 6. which shoe?
7. what men? 8. what a noise[1]! 9. which train? 10.
what a fog[2]! 11. what a pity[3]! 12. which woman?
13. which days? 14. which lamps[4]? 15. which cup[5]?
16. what hats! 17. Whose is this knife[6]? 18. Whose ink

is this ?   19. Whose friends are these ladies ?   20. Whose is this ?   21. What idle[7] boys !   22. What a great mistake[8] !
23. What is the price[9] of this ?   24. What is the number[10] ?

---

1 ruido ; 2 niebla ; 3 lástima ; 4 lámpara ; 5 taza ; 6 cuchillo ; 7 holgazán ; 8 error ; 9 precio ; 10 número.   PRON. 1 rroo-**ee**-do ; 2 ne-**ay**-blah ; 3 **lahss**-te-mah ;   4 **lahm**-pah-rah ;   5 **tah**-thah ;   6 koo-**chee**-l'yo ; 7 oll-gah-**thahn** ;   8 airr-**ror** ;   9 **pray**-the-o ;   10 **noo**-may-ro.

---

36.   The Past Tense can sometimes be rendered in Spanish by the Perfect Tense,* thus :

PAST.	PERFECT.	
he spoke	he has spoken	**ha hablado**
did he speak ?	has he spoken ?	¿ **ha hablado** (él) ?
he did not speak	he has not spoken	**no ha hablado**
did he not speak ?	has he not spoken ?	¿ **no ha hablado** (él) ?

[NOTE CAREFULLY that the Past Participle must be preceded by part of **haber** (to have).   For instance, **Vd. visto, yo escrito**, etc., is an incorrect construction, just as 'you seen,' 'I written,' etc., is impossible in English.]

EXERCISE II.

1. he (has) bought ;   2. have they bought ?   3. I have not bought ;   4. have you not bought ?   5. have they (FEM.) spoken ?   6. the girl has spoken ;   7. has the doctor[2] written[1]?   8. the merchant has not sold[3] ;   9. have not the ships arrived ?   10. I have not dined (=eaten) ;   11. has not the shopkeeper sent ?   12. you have written[1] ;   13. you (PLUR.) have seen[4] ;   14. have they not found ?

---

1 escrito ;   2 médico ;   3 *to sell*, vender ;   4 visto.
PRON. 1 ess-**kree**-to ;   2 may-de-ko ;   3 ven-**dair** ;   4 **viss**-to.

---

37.   When the Object of a Verb is a person or persons, **á** (to) should precede the Object ; as,

I do not understand your friend.	**No comprendo á su amigo.**
Do you believe the boys ?	¿ **Cree Vd. á los muchachos ?**
BUT : I do not understand this letter.	**No comprendo esta carta.**
Do you believe that story ?	¿ **Cree Vd. ese cuento ?**

Tener is an important exception to this Rule, thus :
I have a sister.   **Tengo una hermana.**

---

* The ordinary English Past Tense (I spoke, he wrote, we did not lend, etc.) is usually best rendered by the Spanish Past Definite.   The formation of the Past Definite is explained in Lesson 9 ; students may meanwhile translate the English Past by the Spanish Perfect Tense.

EXERCISE III.

1. We have seen a very celebrated[1] general.[2] **2. Have you** (PLUR.) found your friends ? 3. Has he [any] brothers ? 4. I have seen that gentleman in Madrid. 5. Do you expect[3] your nieces to-day[4] ? 6. We do not expect[3] [any] letters. 7. We are looking[5] for[5] our keys.[6] 8. Are you looking[5] for[5] your nephew[7] ? 9. I have not seen the[b] king[b] to-day.[a]

---

1 célebre ; 2 general ; 3 esperar ; 4 hoy ; 5 buscar (*to seek, look for*); 6 llave (FEM.) ; 7 sobrino.

PRON. 1 **thay**-lay-bray ; 2 *H*ay-nay-**rahl** ; 3 ess-pay-**rar** ; 4 oh-e ; 5 booss-**kar** ; 6 l'**yah**-vay ; 7 so-**bree**-no.

COLLECTIVE EXERCISE.

1. Have you found my brother in the garden ? 2. Which book have you had ? 3. Whose is that horse ? 4. What man does not love[1] his mother? 5. Whose is this umbrella ? 6. Have you (PLUR.) seen the English travellers[2] ? 7. What a cheap watch[3] you[b] have[a] bought[a] this morning[4] ! 8. The clerk[5] has received that money. 9. Who is smoking in this room ? 10. He has not sent the goods[6] in (=to) time.[7] 11. What easy lessons you[b] have[a] !   12. For whom are these letters ? 13. To whom have you lent your knife ? 14. Who are these men ? 15. What people[8] are[9] there[9] in the house ? 16. Have you not called the servant (FEM.) ? 17. Which cups has she broken ? 18. In which room have you found the red[10] ink ? 19. What a bad pen this[b] is[a] !   20. Which [ones] do you want ?   21. Which is the way[11] to the station[12] ?   22. What is the cause[13] of his silence[14] ? 23. What are their plans[15] ? 24. What is that ?

---

1 amar ; 2 viajero ; 3 reloj ; 4 mañana ; 5 dependiente ; 6 géneros (PLUR.) ; 7 tiempo ; 8 gente (FEM.); 9 hay ; 10 rojo ; 11 camino ; 12 estación ; 13 causa ; 14 silencio ; 15 plan.

PRON. 1 ah-**mar** ; 2 ve-ah-*H*ay-ro ; 3 rray-lo*H* ; 4 mah-n'**yah**-nah ; 5 de-**penn**-de-enn-tay ; 6 *H*ay-nay-ros ; 7 te-**em**-po ; 8 *H*enn-tay ; 9 ah'e *or* i ; 10 rro-*H*o ; 11 kah-**mee**-no ; 12 es-tah-the-**on** ; 13 **kah**'oo-sah ; 14 se-**lenn**-the-o ; 15 plahn.

EIGHTH LESSON.

POSSESSIVE PRONOUNS.

38. mine, **mío** ; ours, **nuestro** ; his, hers, theirs, **suyo.**

FAMILIAR FORM : 2nd Pers. thine, **tuyo** ; yours, **vuestro.**

The Feminine is formed by changing the **o** into **a**, and the Plural by adding **s** to the Singular (Ex. **mía, míos, mías, suya, suyos, suyas,** etc.)

PRON. **me**-o, noo'**es**-tro, soo-yo, too-yo, voo'**es**-tro, **me**-os, me-ahs, etc.

Your sister is in London, and mine is in the country.	Su hermana de Vd. está en Londres, y la mía está en el campo.
His friends are English, and ours are Americans.	Los amigos de él son ingleses, y los nuestros son americanos.

These words are preceded by the Definite Article, except when used with **ser**, in a phrase meaning TO BELONG TO.

This pipe is not his ; it is mine.	Esta pipa no es de él (*or* suya),* es mía.
Those pictures are not ours.	Esos cuadros no son nuestros.
This trunk is mine.	Este baúl es mío ; BUT,
Here is your trunk ; where is mine ?	Aquí está su baúl ; ¿ dónde está el mío ?
Mine (FEM.) is on the table.	La mía está sobre la mesa.

NOTE that Possessive Pronouns take the Gender and Number of the Noun they stand for, NOT the Gender and Number of the Possessor.

* **de él, de ella,** etc., being clearer, are preferable to **suyo, suya.**

EXERCISE I.

1. This stick is not mine. 2. Is that house his ? 3. These letters are ours. 4. Your pupils are industrious, and mine are idle. 5. These pencils are hers. 6. Our friend (F.) is here, but hers has not arrived yet. 7. That key is mine. 8. Our lessons are difficult, but theirs are very easy.

39. If any emphasis is placed on the Possessive Adjectives (see par. 14), **mío, suyo,** etc, are used instead, after the Noun :

It is not HIS mistake.	No es error suyo.
It is OUR fault.	Es culpa nuestra.

40. The phrases ' of mine, of ours, of his,' etc. are also usually translated **mío, nuestro, suyo,** etc. ; as,

a relation of mine	un pariente mío
two friends of his	dos amigos suyos

41. Yours (polite form) is translated **suyo**, or (preferably) **el de Vd., la de Vd**s., etc. Examples :

He has brought my letters, but he has forgotten yours.	Ha traido mis cartas, pero ha olvidado las de Vd.
Is this cab ours, or yours (plur.) ?	¿ Es este coche nuestro, ó de Vds. ?
This hat is yours.	Este sombrero es de Vd.*
Are not those cigars yours ?	¿ No son de Vd. esos cigarros ?

42. De **Vd., de él, ae ella**, etc., are usually employed in preference to **suyo, suya, suyos, suyas**, for greater clearness.

my gloves, his and hers, **mis guantes, los suyos y los de ella.**

*Este sombrero es el de Vd. would mean ' This hat is THE ONE WHICH belongs to you ' (in contradistinction to another that does not).

The phrases **el de Vd., la de ella**, etc., must be employed in such phrases as the following :

my house or my father's	**mi casa ó la de mi padre** [amigos
our horses and our friends'	**nuestros caballos y los de nuestros**
neither his mistake nor his servant's	**ni su error ni el de su criado**

EXERCISE II.

1. my oak[1] and mahogany[2] tables ; 2. my dear[3] mother ;
3. an aunt of his ; 4. my wishes, hers, and theirs ; 5. This is
HER work (= a work of-hers). 6. He is a clerk of-mine. 7.
Is this garden yours (PLUR.) ? 8. Those keys are not yours,
they are mine. 9. Is this newspaper yours ? 10. They are
friends of-ours. 11. That is not MY mistake ; it is hers.
12. Neither[4] his shop nor[5] his neighbour's[6] is open.[7]

---

1 roble ; 2 caoba (translate: tables of oak and the of mahogany) ; 3 querido (*beloved*) ; 4 ni ; 5 ni ; 6 vecino ; 7 abierto (translate: are open).

PRON. 1 rro-blay ; 2 kah-o-bah ; 3 kay-ree-do ; 4, 5 ne ; 6 vay-thee-ao ; 7 ah-be-air-to.

THE FUTURE TENSE.

43. The Future Tense of all Regular Verbs is formed by adding to the Infinitive the following terminations :

SING.—1st Pers. 2nd Pers. 3rd Pers.   PLUR.—1st Pers. 2nd Pers. 3rd Pers.

É   ás   **Á**   **EMOS**   éis   **ÁN**

These terminations are the same as those of the Present Tense of **haber.**

The full conjugations are therefore as follow :

I shall speak	hablaré	I shall owe, etc.	deberé	I shall live, etc.	viviré
he will „	hablará		deberá		vivirá
we shall „	hablaremos		deberemos		viviremos
they will „	hablarán		deberán		vivirán

PRON. ah-blah-**ray**, ah-blah-**rah**, ah-blah-**ray**-mos, ah-blah-**rahn** ; day-bay-**ray**, etc. ; ve-ve-**ray**, etc.

Fam. Forms : hablarás, hablaréis ; deberás, deberéis ; vivirás, viviréis.

44. The Future Tense of **tener** is formed by adding these terminations to **tendr**…, and of **haber** by adding them to **habr**…

The Future Tenses of **ser** and **estar** are REGULAR.

The full conjugations are as follow :

I shall have	tendré	habré	I shall be	seré	estaré
he will „	tendrá	habrá	he will „	será	estará
we shall „	tendremos	habremos	we shall „	seremos	estaremos
they will „	tendrán	habrán	they will „	serán	estarán

PRON. ten-**dray**, etc. ; ah-**bray**, etc. ; say-**ray**, etc. ; es-tah-**ray**, etc.

F. Form : tendrás, tendréis ; habrás, habréis ; serás, seréis ; estarás, estaréis.

EXERCISE III.

1. estaremos ; 2. ¿ no tendrá (él) ? 3. ¿ hablarán Vds. ? 4. no recibiré ; 5. Vd. no beberá ; 6. ¿ hallará (ella) ? 7. escribirán. 8. shall I take ? 9. you will not have (**tener**) ; 10. will they be (**ser**) ? 11. We shall not be (**estar**) ; 12. he will divide ; 13. you will not have sold ; 14. they will smoke ; 15. shall we have sent ? 16. shall I have (**tener**) ?

COLLECTIVE EXERCISE.

1. The professor has corrected[1] my exercises,[2] but not yours. 2. Where shall you be to-morrow[3] ? 3. My friend will be [a] doctor. 4. I shall not have enough[4] money. 5. We shall speak to your father. 6. How much will you receive ? 7. My friend has sold his house, and his son's[5] ; he will now[6] live in mine. 8. I shall buy a table and six[7] chairs. 9. That mistake will be very serious.[8] 10. They will break that window.[9] 11. I shall not buy this house. 12 I shall have sent his orders[10] and his neighbours'.   13. His sister has found her gold[11] and her silver[12] rings.[13] 14. Here

is my stick ; where is yours ? 15. We have seen our mother and his, but not hers. 16. It will be his fault,[14] not yours. 17. Why have you brought[15] your umbrella, and not mine ? 18. We shall keep[16] this watch, and (shall) sell the other.[17]

1 corregir ; 2 tema (MASC.) ; 3 mañana ; 4 bastante ; 5 hijo ; 6 ahora ; 7 seis ; 8 grave ; 9 ventana ; 10 pedido ; 11 oro ; 12 plata ; 13 sortija ; 14 falta ; 15 traído ; 16 guardar ; 17 otro.

PRON. 1 kor-rray-*H*eer ; 2 tay-mah ; 3 mah-n'yah-nah ; 4 bahs-tahn-tay ; 5 ee-*H*o ; 6 ah-o-rah ; 7 say-iss ; 8 grah-vay ; 9 ven-tah-nah ; 10 pay-dee-do ; 11 o-ro ; 12 plah-tah ; 13 sor-tee-*H*ah ; 14 fahl-tah ; 15 trah-ee-do ; 16 goo'ar-dar ; 17 o-tro.

NINTH LESSON.

45.   COMPARISON OF ADJECTIVES.

more, **más** ;   less, **menos** ;   than, **que.**

PRON. mahss, may-nos, kay.

EXAMPLES.

Is the Czar more powerful than the German Emperor ?	¿ Es el Zar más poderoso que el emperador aleman ?
These flowers are less beautiful than the others.	Estas flores son menos hermosas que las otras.

The Comparative is always formed with **más**, thus :

She is worse (i.e. more ill) to-day.	Está hoy más enferma.
The climate of Norway is colder than the climate of England.	El clima de Noruega es más frio que el clima de Inglaterra.

THAN is translated by **de** before a Number, and by **de lo que** before a Verb.   Examples :

I have more than ten pounds.	Tengo más de diez libras.
His trunk is heavier than he says.	Su baúl es más pesado de lo que dice.

46.   The following Comparatives are irregular :

great, **grande**	greater, **mayor**	bad, **malo**		worse, **peor**	
small, **pequeño**	smaller, **menor**	high, tall, **alto**		higher, **superior**	
good, **bueno**	better, **mejor**	low, short, **bajo**		lower, **inferior**	

These words can also be compared regularly (**más grande**, etc.) ; but **más bueno** and **más malo** are hardly ever employed.

PRON. **grahn**-day, mah-yor ; pay-kay-n'yo, may-nor ; boo'ay-no, may-*H*or ; mah-lo, pay-or ; ahl-to, soo-pay-re-or ; bah-*H*o, in-fay-re-or

Exercise I.

1. The coffee[1] is colder than the tea.[2] 2. That man is stronger[3] than you. 3. The apples[4] are not riper[5] than the pears[6]. 4. This water is not colder than the other. 5. London is larger than Paris.[7] 6. Is not the city of Madrid smaller than Paris ? 7. This beer is very good, but the wine is better. 8. I shall not receive less than five shillings. 9. This house is cheaper than you believe.

---

1 café ; 2 té ; 3 fuerte ; 4 manzana ; 5 maduro ; 6 pera ; 7 París.

PRON. 1 kah-**fay** ; 2 tay ; 3 foo'**air**-tay ; 4 mahn-**thah**-nah ; 5 mah-**doo**-ro ; 6 **pay**-rah ; 7 pah-**riss**.

---

47. The Superlative is the same as the Comparative, but the former is always preceded by "THE" ; as,

His exercise is the worst.	Su tema es el peor.
The largest towns of France.	Las ciudades más grandes de Francia
They are the least clever of my pupils.	Son los menos hábiles de mis discípulos.

48. When MOST means VERY, EXTREMELY,* it is generally translated **muy.**

NOTE.—A more emphatic way is to add ísimo (-ma, -mos, -mas) to the Adjective, omitting final vowels (see par. 157), thus :

They are most polite.	Son muy cortéses *or* Son cortesísimos
She is most diligent.	Es muy aplicada *or* Es aplicadísima

* i.e., when it is not used in a Comparison.

Exercise II.

1. He is the idlest of your servants. 2. It is most difficult. 3. That picture is the most beautiful in[1] the collection.[2] 4. This water is the clearest.[3] 5. These windows are the smallest. 6. The smallest mistake has at times[4] most serious consequences[5]. 7. Our house is the most convenient.

---

1 IN after a Superlative is **de** : 2 colección ; 3 claro ; 4 vez ; 5 consecuencia.

   2 ko-lek-the-**on** ; 3 **klah**-ro ; 4 veth ; 5 kon-say-koo'**en**-the-ah.

---

49. as…as, tan…**como** ;   as much…as, **tanto**…**como**.

PRON. tahn, **ko**-mo ; **tahn**-to, **ko**-mo.

REMARK I.—**tan** is invariable, and is used before Adjectives and Adverbs ; **tanto** takes the Gender and Number of the following Noun.

REMARK II.—When following a NEGATION, the first AS is generally changed to SO in English ; but the Spanish is the same. The Plural of MUCH is MANY. Examples :

She is as diligent as you.	Es tan aplicada como Vd.
They are not so good as his.	No son tan buenos como los de él.
I eat as much meat as you.	Como tanta carne como Vd.
You have not found so many names as your sister.	Vd. no ha hallado tantos nombres como su hermana.

EXERCISE III.

1. Have you received as much money to-day as yesterday? 2. Your son is as clever as [he is] industrious. 3. These chairs are as cheap as those. 4. Have you as many pens as I [have] ? 5. This lady is not so tall as you. 6. He has brought as many presents[1] as she [has]. 7. We have not bought so much furniture[2] as you.

---

1 regalo ; 2 muebles (PLUR.). PRON. 1 rray-gah-lo ; 2 moo'ay-bless.

---

50. THE PAST DEFINITE is formed by adding to the STEM the following terminations :

	SINGULAR.			PLURAL.	
Verbs ending in AR :	é	aste	ó	amos	asteis	aron
„ „ ER or IR :	í	iste	ió	imos	isteis	ieron

The full conjugation is as follows :

I spoke	hablé	I owed	debí	I lived	viví
he „	habló	he „	debió	he „	vivió
we „	hablamos	we „	debimos	we „	vivimos
they „	hablaron	they „	debieron	they „	vivieron

PRON. ah-**blay**, ah-blo, ah-**blah**-mos, ah-**blah**-ron ; day-**bee**, day-be-o, day-**bee**-mos, day-be-**ay**-ron ; ve-vee, etc.

Fam. Forms : hablaste, hablasteis ; debiste, debisteis ; viviste, vivisteis.

51. The Past Definite Stem of **tener** is **tuv**…, that of **haber** is **hub**…, and that of **estar** is **estuv**…

52. Whenever the STEM of the PAST DEFINITE is irregular, the Singular terminations are the same as those of the **ar** Verbs,* and the Plural terminations the same as those of the **er** and **ir** Verbs. The STRESS in the Singular, however, is regular.

*Except the Familiar Form, where the Termination is **iste**, not **aste**.

Ser is quite irregular (see last column of table).

The full conjugations are as follow :

I	had	tuve	hube	I	was	estuve	fui
he	,,	tuvo	hubo	he	,,	estuvo	fué
we	,,	tuvimos	hubimos	we were		estuvimos	fuimos
they	,,	tuvieron	hubieron	they	,,	estuvieron	fueron

PRON. too-vay, too-vo, too-vee-mos, too-ve-ay-ron ; oo-bay, etc. ;
es-too-vay, etc. ; foo'ee, foo'ay, foo-ee-mos, foo-ay-ron.

Fam. Forms : tuviste, tuvisteis ; hubiste, hubisteis ; estuviste, estuvisteis ;
fuiste, fuisteis.

EXERCISE IV. (on the PAST DEFINITE*).

1. I sold ; 2. did they buy ? 3. you (PLUR.) received ; 4. did she not arrive ?   5. they had not (**tener**) ;   6. was he (**estar**) ? 7· did we fear ? 8. I smoked ; 9. we did not find ; 10. you were not (**ser**) ;   11. did you send ?   12. had I not (**haber**) ?   13. we wrote ;   14. you (PLUR.) had not learned ; 15. were they not in the room ?

---

* This Tense is used in speaking of an event entirely past. The Perfect Tense (see par. 36) can be employed instead, as in English, if a recent past is referred to.   Thus : I (have) received your letter this morning ;

Recibí (or He recibido) su carta esta mañana·

TENTH LESSON.

RELATIVE PRONOUNS.

Relative Pronouns relate or refer to a preceding word or sentence. In Spanish, they are the same as the Interrogative Pronouns (see Paragraphs 33, 34), except that the Relative Pronoun **cual, cuales** is preceded by the Definite Article, and that ' WHOSE,' when Relative, is usually translated **cuyo** (koo-yo), **cuya, cuyos, cuyas,** instead of **de quien.**

the gentleman whose house is there   el señor cuya casa está allí

53.   WHO, WHICH, THAT (relative) are generally translated **que.**

the man who has done this	el hombre que ha hecho esto
the girls who are downstairs	las muchachas que están abajo
the houses which they built	las casas que edificaron
the money that the child has lost	el dinero que el niño ha perdido

☞ Paragraphs 54 and 55 show when **que** is NOT employed.

54. WHOM after a Preposition is translated **quien, quienes;** as,

the person of whom you spoke	la persona de quien Vd. habló
the gentleman with whom we dined	el señor con quien comimos
the lawyer whom I shall consult	el abogado á quien consultaré

WHO is translated **quien, quienes** after part of ' TO BE ' and a Noun or Pronoun ; as,

Is it he who has made the mistake ?	¿ Es él quien ha hecho el error ?
It is this workman who smokes.	Es este obrero quien fuma.
It is we who have spoken to the banker.	Somos* nosotros quienes hemos hablado al banquero.

*Note that **ser** takes the same Number and Person as its SUBJECT.

55. WHO and WHICH, preceded by a comma,* are generally translated **el cual, la cual, los cuales, las cuales ;** as,

Your aunt, who was here yesterday, will return to-morrow.	Su tía, la cual estuvo aquí ayer, volverá mañana.

*i.e., when the Relative Sentence is as important as the Principal Sentence, not subordinate to it.

REMARK I.—If **cuál** is indirectly Interrogative, it is not preceded by the Definite Article ; as,—He does not know which of the two I shall choose, **No sabe cuál de los dos eligiré.**

REMARK II.—WHICH is translated **lo que** if referring to a preceding sentence instead of to a word. He has forgotten the pronunciation, which is not very surprising. **Ha olvidado la pronunciación, lo que no es muy estraño.**

56. The Relative Pronoun can NEVER be omitted as in English :

the man he met	**el hombre á quien encontró**
This is not the hat I bought.	**Este no es el sombrero que compré.**

The Subject in Relative Sentences is frequently put LAST, if the transposition does not make the meaning doubtful (see par. 32) as,

the windows you have broken	**las ventanas que ha roto Vd.**
the goods the shopkeeper sells	**los géneros que vende el tendero**

EXERCISE I.

1. The house you (PLUR.) have bought is more convenient[1] than mine. 2. Is this the captain[2] whose ship you have seen ? 3. The gentleman who spoke with the children is their uncle. 4. We are not sure which [ones] he will keep. 5. The

boy we saw (translate : have seen) is ill. 6. Have you forgotten the name of the gentleman I live with (=with whom I live) ? 7. He has read the letter I received, which is a pity. 8. The horse I have bought is not very strong. 9. I have brought six books, which I shall lend this evening[3] to your brother.   10. No, it is not this gentleman who is smoking.

1 conveniente ; 2 capitán ; 3 tarde (FEM.).
PRON. 1 kon-vay-ne-en-tay ; 2 kah-pe-**tahn** ; 3 **tar**-day.

57. The IMPERATIVE MOOD is formed by adding to the STEM the following terminations :

	SINGULAR.	PLURAL.
Verbs ending in **ar** :	E	emos EN
„ „ **er** or **ir** :	A	amos AN

The Imperative (Familiar Form excepted) can therefore be formed from the Present Indicative, simply by REVERSING THE TERMINATIONS ; that is, by substituting E for A in the **ar** Verbs, and A for E in the others.

The following are the full conjugations :

let us speak **hablemos** | let us owe **debamos** | let us live **vivamos**
speak **hable** (s.), **hablen** (pl.) | owe **deba, deban** | live **viva, vivan**

PRON, ah-**blay**-mos, ah-blay, ah-blen ; day-**bah**-mos, **day**-bah, day-bahn ; vee-**vah**-mos, vee-vah, **vee**-vahn.

Familiar Forms : habla, hablad ; debe, debed ; vive, vivid.

Vd. is generally added to the Polite Form of the Imperative :
Do not read the letters.   **No lea las cartas.**
Send (PLUR.) the goods.   **Manden los géneros.**
more elegantly, **no lea Vd. las cartas, manden Vds. los géneros.**

58. The Imperatives of TO HAVE and TO BE are as follow :

	tener.	haber.		ser.	estar.
let us have	tengamos	hayamos	let us be	seamos	estemos
have	tenga / tengan	haya / hayan	be	sea / sean	esté / estén

PRON. ten-gah, etc.; ah-yah, etc.; say-ah, ete.; es-tay, es-tay-mos, es-ten.
Familiar Forms : ten, tened ; hé, habed ; sé, sed ; está, estad.

59. Such phrases as ' let him speak,' ' let her owe,' ' let them live,' are usually rendered by putting **que** before the 3rd Person of the Imperative, thus :
let him wait   **que espere (él)**
let them send the wine **que manden el vino**

When LET means TO ALLOW, it is translated by **dejar.**

Let the children (=allow them to) play in th:. room.	**Dejen Vds. á los niños jugar en este cuarto.**

EXERCISE II.

1. Bebamos agua. 2. Venda (Vd.) su caballo. 3. No aguardemos. 4. No compre (Vd.) estos cigarros. 5. No guardemos estas muestras. 6. No fumen (Vds.) todavía. 7. Esté (Vd.) en tiempo. 8. ¡ Tenga (Vd.) lástima ! 9. Tome (Vd.) esta silla.

10. Lend your umbrella to my cousin. 11. Let the boy speak = allow the boy to speak. 12. Let us dine now. 13. Let them wait. 14. Let her buy the dress.[1] 15. Be there this evening. 16. Send the parcels[2] to my house. 17. Have the kindness[3] to[4] wait a little[5].

---

1 vestido ; 2 paquete ; 3 bondad ; 4 de ; 5 poco.
PRON. 1 ves-**tee**-do ; 2 pah-**kay**-tay ; 3 bon-**dahd** ; 4 day ; 5 **po**-ko.

COLLECTIVE EXERCISE.

1. Take the umbrella which is in the corner.[1] 2. Do not break the plates[2] I bought yesterday. 3. Do not forget (PL.) to[3] buy [some] tea, coffee, and sugar.[4] 4. Do not lend [any] money to that man. 5. Let us eat this fruit.[5] 6. Look[6] at[6] those shops. 7. Do not break that glass. 8. Do not let us speak to that man. 9. The person[7] for whom he works is here. 10. The officers you (have) found downstairs[8] will be here to-morrow. 11. The bread you ate is as good as this. 12. They have not received the newspapers I sent, which is very strange.[9] 13. Guess[10] which of the girls is the best. 14. I have found several[11] important[12] documents,[13] which I shall send to our lawyer. 15. Do not answer[14] (to) that question.[15] 16. Is it they who are working ? 17. Do not be so impolite.[1]

---

1 rincón ; 2 plato ; 3 de ; 4 azúcar ; 5 fruta ; 6 mirar ; 7 persona ; 8 abajo ; 9 estraño ; 10 adivinar ; 11 varios ; 12 importante ; 13 documento ; 14 contestar ; 15 pregunta ; 16 descortés.

PRON. 1 rrin-kon ; 2 plah-to ; 4 ah-**thoo**-kar ; 5 **froo**-tah ; 6 me-rar ; 7 pair-**so**-nah ; 8 ah-**bah**-*H*o ; 9 es-trah-n'yo ; 10 ah-de-ve-**nar** ; 11 **vah**-re-os ; 12 im-por-**tahn**-tay ; 13 do-koo-**men**-to ; 14 kon-tess-**tar** ; 15 pray-**goonn**-tah ; 16 dess-kor-**tess.**

ELEVENTH LESSON.

REGULAR VERBS—*(continued.)*

The six remaining Tenses are formed according to this simple Rule :

60. In the Imperfect, the Conditional, and the four Tenses of the Subjunctive, the Third Person Singular is like the First. The remainder of the Tense can always be formed by adding to the First Person Singular the following terminations :

SING.—1st Pers. 2nd Pers. 3rd Pers.   PLUR.—1st Pers. 2nd Pers. 3rd Pers.

—   s   —   **MOS**   is   **N**

These endings are the same as in the PRESENT TENSE.

☞ In all parts of the Verb except the three Present Tenses (Indicative, Imperative, and Subjunctive) the STRESS is on the
FIRST SYLLABLE OF THE TERMINATION.

61. THE IMPERFECT TENSE is formed by adding to the STEM the following terminations :

Verbs ending in **ar** : **ABA** ;   Verbs ending in **er** or **ir** : **ÍA.**

The following are the full conjugations :

I ⎫
he ⎬ was speaking *or* used to speak **hablaba**
we were   „   „   „   **hablábamos**
they were   „   „   „   **hablaban**

I was owing *or* used to owe, etc., **debía, debíamos, debían**
I was living *or* used to live, etc., **vivía, vivíamos, vivían**

PRON. ah-blah-bah, ah-blah-bah-mos, ah-blah-bahn ; day-bee-ah, day-bee-ah-mos, day-bee-ahn ; ve-vee-ah, etc.

Familiar Forms : hablabas, hablabais : debías, debíais ; vivías, vivíais.

62. The Imperfect of SER is **era, éramos, eran.**
Fam. Forms : eras, erais.   PRON. ay-rah, ay-rah-mos, ay-rahn.

Tener, haber and estar are regular in the Imperfect, thus :
tenía, etc. ;   **había,** etc. ;   **estaba,** etc.

63. HAD, WAS, WERE are generally rendered by the Imperfect Tense ; as,

he had forgotten, **había olvidado** ;   it was not mine, **no era mío**
we were not writing, **no estábamos escribiendo,** or **no escribíamos**

EXERCISE I. (on the IMPERFECT*).

1. you used to have ; 2. were they not smoking ? 3. I used not to divide ; 4. was she eating ? 5. I used to be (ser) ; 6. we were not (estar) ; 7. had you (PLUR.) not taken ? 8. used you not to smoke ? 9. we used not to be (ser) ; 10. had he dined ? 11. he was listening ; 12. used you to read ? 13. we were working ; 14. were they not calling ? 15. They were friends of mine. 16. He hadn't time. 17. We had forgotten her name.

*The Imperfect Tense is used in referring to a CONTINUOUS, an INCOMPLETE, or a FREQUENTLY REPEATED past action.

---

64. THE CONDITIONAL MOOD is formed by adding ía to the STEM of the Future, thus :

I should speak } hablaría ∣ we should speak **hablaríamos**
he would „ they would „ **hablarían**

I should owe, etc., **debería, deberíamos, deberían**
I should have, etc., **tendría**, etc. ; **habría**, etc.
I should be, etc., **sería**, etc. ; **estaría**, etc.

PRON. ah-blah-ree-ah, ah-blah-ree-ah-mos, ah-blah-ree-ahn ; day-bay-ree-ah, etc. ; ten-dree-ah, etc. ; ah-bree-ah, etc. ; say-ree-ah, etc. ; es-tah-ree-ah, etc. Familiar Forms :
hablarías, hablaríais ; deberías, deberíais ; tendrías, tendríais, etc.

REMARK.—As in the Imperfect, the Stress is invariably on the first Vowel of the Termination.

EXERCISE II. (on the CONDITIONAL).

1. they would receive ; 2. I should not find ; 3. would you believe ? 4. we should have ; 5. I should not have sold ; 6. would he be (ser) ? 7. you would not be (estar) ; 8. would you (PLUR.) not have spoken ? 9. we should break ; 10. she would not write ; 11. we should send ; 12. would you learn ?

DISJUNCTIVE PERSONAL PRONOUNS.
(i.e., NOT Object of the Verb)

65. me, **mí** ; himself, herself, itself, themselves, } **sí**
thee, **ti** ; yourself, yourselves (*Polite Form*)

These forms are used after Prepositions, thus :

for me, **para mi** ; without thee, **sin ti** ; of herself, **de si.**
conmigo is used for **con mi** (with me), **contigo** for **con ti, and
consigo** for **con si.** PRON. mee, tee, see ; kon-**mee**-go, etc.

After Prepositions, the other Pronouns retain the forms given in Paragraph 1 ; but **si** is used in preference for Pronouns of the 3rd Person, and for Vd., Vds., when the person has already been mentioned in the sentence.

by us, **por nosotros** ;   with him, **con él** *or* **consigo**
to her, **á ella** ;   for them, **para ellos** *or* **para si**
      for you, **para Vd.** *or* **para si.**

EXERCISE III.

1. for her ;   2. towards[1] us ;   3. by[2] him ;   4. of you ;   5. without[3] them (FEM.) ;   6. with you (PLUR.) ;   7. in him ;   8. at me ;   9. to her ;   10. from them ;   11. with me ;   12. by us (F.) ?   13. without him ;   14. against[4] you ;   15. among[5] yourselves ;   16. for them ;   17. with her ;   18. for yourself.

1 hacia ; 2 por ; 3 sin ; 4 contra ; 5 entre.
PRON. 1 **ah**-the-ah ; 2 por ; 3 sin ; 4 **kon**-trah ; 5 **en**-tray.

COLLECTIVE EXERCISE.

1. We were working with him.   2. We should study Spanish.   3. The milk[1] was in the jug.[2]   4. Would you speak to the merchant ? 5. The paper[3] was not good, but the pens were very good.   6. They have always[4] been with me.   7. Who used to be the captain of this ship ?   8. Used we not to have seven[5] chairs in this room ?   9. Was (PAST DEF.) it not you who brought this present for me ? 10. The spoons[6] were not ours.   11. It was (**fueron**) these soldiers who won[7] the battle.[8] 12. Was it not early[9] when he arrived ? 13. Would you buy these knives and forks[10] ?   14. I should not keep that dress. 15. He used always[4] to speak of himself. 16. We used not to travel[11] without him.   17. At what time used you to dine[12] ?   18. Take[13] your children with you.

1 leche (FEM.) ; 2 jarro ; 3 papel ; 4 siempre ; 5 siete ; 6 cuchara ; 7 ganar ; 8 batalla ; 9 temprano ; 10 tenedor ; 11 viajar ; 12 comer ; 13 llevar (*convey, carry*).
PRON. 1 **lay**-chay ; 2 *H*ar-rro ; 3 pah-**pel** ; 4 se-**em**-pray ; 5 se-ay-tay ; 6 koo-**chah**-rah ; 7 gah-**nar** ; 8 bah-**tah**-l'yah ; 9 tem-**prah**-no ; 10 tay-nay-**dor** ; 11 ve-ah-*H*ar ; 12 ko-**mair** ; 13 l'yay-**var**.

TWELFTH LESSON.

66. me, to me, **me ;**   us, to us, **nos**

thee, to thee, **te ;**   you, to you (Fam. Form), **os**

him, **lo ;**   her, **la ;**   to him, to her, **le ;**   to them, **les**

it, **lo** (MASC.), **la** (FEM.) **;**   them, **los** (MASC.), **las** (FEM.)

PRON. may, tay, lo, lah, lay ; nos, os, less, loss, lahss.

The above words (called Conjunctive Personal Pronouns) usually
PRECEDE the Verb of which they are the Object.

I have it	**lo tengo**	he does not send me	**no me envía**
do you lend us ?	**¿ nos presta Vd.?**	shall I have them ?	**¿ los tendré ?**
	I should not wait-for her	**No la esperaría**	

In the polite form of address, YOU must be rendered thus :

	MASC. SING.	FEM. SING.	MASC. PLUR.	FEM. PLUR.
YOU	lo	la	los	las
TO-YOU	le	le	les	les

I do not understand you (PLUR.)   **no los** (or **las**) **comprendo**

we send to you (PL.) **les enviamos**   he lends (to) you   **le presta**

In the Masculine Singular, **le** is often used instead of **lo**, as a
translation of YOU or HIM. But this substitution of **le** for **lo** is only
permissible when ONE MALE person is spoken to or of, thus :

Don't you believe him ?	**¿ No lo** (or **le**) **cree Vd. ?**
Don't you believe it ?	**¿ No lo cree Vd. ?**
Don't you believe her ?	**¿ No la cree Vd. ?**
Don't you believe them ?	**¿ No los** (or **las**) **cree Vd. ?**

67. In Compound Tenses, these words PRECEDE the Auxiliary, as :

He has given me ten shillings.	**Me ha dado diez chelines.**
Have you sold him your house ?	**¿ Le ha vendido Vd. su casa ?**
That man had spoken to us.	**Ese hombre nos había hablado.**

EXERCISE I.

1. We have it (F.).   2. He has taken them.   3. Do you
understand me ?   4. I shall buy it to-morrow.   5. The shopkeeper does not believe us.   6. Have you paid[1] him the bill[2] ?
7. We have seen them in the street.   8. I should not wait[3]
for[3] them.   9. Would you have sold it ?   10. My friend
will keep them (F.).   11. Your uncle had forgotten us.
12. I shall speak to you this evening.

---

1 pagar ; 2 cuenta ; 3 aguardar.   1 pah-**gar** ; 2 koo'**en**-tah ; 3 ah-goo'ar-**dar.**

68. When two Pronouns are Objects of the same Verb, the Indirect Object (i.e. the PERSON) is put first.

The Object is always Indirect when preceded by TO, or when TO can be placed before it without altering its meaning. Examples:

Does he sell it (F.) to us?	¿ Nos la vende?
He will lend it (to) me.	Me lo prestará.
My friend has not sent them to me.	Mi amigo no me los ha enviado.

69. When both the Object Pronouns are in the Third Person, the first (i.e. **le** or **les**) is changed to **se**; as,

I used to owe it (F.) to them.	(Yo) se la debía.
We often lend them to her.	Se los prestamos amenudo.
She has brought them to him.	Se los ha traído.
My clerk will send it to you.	Mi dependiente se lo enviará.
We shall not sell them to you.	No se los venderemos.

70. **á él, á ellas, á Vd.** etc., (see page 45) may be placed after the Verb, to make the meaning of **se, le** or **les** clearer, thus:

Why does he not sell it to them?	¿ Por qué no se lo vende á ellos?
The banker will lend them to him.	El banquero se los prestará á él.
Who has given you the key?	¿ Quién le ha dado la llave á Vd?
We do not owe her the money.	No le debemos el dinero á ella.

71. **á mí, á él, á nosotros, á Vd.** etc., MUST be added, as shown in the preceding paragraph, if there is any emphasis on the Indirect Object:

He has written to us and to you.	Nos ha escrito á nosotros y á Vd
I shall lend them to her, but not to her sister.	Se los prestaré á ella, pero no á su hermana.
They owe the money to me, but not to my cousin.	Me deben el dinero á mi, pero no á mi primo.

EXERCISE II.

1. They used to send it to me every day. 2. Has she sent them to us? 3. He has written to her, and (to) her mother. 4. His aunt has spoken to me, but not to you. 5. Did she read it to them yesterday? 6. The banker will lend it to them, but not to their lawyer.[1] 7. Have you explained[2] it to them? 8. I have not explained it to them yet, but I shall explain it to them to-night[3]. 9. We sell to you (PLUR.), not to them. 10. He will sell it (FEM.) to us to-morrow. 11. The clerk has not explained them (FEM.) to me.

---

1 abogado; 2 explicar; 3 *this night* (noche, FEM.).
PRON. 1 ah-bo-**gah**-do; 2 ex-ple-kar; 3 **no**-chay.

72. The Object Pronouns are placed AFTER* the Infinitive and the Present Participle ; and when they follow the Verb, they form one word with it, but do not alter the Stress. Examples :

to find them, **hallarlos**	to lend them to me, **prestármelos**
owing you (PL.), **debiéndoles**	sending it to him, **enviándoselo**

* This is optional when an Auxiliary Verb, or a Verb used as an Auxiliary, precedes. Examples : She was writing to us, **estaba escribiéndonos** ; or, **nos estaba escribiendo** ; I want to speak to you, **deseo hablarle** ; or, **le deseo hablar.**

73. The Object Pronouns are also placed AFTER the Imperative, unless it is in the Negative, thus :

buy them, **cómprelos Vd.**	do not buy them, **no los compre Vd.**
send (PL.) it to me, **envienmelo Vds.**	do not send it to me, **ne me lo envien Vds.**
lend it to her, **présteselo Vd.**	do not lend it to her, **no se lo preste** [**Vd.**

send it to them (F.), and not to me, **envíeselo Vd. á ellas, y no á mí.**

let him read it, **que lo lea** (Subjunctive, therefore Pronoun precedes).

EXERCISE III.

1. Read it to me. **2.** Read me the letter. **3.** Read that letter to us. **4.** Do not read them (FEM.) to us. **5.** Sell them your watch. **6.** Do not send her the letter. **7.** Buy (PLUR.) it. **8.** Was he speaking to you, or to your father ? **9.** Lend it to them. **10.** Do not lend him [any] money. **11.** It is not easy [to] understand him. **12.** Teach[1] (PLUR.) it to them. **13.** Do not teach[1] (PLUR.) it to them. **14.** Let him listen[2] to me.

---

1 enseñar ; 2 escuchar. PRON. 1 en-say-n'**yar** ; 2 es-koo-**char.**

COLLECTIVE EXERCISE.

1. Look at him, not at me. **2.** Let me (i.e. allow me to) have it. **3.** Why have you sold her your ring ? **4.** He will not forget you (PLUR.). **5.** Do they owe it to us ? **6.** Do not listen to him. **7.** He has not brought them (FEM.) to us. **8.** He used to lend money to you, but not to me. **9.** When shall you (PLUR.) buy it ? **10.** Who has done it ? **11.** How much money do we owe him ? **12.** I have lent them to her. **13.** He will have them to-morrow. **14.** Sell (PLUR.) them to him. **15.** Do not send it to me. **16.** Does he owe it to us ? **17.** Let us keep it. **18.** Do you expect him to-day ?

THIRTEENTH LESSON.

74. Adverbs which are formed in English by adding LY to the Adjective are formed in Spanish by adding MENTE to the Feminine Singular of the Adjective. Examples :

Adjectives { dear **caro** / easy **fácil** | Adverbs { dearly **caramente** / easily **fácilmente**

PRON. kah-rah-**men**-tay ; fah-thil-**men**-tay.

NOTE.—If two or more Adverbs ending in **mente** occur together, the termination is added to the LAST only ; as,

They have fought bravely, enthusiastically, and nobly.
Han peleado valiente, entusiástica y noblemente.

EXERCISE I.

1. surely ; 2. cheaply ; 3. heavily ; 4. coldly ; 5. cleverly ; 6. bravely ; 7. gladly[1] ; 8. doubly[2] ; 9. purely.[3]

---

1 glad, **alegre** ; 2 double, **doble** ; 3 pure, **puro**.

75. The Adverb usually follows the Verb (or the Participle in Compound Tenses), and precedes the Noun which is the Direct Object of the Verb.*

* This is customarily the case ; but the position of the Adverb is varied, as in other languages, for emphasis or euphony. It is therefore to a large extent optional. Examples:

The child does not always read.	El niño no lee siempre.
I am now writing to my uncle.	Estoy escribiendo ahora á mi tío
They often used to speak to me.	Me hablaban amenudo.
He will not find the house easily.	No hallará fácilmente la casa.

EXERCISE II.

1. Copy[1] the names carefully. 2. Are they still[2] listening ? 3. Yesterday I bought a watch, and to-morrow I shall sell it. 4. This man does not always work well. 5. Hardly[3] had I finished[4] my work when my friends arrived. 6. We always drink tea and coffee. 7. To-morrow we shall receive eight[5] pounds.[6]

---

1 copiar ; 2 aún ; 3 apenas ; 4 acabar ; 5 ocho ; 6 libra.

76. Adverbs are compared like Adjectives (see 9th Lesson) ; as,

coldly	**friamente**	easily	**fácilmente**
more coldly	**más friamente**	more easily	**más fácilmente**
the most coldly	**lo más friamente**	the most easily	**lo más fácilmente**

most surely, **muy seguramente**, *or* **segurisimamente**

H.S.S. 4.

NEGATIONS.

77. never, **nunca, jamás***; nobody, **nadie**; nothing, **nada:**
neither...nor, **ni...ni**; no, not any, **ninguno, ninguna.**

PRON. **noonn**-kah, *H*ah-**mahs**, nah-de-ay, **nah**-dah; nee, nin-**goo**-no.

When the above words follow a Verb, **no** must precede the Verb, thus:

I have never seen it.	No lo he visto nunca.
He spoke to nobody.	No habló á nadie.
I have neither your pen nor your pen- [cil.	No tengo ni su pluma ni su lápiz.
He has no houses.	No tiene ninguna† casa.

If, however, these words precede the Verb, **no** is not used; as,

Nobody has been here.	Nadie ha estado aquí.
Never will I believe that.	Jamás (*or* Nunca) creeré eso.
To-day no letter has arrived.	Hoy no ha llegado ninguna carta

EXERCISE III.

1. I shall not have any difficulty.[1]   2. Neither my husband[2] nor my son is[3] upstairs.[4]   3. The servant has neither brought coffee nor tea. 4. Nobody is downstairs. 5. I met nobody in the garden.   6. No house would be large[b] enough.[a] 7. Nothing is more certain.[5] 8. This boy understands nothing.

1 dificultad; 2 esposo; 3=*are*; 4 arriba; 5 seguro.

THE SUBJUNCTIVE MOOD.
(for Reference only)

78. The Third Person Singular of the PRESENT Subjunctive is the same as the Imperative, thus:

hable	deba	tenga	haya	sea	esté
hablemos	debamos	tengamos	hayamos	seamos	estemos
hablen	deban	tengan	hayan	sean	estén

Fam. Forms: hables, habléis; debas, debáis; tengas, tengáis; hayas, hayáis; seas, seáis; estés, estéis.

*Jamás is seldom used except with a Future Tense.

† The Plural Forms **ningunos, ningunas**, are not used.

79. The Stem of the IMPERFECT, FUTURE and CONDITIONAL
Subjunctive is obtained by taking **ron** from the 3rd Person
Plural of the Past Definite (see Paragraphs 50 to 52), thus :

habla..., debie..., vivie..., tuvie..., hubie..., fue..., estuvie...

To this STEM the following Terminations are added :

IMPERFECT **se** ; FUTURE **re** ; CONDITIONAL **ra**

The full Conjugations are therefore as follow :

IMPERFECT : hablase, hablásemos, hablasen ; debiese, etc. ;
tuviese, etc. ; fuese, etc.

FUTURE : hablare, habláremos, hablaren; debiere, etc.;
tuviere, etc. ; fuere, etc.

CONDITIONAL : hablara, habláramos, hablaran ; debiera, etc. ;
tuviera, etc. ; fuera, etc.

Fam. Forms : IMPERFECT : hablases, hablaseis, etc. ; FUTURE : hablares,
hablareis, etc. ; CONDITIONAL : hablaras, hablarais, etc.

The STRESS is always on the vowel preceding the termination
se, re *or* **ra**.

NOTE.—The Subjunctive is used under certain conditions, no matter
what the English construction is. We therefore refrain from the mis-
leading custom of giving MAY, MIGHT, etc., as the English of the
Subjunctive, because this would often be a totally incorrect translation.
The use of this Mood is explained in Lesson 24.

COLLECTIVE EXERCISE.

1. I have a blue[1] dress here. 2. He hardly[a] waited[b] a
minute.[2] 3. Perhaps I shall receive some presents to-
morrow. 4. That customer[3] has already[4] bought the lamp.
5. I shall certainly[5] speak to them to-night. 6. Did you
not find my umbrella here ? 7. Nobody is listening. 8.
He firmly[6] refused[7] [to] continue.[8] 9. Sometimes[9] I drink
beer, but I never drink wine. 10. I want principally[10] [to]
speak to him, not to his partner.[11] 11. He spoke clearly and
energetically.[12] 12. Do you expect a letter to-day ? 13. It
is of no consequence. 14. He believes nothing. 15. They
found nobody at home. 16. Never have I read [a] better[b] book.[a]

1 azul ; 2 minuto ; 3 parroquiano ; 4 ya ; 5 de seguro ; 6 firme
(Adjective) ; 7 rehusar ; 8 continuar ; 9 á veces ; 10 principal (Adjective) ;
11 socio ; 12 enérgico (Adjective).

FOURTEENTH LESSON.

80. ## CARDINAL NUMBERS.

(Those printed in **thick type** are all that need be learned.   The
remainder are Compound Numbers formed regularly.)

1 **uno** (M.), **una** (F.)	21 veintiuno*	101 ciento uno, (una, F.)
2 **dos**	veintiuna	200 doscientos (M.), dos-
3 **tres**	22 veintidos	cientas (F.)
4 **cuatro**	23 veintitres	300 trescientos, -tas
5 **cinco**	24 veinticuatro	400 cuatrocientos, -tas
6 **seis**	25 veinticinco	500 **qui**nientos, -tas
7 **siete**	26 veintiseis	600 seiscientos, -tas
8 **ocho**	27 veintisiete	700 **sete**cientos, -tas
9 **nueve**	28 veintiocho	800 ochocientos, -tas
10 **diez**	29 veintinueve	900 **no**vecientos, -tas
11 **once**	30 **treinta**	1,000 **mil**
12 **doce**	31 treintiuno, -na	1,001 mil uno, (una F.)
13 **trece**	32 treintidos,* etc.	1,100 mil cien(to) †
14 **catorce**	40 **cuarenta**	1,101 mil ciento uno
15 **quince**	50 **cincuenta**	1,200 mil doscientos, -tas
16 dieciseis*	60 **sesenta**	2,000 dos mil ‡
17 diecisiete	70 **setenta**	100,000 cien mil
18 dieciocho	80 **ochenta**	200,000 doscientos mil
19 diecinueve	90 **noventa**	1,000,000 un **millon**
20 **veinte**	100 **cien, ciento**	2,000,000 dos millones

PRON. 1 oo-no, oo-nah ; 2 doss ; 3 tress ; 4 koo'ah-tro ; 5 **thin-**ko ;
6 say-iss ; 7 se-**ay**-tay ; 8 o-cho ; 9 noo'**ay**-vay ; 10 de-eth ; i1 on-
thay ; 12 do-thay ; 13 tray-thay ; 14 kah-**tor**-thay ; 15 kin-thay ;
16 de-eth-e-**say**-iss ; 20 vay-in-tay ; 30 **tray**-in-tah, etc.

* The Compound Numbers (17 to 99, except the even tens) can also be
spelt **diez y seis, veinte y dos, cuarenta y cinco,** etc.

† The numbers 1,100, 1,200, etc., cannot be translated **oncecientos,**
etc.   The correct form is **mil cien(to), mil doscientos,** etc.

‡ **mil** employed as a Numeral has no plural ; as,
  6,000 seis mil ; BUT, **300 trescientos ; 8,000,000 ocho millones.**

81. Uno is contracted to **un** if a Noun or an Adjective follows,
and **ciento** to **cien,** unless a Numeral Adjective follows.

one man, **un hombre**	fifty-one books, **cincuentiun libros**
a hundred good sailors	**cien buenos marineros**
a hundred thousand thanks	**cien mil gracias**
a hundred million men	**cien millones de hombres**

mil and **millon** are considered as Nouns.   **de** is always placed
after **millon, millones,** if the Noun immediately follows.

82. All the Cardinal Numbers are invariable except **uno** and **cientos**, which change in the Feminine to **una, cientas :**

one woman, **una mujer** ; four hundred houses, **cuatrocientas casas.**

EXERCISE I.

1. thirty-five children ; 2. nineteen days ; 3. six weeks[1] ;
4. twelve months[2] ; 5. eighty-eight years[3] ; 6. one minute ;
7. one week[1] ; 8. ninety-seven pounds ; 9. twenty-three
shillings ; 10. eighteen pence[4] ; 11. forty-two dollars[5] ;
12. one hundred and seven books ; 13. five hundred and
seventy-three shillings ; 14. thirteen hundred and fifty-one
houses ; 15. five thousand and twelve hours[6] ; 16. sixteen
thousand seven hundred and sixty-four miles[7] ; 17. a hundred million pounds ; 18. a hundred schools[8] ; 19. five
million two hundred and eighty-six thousand four hundred
and fifteen inhabitants.[9]

1 semana ; 2 mes ; 3 año ; 4 penique ; 5 duro *or* peso ; 6 hora ;
7 milla ; 8 escuela ; 9 habitante.

83. The HOUR OF THE DAY is expressed in Spanish thus :

one o'clock, **la una** ; two o'clock, **las dos** ; five o'clock, **las cinco**, etc.
la, las are used because **hora** (hour), which is understood, is feminine.

84. QUARTER is translated **cuarto**, and HALF **media.**

PRON. koo'ar-to, may-de-ah.

Note the following expressions :
a quarter past four, **las cuatro y cuarto**
half past four, **las cuatro y media**
a quarter to five, **las cinco menos cuarto**

twelve minutes past six, **las
seis y doce**
twenty minutes to seven, **las
siete menos veinte**

85. "IT IS" is translated **es** before **la una**, and **son** before
the other hours, thus :

it is one o'clock, **es la una** ; is it half past two ? ¿ **son las dos y media ?**

EXERCISE II.

1. eleven o'clock ; 2. twenty-five minutes to eight ; 3
half past ten ; 4. a quarter to eleven ; 5. five minutes past
one ; 6. ten minutes to eight ; 7. It is a quarter past nine.
8. Is it one o'clock ? 9. It is not twelve o'clock yet. 10.
It is nineteen minutes to three.

86. The names of the Days and Months are as follow.

Sunday, **Domingo**	January, **Enero**	July, **Julio**
Monday, **Lunes**	February, **Febrero**	August, **Agosto**
Tuesday, **Martes**	March, **Marzo**	September, **Septiembre**
Wednesday, **Miércoles**	April, **Abril**	October, **Octubre**
Thursday, **Jueves**	May, **Mayo**	November, **Noviembre**
Friday, **Viernes**	June, **Junio**	December, **Diciembre**
Saturday, **Sábado**		

PRON. do-**min**-go, loo-ness, **mar**-tess, me-**air**-ko-less, *H*oo-**ay**-vess, ve-**air**-ness, **sah**-bah-do ; ay-**nay**-ro, fay-**bray**-ro, **mar**-tho, ah-**bril**, **mah**-yo, *H*oo-ne-o, *H*oo-le-o, ah-**gos**-to, sep-te-**em**-bray, ok-**too**-bray, no-ve-**em**-bray, dee-the-**em**-bray.

COLLECTIVE EXERCISE.

1. What time (trans. hour) is it ? 2. I[1] do not know[1] what time it is. 3. It is half past twelve. 4. The train starts at twenty-three minutes past eight. 5. He has travelled two hundred and eighty-one miles. 6. We have in the bank[2] £1,954 17s. 6d. 7. This country[3] has [a] hundred million inhabitants. 8. I lent them eighteen hundred and fifty pounds. 9. There[4] are[4] not [a] hundred good soldiers in the regiment.[5] 10. He will be here at ten minutes to one. 11. It is a quarter to twelve. 12. That merchant has £500,000. 13. Fourteen thousand eight hundred and fifty soldiers fought[6] in that battle. 14. It is not a quarter past three yet. 15. They have sent [off] ninety-two parcels, haven't[7] they[7] ? 16. How[8] many[8] days are[4] there[4] in a week ? 17. There[4] are[4] seven days, a hundred and sixty-eight hours, or ten thousand and eighty minutes in a week. 18. What are the names of the days ? 19. Sunday, Monday, Tuesday, Wednesday, Thursday, Friday, Saturday. 20. There[4] are[4] twelve months, or three hundred and sixty-five days, in a year. 21. The months are :—January, February, March, April, May, June, July, August, September, October, November, December.

---

1 no sé ; 2 banco ; 3 país ; 4 hay ; 5 regimiento ; 6 pelear ; 7 ¿ no es verdad ? (is it not truth ?) ; 8 cuántos ?

FIFTEENTH LESSON.

87. ORDINAL NUMBERS.

1st **primero**	6th **sexto**	11th undécimo *or* décimo
2nd **segundo**	7th **séptimo**	primero
3rd **tercero**	8th **octavo**	12th duodécimo *or* décimo
4th **cuarto**	9th **noveno, nono**	20th vigésimo [segundo
5th **quinto**	10th **décimo**	21st vigésimo primero, etc.

(The student need only learn the first ten words in the above list. Beyond the 'TENTH,' Cardinal Numbers are nearly always used in preference to the Ordinal, the latter being very lengthy and cumbrous. Thus :
the 36th page, la **página trigésima sexta** ; but better, **la página treintiseis** ; the 27th chapter = chapter 27, **el capítulo veintisiete**).

88. All the ORDINAL NUMBERS form their Feminine and Plural in the usual way, thus :

the fifth street, **la quinta calle** ; the first names, **los primeros nombres**

89. The Cardinal Numbers are used for expressing the DAYS OF THE MONTH, the first (**el primero**) excepted ; as,

the 1st of July **el primero de Julio** ; the 2nd of August **el dos de Agosto** the 11th of March **el once de Marzo** ; „ 30th of May **el treinta de Mayo**

90. In writing the date with figures, no letters corresponding to the English **th** are used after the figure, THE 1ST (1º) again excepted, thus :

London, July 1st.   **Londres, (el) 1º de Julio.**
Madrid, August 21st.   **Madrid, (el) 21 de Agosto.**

Dates can also be written thus : Agosto 21 de 1907, etc.

91. After the names of monarchs, etc., the Ordinal Numbers are used (WITHOUT the article) up to the 10th. Beyond the 10th, Cardinal Numbers are generally employed ; as,

Henry II., **Enrique II.** (segundo) ; Catherine III., **Catalina III.** (tercera) ; BUT—Louis XIV., **Luis XIV.** (catorce).

EXERCISE I.

1. the first inhabitants ; 2. the eighth part[1] ; 3. the tenth mistake ; 4. the fifth shop ; 5. the second classes[2] ; 6. the

seventh street on[3] the right[3] ;   7. the third window on[4] the left[4] ;   8. the 15th of October ;   9. the first of May ;   10. the 25th of August ;   11. Pius[5] the ninth ;   12. Isabella[6] II. ; 13. Charles[7] XII. ; 14. Paris, June 18th, 1907.

1 parte (FEM.) ; 2 clase (FEM.) ; 3 á la derecha* ; 4 á la izquierda* ; 5 Pío ; 6 Isabel ; 7 Carlos.   * Feminine, because **mano** (hand) is Feminine.

INDEFINITE ADJECTIVES AND PRONOUNS.†

92.   The following words form their Feminine and Plural in the usual way (see Paragraphs 20 and 23) :

any, some, **alguno** ;	no, none, not any, **ninguno** ;†
much,‡ **mucho**	how much ? ¿ **cuánto** ?
other, **otro** ; same, **mismo** ;	all, the whole, everything, **todo** ;
too much, **demasiado** ;	little, a few, **poco**.

PRON. ahl-goo-no ; nin-goo-no ; **moo**-cho ; koo'**ahn**-to ; o-tro ; **mis**-mo ; **to**-do ; day-mah-se-ah-do ; **po**-ko.

the other men, **los otros hombres**	much patience, **mucha paciencia**
all the ink, **toda la tinta**	many numbers, **muchos números**
how much money ? ¿**cuánto dinero** ?	the same book, **el mismo libro**
„ many streets ? ¿ **cuántas calles** ?	the same cups, **las mismas tazas**

93.   The following words do not change :

anyone, anybody, **alguien** ; nobody, **nadie** ; each, every, **cada** ; nothing, **nada** ; something, anything, **algo**.

PRON.   ahlg-e-en ; nah-de-ay ; kah-dah ; nah-dah ; ahl-go.

EXAMPLES : every three weeks, **cada tres semanas** ; is (there) any one at home ? ¿ **hay alguien en casa** ?

EXERCISE II.

1. I have found nothing.   2. A rich[1] man always has [a great] many friends.   3. They looked at it every ten minutes.   4. How many pounds[2] do I owe you ?   5. Do not drink all the water.   6. Have you bought any books to-day ? 7. Is[3] there[3] anybody upstairs ?   8. We sold it to them the other day.   9. You have too many dogs.

1 rico ; 2 libra ; 3 hay.

†see foot-notes, pages 27 and 50.   ‡ The Plural of MUCH is MANY.

94. The final o of **primero** (first), **tercero** (third), **bueno** (good), **malo** (bad), **alguno** (some, any), and **ninguno** (no, none), is omitted if a Noun immediately follows ; as,

have you any money ? ¿ tiene Vd. algún dinero ?
the first day, el primer dia ;   a good soldier, un buen soldado
BUT : a good and brave soldier, un bueno y valiente soldado

The final **A** of Feminine Forms is not omitted ; as,

the third door   la tercera puerta
This is not a good pen.   Esta no es una buena pluma.

95. When **grande** (great, large) precedes the Noun, the final de is generally omitted.

grande precedes the Noun when referring to QUALITY instead of to actual size (see Remark to Paragraph 19), thus :

a great queen, una gran reina ; a great friend of mine, un gran amigo mio ; BUT—a great (i.e., large) ship, un buque grande.

96. **Santo** (Saint) is contracted to **San** when preceding the name of a saint ; as,

St. Peter, San Pedro ;   a great saint, un gran santo

EXERCISE III.

1. a bad[a] voyage[1b] ; 2. a great[a] noise[b] ; 3. a great chimney[2]; 4. a great favor[3] ; 5. St. Paul[4] ; 6. the third boy in the first class ; 7. There[5] is[5] a little (of) coffee, but I have neither sugar nor milk. 8. He never spends [any] money here. 9. I have a bad pen, but good paper.

---

1 viaje ; 2 chimenea ; 3 favor ; 4 Pablo ; 5 hay.

COLLECTIVE EXERCISE.

1. Alexander[1] I. died[2] December 1st, 1825. 2. How much ink is[3] there[3] in the inkstands[4] ? 3. This is a good[a] boy,[b] but the others have not done any work.   4. He is the first in[5] his class, which is very large.   5. My cousins (FEM.) are almost[6] always the first in the list,[7] and my sister is the last. 6. Who was (PAST DEF.) the first King of Spain[8] ? 7. Copy every fourth line.[9] 8. How many words[10] have you (PLUR.) written ? 9. Catherine[11] II. was[12] born[12] May 2nd,

1729, and died[2] Nov. 17th, 1796.   10. This is the first time
that I have found anyone at home.   11. The second lesson
is the most difficult.   12. On[13] the contrary,[13] I think[14] that
the first lessons are very easy, and that the eighth is the most
difficult. 13. Do you not think[14] that the last[15a] chapters[16b] of
this book are very amusing[17]? 14. She was (PAST DEF.) a great
queen.[18] 15. This is the first mistake I have made to-day. 16.
I have filled[19] this inkstand,[4] and my brother has filled all the
others. 17. How many brothers have you ? I have only[20] one.

---

1 Alejandro ; 2 murió (see par. 163) ; 3 hay ; 4 tintero ; 5 de ; 6 casi ;
7 lista ; 8 España ; 9 renglón ; 10 palabra ; 11 Catalina ; 12 nació (see
par. 168) ; 13 al contrario ; 14 *use* creer (*to believe*) ; 15 último ; 16 capítulo ; 17 divertido ; 18 reina ; 19 llenar ; 20 solamente.

SIXTEENTH LESSON.

INDEFINITE ADJECTIVES & PRONOUNS (*concluded*).

97. SOME and ANY before a Noun in the Singular are either not
translated, or rendered **un poco** or **un poco de** (A LITTLE) :

He has given me some sugar. **Me ha dado un poco (de) azúcar.**

98. SOME and ANY before a Noun in the Plural (i.e. meaning **A
FEW**) are either not translated, or rendered by **unos** or
algunos ; as,

Have you any nuts ? { **¿ Tiene Vd. nueces ?** (*or* **algunas nueces**,
or **unas nueces**)

99. After a Negation, ANY is translated **ninguno**, and ANY-
BODY (or ANYONE) **nadie**, thus :

They have not built any house[s]. **No han edificado ninguna casa.**
I have not seen anybody. **No he visto á nadie.**

EXERCISE I.

1. Lend him some tools.[1]   2. We have some salt,[2] but we
have neither mustard[3] nor pepper.[4] 3. Have you not met[5]
anybody ?   4. Has the waiter[6] brought [any] bread and
cheese ? 5. My wife[7] has bought some furniture. 6. Haven't
you seen any samples to-day ?   7. This pupil hasn't [any]

ink. 8. That servant (FEM.) has broken some plates, but she has not broken any glass[es]. 9. He has given me some presents for my daughter.[8]

1 herramienta ; 2 sal (FEM.) ; 3 mostaza ; 4 pimienta ; 5 encontrar ; 6 mozo ; 7 esposa (or señora) ; 8 hija.

REFLECTIVE VERBS.

When the Object of a Verb is the same person or thing as its Subject, the Verb is called REFLECTIVE.   Examples :

NOT REFLECTIVE.

He amused me. I amuse him.
The boys amused us.

REFLECTIVE.

He amused himself. I amuse myself.
The boys amused themselves.

100. The Reflective Pronouns MYSELF, THYSELF, OURSELVES, YOURSELVES (Fam. Form), are translated **me, te, nos, os.**

Note that these are the same as the ordinary Object Pronouns (see Par. 66).

himself, herself, itself, one's self,
themselves, yourself, yourselves (Pol. Form) } are all translated **SE.**

101.   These words immediately precede or follow the Verb, in accordance with the Rules in the 12th Lesson, thus :

to wash one's self, **lavarse**
I wash myself, **me lavo**
you wash yourself, **Vd. se lava**
has the boy washed himself ? ¿ **se ha lavado el muchacho**?
wash yourself, **lávese Vd.**
do not wash yourself, **no se lave Vd.**

washing one's self, **lavándose**
we wash ourselves, **nos lavamos**
you wash yourselves, **Vds. se lavan**
the children will not wash themselves **los niños no se lavarán**
let us wash ourselves, **lavémonos***
do not let us wash ourselves, **no nos lavemos,** etc., etc.

* The final S or D of the Imperative is omitted before the Reflective Pronouns **nos** and **os.**   Thus, the Familiar Form for " wash yourselves " is **lavaos,** not **lavados.**

EXERCISE II.

1. I shall wash myself ; 2. we are not washing ourselves ; 3. have they not washed themselves ? 4. you will tire[1] yourself ; 5. she would congratulate[2] herself ;   6. do not tire[1] yourselves ; 7. has he hurt[3] himself ? 8. have you not hurt[3] yourselves ? 9. they congratulate[2] themselves ; 10. wash yourselves ; 11. the workmen used to tire[1] themselves ; 12. we shall congratulate[2] ourselves.

1 cansar ; 2 felicitar ; 3 lastimar.

102. Many Verbs are reflective in Spanish, but not in **English**.

to make a mistake, **equivocarse**	I made a mistake, **me he equivocado**
to get up, **levantarse**	he used to get up, **se levantaba**
to complain, **quejarse**	we do not complain, **no nos quejamos**
to alight, **apearse** *or* **bajarse**	you will alight, **Vd se apeara** *or* bajará

EXERCISE III.

1. do not complain ; 2. my friend has made a mistake ;
3. why do you interfere[1] ? 4. I shall interfere ; 5. they used
not to interfere ; 6. has the man escaped[2] ? 7. get up immediately[3] ! 8. I am getting[4] tired[4] ; 9. has he not alighted
yet ? 10. we should get up ; 11. let us rejoice[5] ; 12. get down
(=alight) here ; 13. they have got married.[6]

---

1 *to interfere*, meterse ; 2 *to escape*, escaparse ; 3 inmediatamente ;
4 *to get tired*, cansarse ; 5 *to rejoice*, alegrarse ; 6 *to get married*, casarse.

COLLECTIVE EXERCISE.

1. That clerk is very careless,[1] but he thinks[2] that he
never makes a mistake. 2. They alighted at the door[3] of the
church. 3. I do not complain of this, but[4] of that. 4. Why
does that boy not wash himself ? 5. I have not made a mistake
this time.[5] 6. We get up every day at half past six. 7. We
shall not interfere in that. 8. The children have behaved[6]
themselves[6] very well. 9. Your friend congratulated himself
too[7] soon.[8] 10. Do not tire yourselves. 11. We do not want
[to] tire ourselves. 12. Let us get out (= alight) at[9] this
station. 13. They sold me some good tobacco,[10] and him
some very[b] good[b] cigars.[a] 14. This is a good pupil ; he
rarely[11] makes a mistake. 15. At what time do they get up ?
16. We shall alight at the door[3] of the hotel.[12] 17. He
always gets up too[7] late.[13] 18. Don't interfere in these
matters.[14] 19. When will they get married ? 20. They
have already got married. 21. Why don't you get up ?

---

1 descuidado ; 2 creer (*to believe*) ; 3 puerta ; 4 sino (see par. 115) ;
5 *time=occasion*, vez ; 6 comportarse ; 7 demasiado ; 8 pronto ; 9 =*in* ;
10 tabaco ; 11 raramente ; 12 hotel ; 13 tarde ; 14 asunto.

SEVENTEENTH LESSON.

THE PASSIVE VOICE.

A Verb is made Passive by changing its Object into the Subject, thus:

ACTIVE VOICE.	PASSIVE VOICE.
Our mother loves us	We are loved by our mother
I did not write the letter	The letter was not written by me

103. The Passive Voice is formed in Spanish with **ser**, the Past Participle taking the Gender and Number of the Subject.

I (M.) am respected, **soy respetado**	they (F.) are not respected, **no son respetadas**
I (F.) am respected, **soy respetada**	
will she be respected? **¿ será respetada?**	were we (M.) not respected?
is he not respected? **¿ no es respetado?**	**¿ no éramos respetados?**

EXERCISE I. (on the PASSIVE VOICE).

1. they are not believed; 2. are you (FEM. SING.) not feared? 3. we were called; 4. is she loved? 5. the glasses will be broken; 6. the window was broken by the servant; 7. the queen is loved; 8. am I not believed? 9. they are not loved.

---

104. After the Passive Voice, BY is usually translated **de** if the Verb expresses a MENTAL action; otherwise **por** is used.

He was respected by all his family	**Fué respetado de toda su familia**
The houses were built by these masons	**Las casas fueron construídas por estos albañiles**

105. The Passive Voice is not much used in Spanish, the Reflective Form (or the Active Voice) being generally employed instead, thus:

it is believed	**se cree**
Spanish spoken	**se habla* español**
that house was sold	**esa casa se vendió**

* In such phrases, the Subject is often placed after the Verb.

106. The Reflective Form is also generally used in phrases like PEOPLE BELIEVE, THEY (not meaning certain persons) BELIEVE, etc.

they expect, people expect, it is expected = it expects itself, **se espera**

NOTE.—The Reflective Form should be avoided if the Verb expresses a mental action. For instance, 'the Queen is loved' is better translated **la reina es amada**, because **la reina se ama** means 'the Queen loves herself.'

Exercise II.

(In translating this Exercise, only use the Passive Voice before BY.)

1. Foreign[1] money is changed[2] in that shop.   2. Are these books lent to[3] read[3]?   3. People believe that the queen is very ill.   4. These oranges[4] are sold at sixpence a[5] dozen.[6]   5. Those masters[7] are respected[8] by their servants.   6. Milk[c] sold[b] here.[a]   7. Cigars[c] sold[b] here.[a]   8. The box[9] was (PAST DEF.) made[10] by this carpenter.   9. It is feared that the accident[11] will be serious.   10. Money lent.   11. The letters will be written by the clerk.   12. It is hoped that he will arrive to-morrow.

---

1 extranjero ;   2 cambiar ;   3 para leer = *for read(ing)* ;   4 naranja ;
5 = *the* ;   6 docena ;   7 amo ;   8 respetar ;   9 caja ;   10 hecho ;   11 accidente.

Remarks on the Stem of Regular Verbs.

107. The spelling of the STEM of some Regular Verbs is slightly altered in certain parts of the Conjugation, so that the ORIGINAL PRONUNCIATION may be preserved.   These alterations are :

VERBS ENDING IN					EXAMPLES.
car	change the **C** into **QU** before	**e**			to look for, **buscar** ; I looked for, **busqué**
gar	„	**G** „ **GU**	„	**e**	to pay, **pagar** ; let him pay, **que pague**
zar	„	**Z** „ **C**	„	**e**	to attain, **alcanzar** ; let us attain, **alcancemos**
cer or cir „		**C** „ **Z**	„	**a or o**	to conquer, **vencer** ; I conquer, **venzo**
ger or gir „		**G** „ **J**	„	**a or o**	to direct, **dirigir**; let us direct, **dirijamos**
quir	„	**QU** „ **C**	„	**a or o**	to transgress, **delinquir** ; I trangress, **delinco**
eer	change the unstressed **i** of the termination into **y**, whenever it occurs between two vowels,—see page 28.				to read, **leer** he read, **leyó** BUT : he used to read, **leía**

Exercise III.

1. they believed ;   2. let us pay[1] ;   3. Do not let us pick[2] it up[2] ;   4. I attained[3] ;   5. Let us touch[4] ;   6. let him pick[2] it up[2] ;   7. do I conquer[5] ?   8. he read ;   9. I did not read ;   10. I enjoyed[6] ;   11. touch[4] them ;   12. do not touch (PLUR.) them ;   13. do not arrive too late ;   14. pay[1] me ;   15. let

him pay ; 16. I touched ; 17. Let us conquer[5] this difficulty.
18. Pick[2] up[2] that apple.   19. Let us look for a cab.   20.
Direct[7] the letters.   21. Do not touch those books.

1 pagar ; 2 recoger ; 3 alcanzar ; 4 tocar ; 5 vencer ; 6 gozar ; 7 dirigir.

COLLECTIVE EXERCISE.

1. Newspapers sold here.   2. Pay the carpenter.[1]   3. This
window was not broken yesterday.   4. I arrived [on] the
tenth of December. 5. As[2] soon as[2] I overtook[3] him, I spoke
to him. 6. Pick up that stone ; I want [to] examine[4] it.
7. They believed that I had made a mistake. 8. Without
doubt[5] the parcels[6] will be found by the boy. 9. The message[7]
was sent to the captains.   10. Let us take[8] hold of[8] this rail[9] ;
the staircase[10] is not very safe.[11] 11. Do not let us touch the
papers, because we shall disarrange[12] them. 12. He addressed[13]
himself to his friend, but received no answer.[14] 13. It is
believed that a ship has been wrecked.[15]   14. A good
mother is loved by her children.   15. They were wounded
by the soldiers.   16. It is doubted[16] whether[17] he will have
enough patience.   17. I advanced[18] carefully towards
the horse's head.[19]   18. People believed (IMPERF.) that the
message[7] had arrived.   19. Luggage[20] is not received here.

1 carpintero ; 2 luego que or tan pronto como ; 3 alcanzar ; 4 examinar ;
5 duda ; 6 paquete ; 7 parte ; 8 coger; 9 barandilla ; 10 escalera ; 11 seguro ;
12 desarreglar ; 13 dirigir ; 14 contestación ; 15 to be wrecked, nau-
fragar ; 16 dudar; 17 si ; 18 avanzar ; 19 cabeza ; 20 equipajes (PLUR.).

EIGHTEENTH LESSON.

VERBS SLIGHTLY IRREGULAR.

108. Many Verbs change the VOWEL OF THE STEM whenever it
takes the STRESS,* but are otherwise quite Regular. These
Verbs consist of the following two classes :
    (1) Verbs which change the **E** of the Stem to **IE**
    (2)   ,,   ,,   **O** ,, ,, **UE**

* i.e., in all the Persons of the Singular, and in the Third Person Plural,
of the IMPERATIVE, PRESENT INDICATIVE and PRESENT SUBJUNCTIVE.
The remaining Tenses are perfectly Regular, as the Stress is ON THE TER-
MINATION,—see par. 60.

EXAMPLES.

to shut, **cerrar** ; to lose, **perder** ; to cost, **costar** ; to move, **mover.**

		SINGULAR.		PLURAL.	
PRES. INDIC.	I shut, etc.,	cierro	cierra	cerramos	cierran
	I lose, etc.,	pierdo	pierde	perdemos	pierden
	I cost, etc.	cuesto	cuesta	costamos	cuestan
	I move, etc.,	muevo	mueve	movemos	mueven
IMPERATIVE	shut, etc.		cierre	cerremos	cierren
	lose, etc.,		pierda	perdamos	pierdan
	cost, etc.,		cueste	costemos	cuesten
	move, etc.,		mueva	movamos	muevan
PRES. SUBJ.	that I shut, etc.,		cierre	cerremos	cierren
	,, I lose, etc.,		pierda	perdamos	pierdan
	,, I cost, etc.,		cueste	costemos	cuesten
	,, I move, etc.		mueva	movamos	muevan

The Familiar Form changes the stem vowel in the Singular, being stressed (cierras, pierdes, etc.) ; but not in the Plural, as the termination takes the Stress (cerráis, perdéis, etc.).

THE CONJUGATION OF THESE VERBS REQUIRES NO LEARNING, their terminations being perfectly regular. When once it is known that the Verb belongs to one of these groups, it is simply necessary to change the stressed vowel of the stem always,—the unstressed vowel never.

Complete lists of these groups are given in Hugo's ' Spanish Verbs Simplified.'

109. The following are the principal Verbs conjugated like **cerrar** or **perder :**

to begin, empezar	to freeze, helar*	to snow, nevar*
to commence, comenzar	to light, encender [dar	to think, pensar
to defend, defender	to recommend, recomen-	to understand, entender
to deny, negar	to sit down, sentarse	to warm, calentar

110. The following are the principal Verbs conjugated like **costar** or **mover :**

to approve, aprobar	to meet, encontrar	to remember, acordarse
to dream, soñar	to prove, probar	to return, come back, vol-
to fly, volar	to rain, llover *	to show, mostrar [ver
to go to bed, acostarse	to relate, contar	to thunder, tronar*

*Impersonal Verbs are only used in the 3rd Pers. Sing.,—see par. 129.

EXERCISE I.

1. let us shut ; 2. do not shut ; 3. it costs ; 4. they will cost ; 5. I do not move ; 6. do we move ? 7. they lose ; 8. we do not lose ; 9. it rains ; 10. is it not raining ? 11. I shall return ; 12. were you not relating ? 13. does the

child show ?   14. do not show us ;   15. we should think ;
16. do you think ? 17. I do not deny it. 18. show me ; 19.
let us sit down ;   20. Why do you not sit down ?   21. Do
you think[1] (that) it will freeze to-morrow ? 22. Let us return
home[2] ; it[b] will rain[b] soon.[a] 23. If[3] I meet him, I shall speak
to him. 24. They would come back at half past nine. 25.
It does not thunder now.   26. Why does not your servant
come back ? 27. If they deny it, I shall not believe them. 28.
Has he not lighted the fire yet ?   1 *use* creer ; 2 á casa ; 3 si.

REMARKS ON PREPOSITIONS AND CONJUNCTIONS.

111. Verbs immediately preceded by a Preposition must be in
the Infinitive ; as,

in speaking, **en hablar** | without arriving late, **sin llegar tarde**
before reading, **antes de leer** | after having seen,**después de haber visto**

112. FOR (para) is translated **por** when referring to an
EXCHANGE or EQUIVALENT ; i.e., when meaning in exchange
for, in return for :

He has given me his watch for mine. | **Me ha dado su reloj por el mio.**
I shall change this shilling for twelve pennies. | **Cambiaré este chelín por doce peniques.**

113. AND (y) is translated **é** before words commencing with **i** or
hi ; as,

He is very clever and ingenious. | **Es muy hábil é ingenioso.**
The poems and stories of this author. | **Las poesías é historias de este escritor.**

114. OR (ó) is translated **ú** before words commencing with **o** or
ho ; as,

Lend me seven or eight pounds. | **Présteme Vd. siete ú ocho libras**
Did you break it yesterday or to-day? | **¿ Lo rompió Vd. ayer ú hoy ?**

115. BUT (pero) is translated **sino** after a Negation, unless
a Verb follows ; as,

I have not seen him, but his wife. | **No le he visto á él, sino á su esposa.**   [á su socio.
BUT—I have not seen him, but I have seen his partner. | **No le he visto á él, pero he visto**

116. The Conjunction **que** (that) should not be omitted in
Spanish ; as,

I am sure it does not freeze. | **Estoy seguro que no hiela.**

H.S.S. 5.

Exercise II.

1. in working;   2. after[1] having waited;   3. silver or gold;   4. sons and daughters;   5. sons or daughters;   6. before[2] starting;   7. without drinking;   8. before[2] lending it;   9. brothers and sisters;   10. after having shown me his music[3] and instruments[4];   11. in showing them to him; 12. ten or eleven shillings;   13. Change this cup for the other.   14. It is not my fault,[5] but his.   15. The boat has not arrived to-day, but perhaps it will arrive to-morrow.

1 después de ; 2 antes de ; 3 música ; 4 instrumento ; 5 culpa.

COLLECTIVE EXERCISE.

1. His master[1] does not approve [of] his conduct.[2] **2.** Before recommending the book, I shall examine it. 3. They bought it without examining it. 4. I believed it would rain. 5. After having sat down, I related the facts[3] and incidents[4] of my voyage.   6. Is your room light[5] or dark[6]?   7. He did not show his ticket[7] to me, but to you.   8. Do you deny that the discoveries[8] and inventions[9] of this century[10] have been very useful[11]?   9. Let us begin now.   10. Do not begin yet; I am not ready.   11. Do not light the fire in my room, but shut the windows.   12. If I return in time, I will explain all my opinions[12] and ideas.[13]   13. Show me what[14] you have in your (translate : the) hand.   14. I have seven or eight shillings in my pocket.[15]   15. He sold me his ring for sixty dollars.   16. He returned last[16] week.[16]   17. Do not come back without speaking to him.   18. Warm yourself before starting.   19. How much did you receive for your watch?   20. After having done their work, they will come back.   21. He recommended a grammar[17] to us, but we have forgotten the title.[18]   22. My breakfast[19] costs me about[20] two shillings a[21] day.   23. Mine costs me more.

1 amo ; 2 conducta ; 3 hecho ; 4 incidente ; 5 claro ; 6 obscuro ; 7 billete ; 8 descubrimiento ; 9 invención ; 10 siglo ; 11 útil ; 12 opinión ; 13 idea ; 14 lo que (= *that which*) ; 15 bolsillo ; 16 la semana pasada ; 17 gramática ; 18 título ; 19 almuerzo ; 20 aproximadamente ; 21=*each*.

NINETEENTH LESSON.

IRREGULAR VERBS.

117. Verbs which differ in any respect from the regular Conjugations, either in stem or termination, are called IRREGULAR. Even the irregularities, however, are subject to certain rules; and when these rules are mastered, the Irregular Verbs present little difficulty. The following are the chief points to be remembered :—

I.—The Terminations of every Tense except the PRESENT INDICATIVE are QUITE REGULAR.*

II.—The Stem of the IMPERFECT is regular.

> Exceptions : **ir**, to go ; **ver**, to see ; **ser**, to be.

III.—The PAST DEFINITE follows the Rule in Paragraph 52.†

Exception : **ir**, to go, the Past Definite of which is the same as that of **ser**.

IV.—The IMPERATIVE (polite form) is formed by changing the final vowel of the FIRST PERSON SINGULAR of the PRESENT INDICATIVE.

> Exceptions : **ir**, to go ; **dar**, to give ; **saber**, to know.

V.—The CONDITIONAL and SUBJUNCTIVE are always formed according to the Rules in Paragraphs 64, 78, 79,—no exceptions.

☞ Therefore, to be able to conjugate any Irregular Verb in full, the Student WHO HAS LEARNT THE REGULAR CONJUGATIONS, AND THE ABOVE RULES, need only know the irregularities in the PRESENT INDICATIVE, the FUTURE and PAST DEFINITE STEMS, the Singular (familiar form) of the IMPERATIVE, and the PARTICIPLES.

We now proceed to give the important Irregular Verbs. All the irregularities are printed in **thick type**, the few exceptions to the above Rules being indicated by **CAPITALS**, and given in this lesson. TENSES FORMED ACCORDING TO OUR RULES ARE OMITTED HERE; the full conjugation of every Irregular Verb is given for reference in Hugo's 'Spanish Verbs Simplified.'

118.   to give, **dar.**

PRES. INDIC.   I give, etc., **doy**, das, da ; damos, dais, dan.
PAST DEF.   I gave, etc., **di**, **diste**, **dió** ; **dimos**, **disteis**, **dieron.**

---

* Excepting also the Singular (familiar form) of the Imperative, the final vowel of which is sometimes omitted.

† A few Verbs ending in **ir** change the Vowel of the Stem in the Third Person of the Past Definite. These will be found in the 23rd Lesson.

119.   to know, **saber.**

PRES. INDIC. I know, etc., sé, sabes, sabe ; sabemos, sabéis, saben.
PAST DEF. I knew, etc., supe, supiste, supo ; supimos, supisteis, supieron
FUTURE   I shall know, etc., sabré, sabrás, sabrá ; sabremos, sabréis,
IMPERATIVE know, etc., sabe, sEPa ; sepamos, sabed, sepan.   [sabrán.

120.   to go, **ir** (to go away, **irse**).

PRES. PARTIC. going, yendo.   PAST PARTIC. gone, ido.
PRES. INDIC. I go, etc., voy, vas, va ; vamos, vais, van.
IMPERFECT   I used to go, etc., iBa, ibas, iba ; íbamos, ibais, iban.

PAST DEF.   I went, etc., fuí, fuiste, fuÉ ; fuimos, fuisteis, fueron.
IMPERATIVE go, etc., Vé, VAYa ; vamos, id, vayan.

121. Such phrases as ' I am going ' cannot be rendered by
yendo preceded by part of **estar.** The simple Tense of **ir**
must be used, thus :

Was he not going to speak ?   ¿ No iba él á hablar ?

122. TO or AND, if preceded by part of **ir,** and followed by
another Verb, is translated **á.**

I am going to smoke, voy á fumar ; go and look for it, Vaya á buscarlo.

EXERCISE I.

1. I gave ;   2. I shall not give ;   3. do you know ?   4. he
did not go ;   5. will they know ?   6. I do not give ;   7. they
knew ;   8. let us go ;   9. I do not know;   10. going;   11. I
go ;   12. you used not to give ;   13. used they to know ?   14.
go away !   15. do you go away ?   16. we do not give ;   17. do
not give (PLUR.) ;   18. know !   19. go away (PLUR.) !   20. Let
us give him this grammar.   21.The professor is giving a lesson.
22. Go (PLUR.) to his house the[1] day after to-morrow.[1]   23.
Give it to us soon.   24. We gave it to you last[2] week.[2]   25.
Will your cousin not go to-night[3] ?   26. Do you know it ?
27. I do not know who has gone to buy them.

1 pasado mañana ; 2 la semana pasada (*past*); 3=*this night.*

123.   to say, to tell, **decir.**

PRES. PARTIC. saying, diciendo ;   PAST PARTIC. said, dicho.
PRES. INDIC. I say, etc., digo, dices, dice ; decimos, decís, dicen.
PAST DEF.   I said, etc., dije, dijiste, dijo ; dijimos, dijisteis, dijeron.
FUTURE   I shall say, etc., diré, dirás, dirá ; diremos, diréis, dirán.
IMPERATIVE say, etc., dI, diga ; digamos, decid, digan.

124.   to see, **ver.**

PRES. PARTIC.   seeing, viendo ;   PAST PARTIC.   seen, vis**to** ;
PRES. INDIC.   I see, etc., v**eo**, ve**s**, ve ;   vemos, veis, ven.
IMPERFECT   I used to see, etc., v**Eía**, ve**ías**, ve**ía** ;   ve**íamos**, ve**íais**, ve**ían**.
IMPERATIVE   see, etc.,   ve, ve**a** ;   ve**amos**, ved, vean.

125.   to err, **errar** (very rarely employed).

PRES. INDIC.   I err, etc.,   **y**erro, **y**erras, **y**erra ;   erramos, err**áis**, **y**erran.
IMPERATIVE   err, etc., **Y**erra, **y**erre ;   erremos, errad, **y**erren.

EXERCISE II.

1. let us see ;   2. they said ;   3. I do not see ;   4. shall we not tell ?   5. they say ;   6. he used to see ;   7. we do not see ;   8. what is he saying ?   9. you saw ;   10. we have told ; 11. do not say ;   12. seeing ;   13. did we say ?   14. do not see ; 15. I do not say ;   16. Go and see who is in the garden.   17. Tell me whether you are tired.   18. He has told me nothing.

COLLECTIVE EXERCISE.

1. The captain did not give anything to the sailors.   2. They told me that their clerk had no experience.[1]   3. Let us tell them what[2] we think.   4. I do not know whether they go every day by rail.[3]   5. When I go into[4] the country, I see them.   6. Let us see who has gone home.   7. He does not understand what[2] they are saying.   8. I am going to explain it to him.   9. We are going to see our uncle.   10. Go and see who is at the door.   11. He used to know several languages,[5] but he has forgotten them.   12. Tell me when he will come back. 13. Why do they not tell us the truth[6] ?   14. Go home ; your father wants to see you.   15. If I see the man, I will tell him what[2] you want. 16. We went to London last[7] year.[7] 17. They used often to go to the theatre.[8]   18. We never see our friends until[9] (the) evening.[10]   19. Why do you not give him a chair ?   20. Who told her that ?   21. I tell you it is true.[11] 22. When I saw him, he was going home. 23. I shall soon know it. 24. I never give it to him. 25. I shall go to the station to-morrow.   26. Do not give it to him, but to me.

---

1 experiencia ;   2 *what=that which* is translated ' lo que ' ;   3 ferro-carril ;   4=*to* ; 5 idioma (MASC.) ; 6 verdad ; 7 el año pasado ; 8 teatro ; 9 hasta ; 10 noche (FEM.) ; 11=*truth*, verdad.

TWENTIETH LESSON.

126.   to do, to make, **hacer.**

PAST PARTIC.   done, made, hecho.
PRES. INDIC.   I do, I make, etc., hago, haces, hace ; hacemos, hacéis, hacen.
PAST DEF.   I did, I made, etc., hice, hiciste, hizo ; hicimos, hicisteis, hi-
FUTURE   I shall do *or* make, etc., haré, harás, hará, etc.   [cieron
IMPERATIVE   do, make, etc., haz, haga ; hagamos, haced, hagan.

127.   to put, **poner.**

PAST PARTIC.   put, puesto.
PRES. INDIC.   I put, etc., pongo, pones, pone ; ponemos, ponéis, ponen.
PAST DEF.   I put, etc., puse, pusiste, puso ; pusimos, pusisteis, pu-
FUTURE   I shall put, etc., pondré, etc.   [sieron
IMPERATIVE   put, etc., pon, ponga ; pongamos, poned, pongan.

128.   to be worth, **valer.**

PRES. INDIC.   I am worth, etc., valgo, vales, vale ; valemos, valéis, valen.
FUTURE   I shall be worth, etc., valdré, etc.
IMPERATIVE   be worth, etc., val *or* vale, valga ; valgamos, valed, valgan.

EXERCISE I.

1. he would put ;   2. I do not make ;   3. let us do ;   4. do not put (PLUR.) ;   5. am I worth ?   6. they are not worth ; 7. you have put ;   8. we shall make ;   9. will it be worth ? 10. putting ;   11. they did not make ;   12. we do ;   13. did you put ?   14. I do not put ;   15. let us be worth ;   16. would it not be worth ?   17. Where shall we put them ?   18. Do not do it yet.   19. Put them in the corner.   20. Does he put his letters here ?   21. He used not to make them.   22. What have you done this morning ?   23. I am not doing anything.

IMPERSONAL VERBS.

129.   Impersonal Verbs have no person or thing as their subject, and are only used in the Third Person Singular ; as,

it is growing dark, **anochece**   it is raining, **llueve**
it does not appear, **no parece**   it thunders, **truena**

130.   Impersonal expressions are frequently constructed with **hacer, ser,** and other Verbs. Note the following :

it is hot, **hace calor** ;   it is cold, **hace frio** ;   it is windy, **hace viento**
it is certain, **es cierto** ;   it is true, **es verdad** ;   it is necessary, **es menester**

All such phrases can of course be used in any Tense, negatively and interrogatively, thus : will it be windy ? ¿ **hará viento** ? it was not true, **no era verdad** ;   is it not cold ? ¿ **no hace frio** ?

131. THERE IS, ARE, WAS, WERE, WILL BE, WOULD BE, etc., are
translated by the Third Person Singular of **haber**; but in
the Present Tense, **hay** is used instead of **ha**. Examples:

there is, there are, **hay**	there is not, there are not, **no hay**
is there? are there? ¿ **hay**?	is there not? are there not? ¿ **no hay**?
will there be? ¿ **habrá**?	there was or were not, **no habia**

there would be a great many men there, **habria alli muchos hombres**
there is no ink or there is not any ink, **no hay tinta**
there will not have been time, **no habrá habido tiempo**

NOTE.—**hay** simply expresses EXISTENCE. If anything has to be POINTED
OUT, **alli está** (there is), or **alli están** (there are) is employed.

132. If SOME, ANY (not followed by a Noun), or NONE, is
preceded by THERE IS, WAS, WILL BE, etc., it is translated like
IT or THEM. Examples:

We shall buy some cakes, if there are any. [none.	Compraremos algunos paste-les, si los hay.
I looked for some ink, but there was	Busqué tinta, pero no la habia.

133. AGO is translated **hace** (or **há***), thus:

a month ago, **hace un mes**;   three years ago, **hace tres años**

* **há** can only be used at the end of the sentence; as,

a long time ago, **mucho tiempo há**

EXERCISE II.

1. twenty years ago;   **2.** it would be worth more;   **3.**
there is no difficulty;   **4.** *there* is your hat;   **5.** was* it [the
weather] hot?   **6.** there was* no chair;   **7.** was* there a
train?   **8.** will it not be worth?   **9.** an hour ago;   **10.** *there*
are our cousins;   **11.** is it not certain?   **12.** will it be windy?
13. there will not be enough bread;   **14.** it is not hot to-day;
15. there was* no mistake;   **16.** is it [the weather] cold?   **17.**
was* it not worth more?   **18.** is there [any] water?   **19.** *there*
is the station;   **20.** six months ago;   **21.** He wanted* [some]
money, but he had* none.

---

134. mucho (much) is used with VERBS and NOUNS.

it was very hot=it made much heat   **hacia mucho calor**
it is not very windy=it does not make much wind, **no hace mucho viento**
he has not hurt me much   **no me ha lastimado mucho**

* Use the Imperfect in all these cases,—see Note on page 44.

135. muy (very) is used with ADVERBS and ADJECTIVES, and with Past Participles used as ADJECTIVES.† Examples :

Are you much hurt ?	¿ Está Vd. muy lastimado ?
The window was not much broken.	La ventana no estaba muy rota.
The prince is much beloved.	El príncipe es muy amado.

† i.e., when the Past Participle is preceded by part of ser or estar.

mucho is used instead of muy when the Participle or Adjective PRECEDES :
they are celebrated, but not very, son celebrados, pero no mucho

136. tan (see par. 49) follows the same Rules as muy, and tanto the same Rules as mucho ; as,

it is not so certain   no es tan seguro
it is as cold=it makes as much cold   hace tanto frío

137. Adjectives qualified by muy follow the Noun, thus :

it is a good pen   es una buena pluma
BUT—it is a very good pen   es una pluma muy buena

EXERCISE III.

1. they are much esteemed ; 2. are you (FEM.) fatigued[1] ? not very ; 3. a bad boy ; 4. a very bad boy ; 5. is it as windy as [it was] yesterday ? 6. I am not so satisfied as you ; 7. a very celebrated[2] painter[3] ; 8. It will be very cold ; 9. Was it not very hot ? 10. He was not much applauded[4]. 11. Is the queen much loved ? 12. I have not so much money. 13. He was as much hated[5] as his father.

---

1 fatigar ; 2 célebre ; 3 pintor ; 4 aplaudir ; 5 odiar.

COLLECTIVE EXERCISE.

1. Do me the favor[1] to wait a little. 2. Is this picture worth as much as the other ? 3. There were several[2] children who were making [a] noise. 4. Put [some] wine on the table. 5. I hope it will not be so windy. 6. I shall do it to-morrow, if I have time. 7. This beautiful[a] furniture[b] was made a hundred years ago. 8. He will put some flowers in the window. 9. The king is not so much esteemed as the queen. 10. I believe it will be very hot to-morrow. 11. I put them in the box a week ago. 12. There is no room[3] to[4] put our hats. 13. Have you put it here ? 14. There is the

stick ; give it to him.   15. There will not be enough time to[4] do it.   16. I never do it.   17. There was one picture which was very much admired[5].   18. Those are the pictures that were so much admired.   19. The travellers[6] were (IMPERF.) tired, but not very.   20. I have not put anything in the boxes.   21. What is he putting inside[7] the drawer ?   22. Why does he not do his work ?   23. I put it there now.

---

1 favor ;   2 varios ;   3 sitio ;   4 para ;   5 admirar ;   6 viajero ;   7 dentro de.

TWENTY-FIRST LESSON.

138.   to be willing to, to like *or* wish to, to like to have, **querer.**

PRES. INDIC.   I wish, I am willing, etc., quiero, quieres, quiere ; quere-
                  mos, queréis, quieren.   [mos, quisisteis, quisieron.
PAST DEF.   I wished, I was willing, etc., quise, quisiste, quiso ; quisi-
FUTURE   I shall wish, I shall be willing, etc., querré, etc.
IMPERATIVE   wish, etc., quiere, quiera ; queramos, quered, quieran.

WILL in the sense of TO BE WILLING TO is translated by **querer** ; as,
Will you lend me your umbrella ? ¿ **Quiere Vd. prestarme su paraguas?**

139.   to be able to, **poder.**

PRES. PARTIC.   being able, pudiendo.
PRES. INDIC.   I can, I am able to, etc., puedo, puedes, puede ; podemos,
                   podéis, pueden.   [pudisteis, pudieron.
PAST DEF.   I could, I was able to, etc., pude, pudiste, pudo ; pudimos,
FUTURE   I shall be able to, etc., podré, etc.

140.   CAN (and sometimes MAY) is translated by the Present
        Tense of **poder** ; as,

We cannot see the light.	No podemos ver la luz.
May I speak to you ?	¿ Puedo hablarle á Vd. ?

141.   COULD is translated by the Past of **poder** :

Could you find the house ?	¿ Pudo Vd. hallar la casa ?
They could not come yesterday.	No pudieron venir ayer.

COULD=SHOULD or WOULD BE ABLE TO is rendered by the Conditional of **poder** :   they could come to-morrow, **podrían venir mañana.**

When CAN, COULD, SHALL BE ABLE, etc., refer to an accomplishment that has to be ACQUIRED, **saber** is usually employed instead of **poder.**

Can you swim ? ¿ Sabe Vd. nadar ?   I cannot paint, No sé pintar.
They could not (=did not know how to) write, No sabían escribir.

Exercise I.

1. liking; 2. I do not want to; 3. was he able to? 4. we shall not be willing to; 5. can he? 6. will they not like to? 7. were you willing to? 8. we could (= were able to); 9. we could (= should be able to); 10. being able to; 11. do you (PLUR.) not wish to? 12. I used to be able to; 13. we do not wish to; 14. he will not be able to; 15. would she like to? 16. may we? 17. you cannot; 18. they used to like to; 19. will you? 20. would she not be able to? 21. we cannot; 22. You cannot doubt it. 23. I was not able to arrive in time. 24. He could not speak Spanish. 25. Can't the child read?

Translation of "to" before an Infinitive.

The second of two Verbs coming together must be in the Infinitive* ; as,

| I am beginning to understand it. | Empiezo á comprenderlo. |
| Do not forget to send them to us. | No olvide Vd. de enviárnoslos. |

* The Auxiliaries 'to be' and 'to have' are immediately followed by a Participle; but this Rule is otherwise invariable.

142. to before an Infinitive is generally translated **de**, unless meaning IN ORDER TO, when it is rendered by **para**.

It is time to begin.	Es tiempo de empezar.
I shall not refuse to give it to him.	No rehusaré de dárselo.
That gentleman was waiting (in order) to see you.	Ese caballero estaba esperando para verle.
He said it to prove I had made a mistake.	Lo dijo para probar que me había equivocado.
Did he bring the pictures to sell them to you?	¿Ha traído los cuadros para vendérselos á Vd.?

143. to is translated **á** after certain Verbs, of which the principal are the following:

to authorize, **autorizar**	to continue, **continuar** [**convidar**	to learn, **aprender**
to begin, **empezar**	to invite, **invitar,**	to persuade, **persuadir**
to commence, **comenzar**		to teach, **enseñar**

Also Verbs of MOTION, such as :

to run, **correr**; to go out, **salir** (IRREG.); to walk, **andar** (IRREG.); to come back, **volver** (IRREG.); to come, **venir** (IRREG.),

The ladies began to sing.	Las señoras empezaron á cantar.
I shall teach him to write.	Le enseñaré á escribir.
He ran to see who was there.	Corrió á ver quién estaba allí.

NOTE.—Paragraphs 121 and 122 apply to all Verbs of MOTION; as,
He is coming to see me to-night. **Viene á verme esta noche.**

144. TO is not translated at all after certain Verbs, of which the principal are the following :

to be able, **poder**	to make, **hacer**
to allow, to let, **dejar**	to order, to command, **mandar**
to appear, **parecer**	to owe (must, ought), **deber**
to desire, to want, **desear**	to permit, **permitir**
to fear, **temer**	please = have the kindness to, **servirse** (see par. 160.)
to feel, **sentir**	
to hear, **oir**	to promise, **prometer**
to hope, **esperar**	to see, **ver**
to intend, **intentar**	to be willing, etc., **querer**
to know (how to), **saber**	

EXAMPLES.

Was he not able to understand you ?	¿ No pudo comprenderle ?
They want to speak to us.	Desean hablarnos.
Please walk in.	Sírvase Vd. entrar.
He promised to bring it to me.	Prometió traermelo.

EXERCISE II.

1. We have invited them to dine with us. 2. It began to rain. 3. I cannot answer. 4. Will you give me your card[1] ? 5. I wrote to him yesterday to tell him you had arrived. 6. We went to see your uncle yesterday. 7. It appears to be impossible.[2] 8. He did not intend to look at them. 9. She has brought the letter home to read it. 10. I used to teach my[b] children[b] to[a] swim.[3a] 11. Do me the favor to give me a glass of water. 12. Leave off (PLUR.) talking (=cease[4] to speak).

1 tarjeta ; 2 imposible ; 3 nadar ; 4 cesar.

145. Deber used before another Verb expresses DUTY, or (a certain amount of) COMPULSION.

Tener que (or **haber de**) expresses a stronger degree of compulsion,—see Hugo's 'Spanish Verbs Simplified,' page 93.

MUST (or HAVE TO) is rendered by the PRESENT TENSE of **deber,** or by **tener que, haber de,** thus :

I must speak to them.	Debo hablarles.
I have to speak to them.	{ Tengo que hablarles. / He de hablarles. }
Must you (or are you to) copy this letter ?	¿ Debe Vd. copiar esta carta ?
Have you [got] to copy this letter ?	{ ¿ Tiene Vd. que copiar „ „ ? / ¿ Ha de copiar Vd. „ „ ? }

These expressions can be used with the same meaning in other Tenses, thus :

The servant will have to fill it.	El criado tendrá que (or habrá de) llenarlo. [bajar ?
Would they not have to work ?	¿ No tendrían que (or habrían de) tra-
I shall have to sell them=the right thing for me to do will be to sell them	deberé venderlos

146. OUGHT is rendered by the CONDITIONAL of **deber**.

In such cases, the Conditional Subjunctive is generally employed in preference to the Conditional Indicative ; but either is correct.

You ought to sell them to him.	Vd. debiera (better than debería) ven-
The children ought not to make so much noise.	dérselos. [ruido.
	Los niños no debieran hacer tanto

EXERCISE III.

1. We must go home.   2. You ought not to do that.   3. You will have to wait until (the) evening.   4. How much work have you to do ?   5. They had to start without buying their tickets.   6. Must you copy it ?   7. He has several things to do.   8. We should not have to pay so much money as you.   9. They ought not to smoke so much.

COLLECTIVE EXERCISE.

1. The soldiers ought to obey[1] the officer, but they do not always do it.   2. Why will you not show me the picture ?   3. I do not like to put it here.   4. Will you tell him your name ?   5. I cannot lend you this book ; it is not mine.   6. He had nothing to do.   7. I must teach him to speak more correctly.[2]   8. We were able to finish[3] it yesterday.   9. We could finish it to-morrow.   10. They have not been able to find them yet.   11. We (have) said it to persuade[4] him.   12. They wanted to learn to speak Spanish.   13. Run[5] and see who is at the door.   14. We could not wait to see him ; we had to go away.   15. He wanted to keep all the money for himself. 16. He will not like to come back without receiving a reply.[6]   17. You ought to give me more time.   18. Could the lawyer understand ?   19. We expect to receive a reply[6] to-morrow.   20. He wrote to me to say he had made a

mistake. 21. Would you be able to send us the goods to-day ? 22. We must ask our master now. 23. I am going to give them to him, to show[7] him that I am not offended.[8] 24. You must not sing[9] so loud.[10] 25. Cannot your friend speak German ? 26. Ought you not to invite them to dine ? 27. When shall I be able to draw[11] as well as you ? 28. I cannot play[12] the piano.[13]

---

1 obedecer ; 2 correctamente ; 3 acabar ; 4 persuadir ; 5 correr; 6 respuesta ; 7 demostrar (*demonstrate*) ; 8 ofendido ; 9 cantar ; 10 alto (*high*) ; 11 dibujar ; 12=*touch* (tocar) ; 13 piano.

TWENTY-SECOND LESSON.

147.   to come, venir.

PRES. PARTIC. coming, viniendo.
PRES. INDIC. I come, etc., vengo, vienes, viene ; venimos, venís, vienen.
PAST DEF. I came, etc., vine, viniste, vino ; vinimos, vinisteis, vinieron.
FUTURE I shall come, etc., vendré, etc.
IMPERATIVE come, etc., ven, venga ; vengamos, venid, vengan.

148.   to go out, salir.*

PRES. INDIC. I go out, etc., salgo, sales, sale ; salimos, salís, salen.
FUTURE I shall go out, etc., saldré, etc.
IMPERATIVE go out, etc., sal, salga ; salgamos, salid, salgan.

149.   to walk, andar.

PAST DEF. I walked, etc., anduve, anduviste, anduvo ; anduvimos, anduvisteis, anduvieron.

150.   to hear, oir.

PRES. PARTIC. hearing, oyendo.   PAST PARTIC. heard, oído.
PRES. INDIC. I hear, etc., oigo, oyes, oye ; oímos, oís, oyen.
PAST DEF. I heard, etc., oí, oiste, oyó ; oímos, oísteis, oyeron.
IMPERATIVE hear, etc., oye, oiga ; oigamos, oíd, oigan.

EXERCISE I.

1. I hear ; 2. do not come ; 3. did they walk ? 4. you will not go out; 5. they will come ; 6. I came ; 7. we used to walk ; 8. gone out ; 9. coming ; 10. did we hear ? 11. do not let us go out ; 12. walking ; 13. I do not come ; 14. do you (PLUR.) come ?   15. they did not hear ;   16. you will

---

*conjugated like valer.

78

hear; 17. hearing; 18. we used to come; 19. let us hear; 20. does she not go out? 21. do we come? 22. I should come; 23. do not go out (PLUR.) now. 24. I have come to see you. 25. He has heard me speak. 26. He walked very quickly.[1] 27. I am going out to see the town. 28. We shall come next[2] week.[2] 29. He heard me perfectly,[3] because I spoke slowly.[4] 30. I am coming to explain it to you. 31. Try[5] to hear what[6] is being said. 32. The noise is not often heard from[7] here.

---

1 deprisa; 2=*the week which comes*; 3 perfectamente; 4 despacio; 5 tratar; 6 lo que (WHAT is translated lo que when Relative); 7 desde.

---

151. to bring, **traer.**

PRES. INDIC. I bring, etc., traigo, traes, trae; traemos, traéis, traen.
PAST DEF. I brought, etc., traje, trajiste, trajo; trajimos, trajisteis, tra-
IMPERATIVE bring, etc., trae, traiga; traigamos, traed, traigan. [jeron.

152. to fall, **caer.**

PRES. INDIC. I fall, etc., caigo, caes, cae; caemos, caéis, caen.
IMPERATIVE fall, etc., cae, caiga; caigamos, caed, caigan.

153. to be able to be contained, **caber.***

PRES. INDIC. quepo, cabes, cabe; cabemos, cabéis, caben.
PAST DEF. cupe, cupiste, cupo; cupimos, cupisteis, cupieron.
FUTURE cabré, etc.
IMPERATIVE cabe, quepa; quepamos, cabed, quepan.

*The following examples show how this difficult Verb is employed:
This room used to hold all his furniture=All his furniture was able to be contained in this room. **Todos sus muebles cabían en este cuarto.**
There is room for me here=I am able to be contained here. **Quepo aquí.**

154. to play, **jugar.**

PRES. INDIC. I play, etc., juego, juegas, juega; jugamos, jugáis, juegan.
IMPERATIVE play, etc., juega, juegue; juguemos, jugad, jueguen.

155. The following Verbs have irregular Past Participles:

INFINITIVE.	PAST PARTICIPLE.	INFINITIVE.	PAST PARTICIPLE
to absolve, absolver	absuelto	to print, imprimir	impreso
to cover, cubrir	cubierto	to resolve, resolver	resuelto
to dissolve, disolver	disuelto	to return, come back, volver	vuelto
to open, abrir	abierto	to write, escribir	escrito

REMARK.—These eight Verbs are otherwise quite Regular, except those ending in OLVER, which are conjugated like **mover** (see paragraph 108).

156. Many Spanish Verbs have a regular and an irregular form for the Past Participle. The Irregular Form, however, is generally used as an Adjective only, the Regular Form being employed in the Compound Tenses. For complete list, see Hugo's 'Spanish Verbs Simplified,' pages 62 to 64.

to join, **juntar** : we have joined them, **los hemos juntado** ;
it is not joined, **no está junto** or **junta**

Exercise II.

1. we play; 2. do you not play? 3. I used to write; 4. have they opened? 5. we do not bring; 6. do not bring (PLUR.); 7. it is able to be contained; 8. they were not able to be contained; 9. we have not printed; 10. do not fall; 11. you have not brought; 12. it is covered; 13. hasn't he come back yet? 14. let us print it; 15. I do not open them; 16. it will not be able to be contained; 17. I have brought; 18. I do not bring; 19. you will fall; 20. do not play; 21. cover them; 22. I fall; 23. There is room[1] for all the money in this box. 24. Bring it to me now. 25. I expect they will fall. 26. Will you open the window? It is already open(ed). 27. There is not room[1] for me in this carriage. 28. Every[2] kind[2] of foreign books printed here. 29. Bring us the answer as[3] soon as possible.[3] 30. Why do you not put[4] your hat on[4]?

---

1 *use* caber ; 2=*all class* ; 3 lo antes posible ; 4 *cover yourself.*

Superlative of Adjectives and Adverbs.

157. MOST (meaning VERY, EXTREMELY) can be expressed by affixing **ísimo** (-ma, -mos, -mas) to the Adjective, omitting the final vowel. Adverbs can be formed by affixing **mente** to the Feminine Singular of the Superlative.

very difficult	dificilisimo	very easily	facilisimamente
very rare	rarísimo	very rarely	rarisimamente

The termination **ble** is changed to **bil, co** to **qu, go** to **gu,** and **z** to **c,** thus :

noble	noble	very noble	nobilísimo
nobly	noblemente	very nobly	nobilisimamente
bitter	amargo	very bitter	amarguísimo
richly	ricamente	very richly	riquisimamente

158. The most important Irregular Superlatives are as follow :

celebrated	célebre		very celebrated	celebérrimo
faithful	fiel		very faithful	fidelísimo
good	bueno		very good	bonísimo
new	nuevo		very new	novísimo
strong	fuerte		very strong	fortísimo
wise	sabio		very wise	sapientísimo

Many Adjectives, such as those of more than three syllables ending in **ble**, cannot take the **ísimo** termination, which is given here for Reference only. The Student should employ **muy**, except in the following Exercise.

EXERCISE III. (on the **ísimo** Termination).

1. most certainly ; 2. extremely happy[1] (MASC. SING.) ; 3. very happily ; 4. most rare[1] (MASC. PLUR.) ; 5. extremely good (FEM. PLUR.) ; 6. most honorable[2] (MASC. PLUR.) ; 7. with very much pleasure[3] ; 8. My dogs are most faithful. 9. These children are extremely good. 10. His answer is extremely useful. 11. It is an extremely easy [piece of] work.

---

1 raro ; 2 honorable ; 3 gusto.

COLLECTIVE EXERCISE.

1. Bring them to me as[1] soon as possible[1]. 2. He never comes very early. 3. We ought to give it to him. 4. You ought to wait a little. 5. He will not come[2] back[2] before six o'clock. 6. They came back last[3] month.[3] 7. We shall come back to-morrow[4] morning.[4] 8. We shall have to open all the windows at[5] once.[5] 9. Open the drawers. 10. There will be room[6] for the things in this box. 11. I hope they will come back soon. 12. He will have to bring it to me to-morrow[4] morning.[4] 13. At what time will the carriage come back ? 14. I have to go out to buy several things. 15. Why do you walk so slowly ? 16. I hope they will come to see us next[7] week.[7] 17. It is almost impossible to hear the noise. 18. The children are playing downstairs. 19. The train always leaves[8] at half past eight. 20. He never brings them early[b] enough.[a]

---

1 lo antes posible ; 2 volver ; 3 el mes pasado ; 4 mañana por la mañana ; 5 enseguida ; 6 *use* caber ; 7 *the week which is-coming* ; 8 *goes out.*

TWENTY-THIRD LESSON.

(The Verbs in this Lesson change the Vowel of the Stem whenever it takes the Stress, like those in Lesson 18 ; but their PRESENT PARTICIPLE, PAST DEFINITE (3rd Person), and PRESENT SUBJUNCTIVE and IMPERATIVE (1st Person Plural), contain a further irregularity in the Vowel of the STEM. For complete list, see Hugo's ' Spanish Verbs Simplified.'

159. to ask, to request, **pedir.**

PRES. PARTIC. asking, pidiendo.
PRES. INDIC. I ask, etc., pido, pides, pide ; pedimos, pedís, piden.
PAST DEF. I asked, etc., pedí, pediste, pidió ; pedimos, pedísteis, pi-
IMPERATIVE ask, etc., pide, pida ; pidamos, pedid, pidan.   [dieron.
PRES. SUBJUNC. I ask, etc., pida, pidas, pida ; pidamos, pidáis, pidan.

160. The principal Verbs conjugated like **pedir** are as follow :

to choose, **elegir**	to follow, **seguir**	to repeat, **repetir**
to clothe, **vestir**	to laugh, **reir**	to rule, **regir**
to correct, **corregir**	to measure, **medir**	to serve, **servir**
to dye, **teñir**	to prevent, **impedir**	to smile, **sonreir**

In Verbs conjugated like **pedir**, the UNACCENTED i of the termination is omitted after i or ñ, thus : laughing, **riendo** ; he laughed, **rió** ; dyeing, **tiñendo** ; they dyed, **tiñeron** ; BUT—he used to laugh, **reía** ; we used to dye, **teñíamos**, etc.

EXERCISE I.

1. you asked ; 2. we did not repeat ; 3. will he laugh ? 4. do not choose (PLUR.) ; 5. smiling ; 6. you used to laugh ; 7. do you not rule ? 8. we follow ; 9. It is not known whether he can prevent it. 10. Why are you laughing ? 11. Do not laugh. 12. Follow us.

161. to feel, to be sorry, **sentir.**

PRES. PARTIC. feeling, sintiendo.
PRES. INDIC. I feel, etc., siento, sientes, siente ; sentimos, sentís, sienten.
PAST DEF. I felt, etc., sentí, sentiste, sintió ; sentimos, sentisteis, sin-
IMPERATIVE feel, etc., siente, sienta ; sintamos, sentid, sientan. [tieron.
PRES. SUBJUNC. I feel, etc., sienta, sientas, sienta; sintamos, sintáis, sientan

162. The principal Verbs conjugated like **sentir** are as follow :

to consent, **consentir**	to (tell a) lie, **mentir**	to require, **requerir**
to defer, **diferir**	to prefer, **preferir**	to suggest, **sugerir**
to divert, **divertir**	to repent, **arrepentirse**	to wound, **herir**

H.S.S. **6.**

Exercise II.

1. did he consent ? 2. I did not suggest; 3. what did you suggest ? 4. we did not wound ; 5. they will consent also[1] ; 6. Do not defer it. 7. Which of the two do you prefer ? 8. Used he not to tell lies ? 9. He is[b] now[a] repenting. 10. Did you not feel the blow[2] ? 11. Let us repent. 12. We[3] are very sorry for it.[3] 13. I am very sorry [to] disturb[4] you.

1 también ; 2 golpe ; 3=*we feel it much* ; 4 molestar.

163. to die, **morir.**

Pres. Partic.	dying, muriendo. Past Partic. died, muerto.
Pres. Indic.	I die, etc., muero, mueres, muere; morimos, morís, mueren
Past Def.	I died, etc., morí, moriste, murió ; morimos, moristeis, mu-
Imperative	die, etc., muere, muera ; muramos, morid, mueran. [rieron.
Pres. Subjunc.	I die, etc., muera, mueras, muera ; muramos, muráis, mueran.

164. **dormir**, to sleep, is conjugated exactly like **morir**, except that its Past Participle (slept, **dormido**) is regular ; **dormirse** means to fall asleep, go to sleep.

165. Irregular Verbs and their compounds are usually conjugated alike. Examples :

suponer (to suppose)	is conjugated like	**poner**
convenir (to agree)	„	„	**venir**
contrahacer (to counterfeit)	„	„	**hacer***

* **satisfacer** (to satisfy) is also conjugated like **hacer** ; but the Singular Familiar Form of the Imperative is sometimes regular (**satisface**).

Exceptions.—All the Compounds of decir (contradecir, to contradict ; predecir, to predict, etc.) take dice instead of di in the Singular Familiar Form of the Imperative, thus : contradice. The Past Participle and the Future Stem of the Compounds of decir are regular.

Exercise III.

1. he will contradict ; 2. don't go to sleep ; 3. we sleep ; 4. they died ; 5. they did not agree ; 6. dying ; 7. I slept ; 8. you would die ; 9. used you (PLUR.) not to sleep ? 10. had he supposed ? 11. do not let us counterfeit ; 12. He died rather[1] young.[2] 13. Do you ever[3] sleep in[4] the afternoon[5] ? 14. Are the children not sleeping ? 15. I suppose so.[6]

1 algo ; 2 joven ; 3 alguna vez ; 4 por ; 5 tarde (FEM.) ; 6=*that yes.*

THE FAMILIAR FORM.

The Second Person of Verbs and Pronouns is used by Spaniards in addressing near relations, intimate friends, children, servants, and animals. A knowledge of this form of address is therefore essential, as it is of frequent occurrence in books ; but FOREIGNERS SHOULD NOT EMPLOY THE FAMILIAR FORM. Its formation has been explained in previous lessons.

EXERCISE IV. (on the FAMILIAR FORM)

1. buy (SING.) ; 2. fear (PLUR.) ; 3. thou findest ; 4. do you owe ? 5. thou dost not fear ; 6. you used to send ; 7. thou wilt break ; 8. thou wouldst not do ; 9. you have come ; 10. art thou (FEM.) ready ? 11. hast thou not put ? 12. what hast thou ? 13. you went ; 14. write (PLUR.) ; 15. are you listening ? 16. are you willing to come ? 17. you will not have ; 18. thou hadst not ; 19. had you waited ? 20. show (SING.) it to me ; 21. do (PLUR.) it ; 22. art thou not English ? 23. you are not workmen.

---

166. The Familiar Form of the Imperative cannot be used in the negative. The Present Subjunctive* (see Paragraph 78) is employed instead, thus :

speak (SING.), **habla**	do not speak (SING.), **no hables**
drink (PLUR.), **bebed**	do not drink (PLUR.), **no bebáis**

167. When the Reflective Pronoun **os** is added to the Plural Familiar Form of the Imperative, the final **d** is omitted,† thus :

wash yourselves, **lavaos** (*not* lavados) ; rejoice, **alegraos** (*not* alegrados)

EXERCISE V. (on the FAMILIAR FORM).

1. take (PLUR.) ; 2. do not take (PLUR.) ; 3. write (SING.) ; 4. do not write (SING.) ; 5. go away (SING.) ; 6. go away (PLUR.) ; 7. speak to me (SING.) ; 8. do not speak (SING.) to us ; 9. do not tire yourself ; 10. do not tire yourselves ; 11. learn (PLUR.) ; 12. do not learn (PLUR.). 13. Buy (SING.) this watch. 14. Do not sell (SING.) this watch. 15. Lend (PLUR.) me your umbrella. 16. Do not read the letter. 17. Read it (F.).

---

* The Polite Form is really the Subjunctive used as an Imperative.
† The only exception is **irse** (to go away), the Plur. Impera. of which is **idos**.

COLLECTIVE EXERCISE.

1. He asked me [for] five shillings. 2. I shall give them
to him this evening. 3. Show me what you have chosen.
4. Please[1] take [a] seat.[2] 5. When I arrived, the children
were asleep.[3] 6. I shall ask him [for] something. 7. Repeat
it. 8. Will you follow me ? 9. He never corrects us
when we make a mistake. 10. Please[1] (PLUR.) wait a little.
11. One of the two has been[4] telling lies,[4] but I don't know
which. 12. I find[5] it extremely difficult. 13. He is very sorry
he will not be able to come to-night. 14. When did he die ?
15. Please tell me the exact[6] time. 16. I cannot tell you (it);
my watch isn't going.[7] 17. I am very sorry for (=I feel much)
that accident. 18. Don't make any noise ; they are both[8]
asleep.[3] 19. I suppose they will arrive soon. 20. Repeat what
you (have) said. 21. He consented at once. 22. They laughed[9]
when we told them that. 23. He prevented us from[10]seeing it.

---

1 *Imperative of* servirse ; 2 asiento ; 3 dormido (*or* durmiendo) ; 4 *lied* ;
5 encontrar ; 6 exacto ; 7 andar ; 8 ambos ; 9 reirse ; 10 de.

TWENTY-FOURTH LESSON.

168. Verbs ending in **acer,*** **ecer, ocer,*** or **ucir,** change
the C into ZC before A or O.

to know (to be acquainted with), **conocer.**

PRES. INDIC. I know, etc., conozco, conoces, conoce ; conocemos, etc.
IMPERATIVE know, etc., conoce, conozca ; conozcamos, conoced, co-
nozcan.

169. The Verbs ending in **ducir** are also irregular in the Stem
of the Past Definite.

to translate, **traducir.**

PRES. INDIC. I translate, etc., traduzco, traduces, traduce ; traducimos, etc.
IMPERATIVE translate, etc., traduce, traduzca ; traduzcamos, traducid,
traduzcan.
PAST DEF. I translated, etc., traduje, tradujiste, tradujo ; tradujimos,
tradujisteis, tradujeron.

---

*Except **hacer** and its Compounds, and **cocer** (to cook), which is conjugated like **mover** (cuezo, cueces, cuece ; cocemos, cocéis, cuecen).

Exercise I.

1. I grow[1] ; **2.** does he not grow[1] ? **3.** it did not shine[2]; **4.** do they cook[3] ? **5.** I do not know[4] ; **6.** do not recognize[5] ; **7.** they were born[6] ; **8.** we produced[7] ; **9.** let us translate[8] ; **10.** do I not cook[3] ? **11.** shine[2] ! **12.** they deducted[9] ; **13.** used you to cook[3] ? **14.** When were you born[6] (PAST DEF.) ? **15.** Do I appear[10] to be tired ? **16.** They will translate[8] this letter in half [an] hour. **17.** I do not know[4] the price. **18.** Do you know[4] this gentleman ? **19.** I do not recognize[5] him.

1 crecer ; 2 lucir ; 3 cocer ; 4 conocer ; 5 reconocer ; 6 *to be born,* nacer ; 7 producir ; 8 traducir ; 9 deducir ; 10 parecer .

---

170. Verbs ending in **uir*** are conjugated like the following example : to destroy, **destruir.**

PRES. INDIC. I destroy, etc., destruyo, destruyes, destruye ; destruimos, destruís, destruyen.

IMPERATIVE destroy, etc., destruye, destruya ; destruyamos, destruid, destruyan.

Exercise II.

1. do you distribute[1] ? **2.** they fled[2] ; **3.** following[3] ; **4.** I do not attribute[4] ; **5.** I follow[3] ; **6.** we did not follow[3] ; **7.** you will destroy[5] ; **8.** would you (PLUR.) not distinguish[6]? **9.** I argue[7] ; **10.** you used not to distribute[1] ; **11.** Please[8] follow[3] them. **12.** Do not destroy[5] these documents.

1 distribuir ; 2 huir ; 3 seguir (see Par. 160) ; 4 atribuir ; 5 destruir ; 6 distinguir ; 7 argüir ; 8 servirse (see Pars. 144, 160).

THE INTERJECTIONS.

171. The principal Interjections are :

¡ ah ! ¡ oh ! OH ! (denoting grief)
¡ ay ! ¡ oh ! OH ! (denoting pain)
¡ chito ! ¡ chitón ! SILENCE !
¡ cuidado ! TAKE CARE !
¡ de veras ! INDEED !
¡ ea ! ¡ ánimo ! WELL ! COME ON !

¡ ha ! ¡ he ! AH ! (denoting joy)
¡ ho ! ¡ hola ! HI ! HULLO !
¡ hombre ! DEAR ME !
¡ o ! ¡ oh ! OH ! (denoting surprise)
¡ ojalá ! WOULD TO GOD !

*This form of conjugation only applies to Verbs where the **u** is pronounced ; not to such as **distinguir** (to distinguish).

THE SUBJUNCTIVE MOOD.

Write out the four Tenses of the Subjunctive Mood of the following Verbs
(see paragraphs 78, 79).

EXERCISE III.

1. tener, to have ; **2. haber,** to have ; **3. ser,** to be ; **4. estar,** to be ; **5. tomar,** to take ; **6. beber,** to drink ; **7. dar,** to give (paragraph 118) ; **8. escribir,** to write ; **9. ver,** to see (par. 124) ; **10. venir,** to come (par. 147) ; **11. poder,** to be able to (par. 139) ; **12. ir,** to go (par. 120) ; **13. decir,** to say (par. 123) ; **14. morir,** to die (par. 163).

TWENTY-FIFTH LESSON.

INTRODUCTORY REMARKS ON THE SUBJUNCTIVE.

The employment of this mood is largely a matter of taste. The Indicative would sometimes be equally correct ; and even when the Subjunctive ought to be employed, the omission to do so seldom destroys or alters the meaning of the sentence. The proper use of the Subjunctive is a GRAMMATICAL NICETY, which foreigners need not study too deeply.

The second of two Verbs connected by que must be put in the Subjunctive under certain conditions, explained in Paragraphs 172 to 190, NO MATTER WHAT THE ENGLISH WORDING IS ; and if the second Verb in English is not preceded by 'that,' the alteration in construction must be made before translating, thus :

CHANGE	INTO	
We deny their having said that.	We deny that they have said that.	Negamos que hayan dicho eso.
It is impossible for him to do it.	It is impossible that he [should] do it.	Es imposible que lo haga.
It is not fair for us to keep them.	It is not fair that we [should] keep them	No es justo que los guardemos.

The sentence following 'that' is called the DEPENDENT sentence.

EXAMPLES OF
PRINCIPAL SENTENCES and DEPENDENT SENTENCES.

it is necessary (es menester) that he should read it (que lo lea)

I am sorry (Siento) that they are not here (que no estén aqui)

☞ If the Subject of the Verb in the dependent sentence would be the same as in the principal sentence, the Infinitive, a simpler construction, is employed in preference, thus :

We deny having said that.	} Negamos haber dicho eso.
We deny that we said that.	
I am very pleased to have met you.	} Me alegro mucho de haberle
I am very pleased that I have met you.	encontrado.

EMPLOYMENT OF THE SUBJUNCTIVE MOOD.

172. The Subjunctive is used after most Verbs expressing a MENTAL ACTION OR EMOTION. Examples :

We cannot allow you to keep it (=allow that you keep it).	No podemos dejar que Vd. lo guarde.
I want them to tell me (= I wish that they tell it to me).	Quiero que me lo digan.

EXERCISE I.

1. Does he want her to read it* ? 2. They want you to accept[1] this. 3. They will not want us to keep it. 4. She wants us to stay[2] there. 5. We do not want them to hear us. 6. Do you want me to shut the door ? 7. What does he want me to do ? 8. They want us to pay the bill at[3] once.[3]

---

1 aceptar ; 2 quedarse (*to stay, to remain*) ; 3 enseguida.

* Translate : ' Does he want that she read it ?' and use the same construction (**desear**, followed by **que** and the Subjunctive) throughout the above Exercise. In all cases where the Subjunctive Mood is required in this Lesson, the PRESENT Subjunctive is to be employed.

173. The Subjunctive is used after most IMPERSONAL VERBS and expressions. Examples :

It is necessary for us to give it to them (=that we give it to them).	Es menester que se lo demos.
Is it right that the prisoners [should] be punished ?	¿ Es justo que los presos sean castigados ?
It is better that we [should] send the answer by post.	Es mejor que enviemos la respuesta por el correo.

EXERCISE II.

1. It is not necessary[1] for him to pay us (= that he pay us) much. 2. It is necessary that he [should] start[2] directly.[3] 3. It is possible that the money is his. 4. We are[4] sorry[4] that he has not found us. 5. She is[5] afraid[5] he will come. 6. Is it necessary for us to write to them ? *or*, that we [should] write to them ? 7. Do you wish[6] me to open the windows ? 8. Does he wish[6] us to put it here ?

---

1 necesario ; 2 salir (*see par.* 148) ; 3 al instante ; 4 sentir ; 5 *fears* ; 6 querer.

174. The Subjunctive is used after certain Conjunctions, of which the principal are :

after, después que ;   before, antes que ;   unless, á menos que ; in order that, á fin de que, para que ; until, hasta que ; when, cuando.

EXAMPLES :

until he arrives	hasta que llegue
before he telegraphs	antes que telegrafíe
when they send (at some future time)	cuando envíen

Cuando is only followed by the Subjunctive when it is not Interrogative, and refers to the future, thus :

When I have time, I shall do it. **Cuando tengA tiempo, lo haré.** BUT : When[ever] I have time, I do it. **Cuando tengo tiempo, lo hago.** I used to do it when I had time. **Lo hacía, cuando tenía tiempo.** I did it when I had time.   **Lo hice cuando tuve tiempo.**

EXERCISE III.

1. after he comes to see us ; 2. in order that it [may] not cost too much ; 3. before they do the work. 4. When I receive his answer, I shall show it to you. 5. I shall expect you, unless it rains. 6. When he arrives, I shall speak to him. 7. We shall send them the goods when we have time. 8. Let[1] me know[1] when you are disengaged.[2] 9. Wait until they are ready. 10. We shall pay them before they have finished[3] it. 11. They will pay his bill[4] when they have more money. 12. When he comes to see me, he never stays[5] very[6] long.[6] 13. When they come back, I shall explain it to them. 14. He always speaks to me when he sees me.

---

1 *to let know = advise, inform,* avisar ; 2 desocupado ; 3 terminar ; 4 cuenta ; 5 permanecer ; 6 *much time.*

175. The Subjunctive is generally used after the NEGATIVE FORM of Verbs.

IMPORTANT EXCEPTION : The Negative Forms of **saber** and **decir** are not followed by the Subjunctive, thus :

Don't you know he will be there ?   ¿ No sabe Vd. que estará allí ?

EXERCISE IV.

1. I do not believe he wants to go out. 2. He did not say whether he would be able to do it. 3. We do not believe he will receive any reward.[1] 4. Is it not probable[2]

that they will be able to see it ?   5. Don't you expect that his cousin will come the[3] day after to-morrow[3] ?   6. We don't expect they will bring it.   7. It is not necessary for us to copy the addresses[4] he gave us.

---

1 premio : 2 probable ; 3 pasado mañana ; 4 dirección.

TWENTY-SIXTH LESSON.

USE OF THE TENSES OF THE SUBJUNCTIVE.

176.   If the first Verb is PRESENT or FUTURE, the PRESENT Subjunctive is employed, as shown in the previous lesson.

177.   If the first Verb is PAST or CONDITIONAL, the IMPERFECT Subjunctive is employed.

We were afraid you would not receive it.	**Temimos que Vd. no lo recibiese.**
Would you like me to copy it (=would it please you that I copied it) ?	**¿ Le gustaría que lo copiase ?**

REMARK I.—The Conditional Subjunctive can often be used in place of the Imperfect Subjunctive, and *vice versâ* ; but the Imperfect is preferable after the Conjunctions mentioned in par. 174, and after Relative Pronouns.

REMARK II.—The Conditional Subjunctive is frequently substituted for the Conditional Indicative (see par. 146).

Who would have guessed that ?	**¿ Quién hubiera adivinado eso ?**
You ought to explain it to them.	**Vd. debiera explicárselo.**

EXERCISE I.

1. I didn't think[1] he had come.   2. We wish[2] they hadn't begun.   3. I wish[2] she were not here.   4. Did he want[3] me to do it ?   5. It was not necessary for them to speak. 6. He would have denied that his brother was there. 7. I should like to have more money.

---

1 use 'creer' ; 2 render as 'should like' (Conditional of 'desear') ; 3 Imperfect of 'desear.'

---

178.   The Imperfect Subjunctive is used after **si** (if), when the other clause of the sentence is in the Conditional.

We should give them a prize, if they were more industrious.	**Les daríamos un premio, si fuesen más aplicados.**

179. When **si** (if) means 'whether,' it is followed by the Conditional of the INDICATIVE. Examples:

I did not know if they would come.	**No sabia si vendrian.**
He asked me if I could lend him ten pounds.	**Me preguntó si podria prestarle diez libras.**

180. The FUTURE Subjunctive may be used, if it refers to the future ; but this Tense is very seldom employed.

I will do it, if I can. **Lo haré si pudiere** (*far better*, **si puedo**).

EXERCISE II.

1. I should help[1] him, if I were less busy.[2] 2. He would copy it, if he had more time. 3. We should pay them at once, if we had enough money. 4. If he were here, I should give them to him. 5. I should work better, if I had better tools.[3] 6. Ask them if (=whether) they will be at[4] the station to-night. 7. Do you know if he lives in Madrid now ?

1 ayudar ; 2 ocupado ; 3 herramienta ; 4 en.

AUGMENTATIVE AND DIMINUTIVE TERMINATIONS

are added to Nouns (and occasionally to Adjectives) to qualify their meaning ; but as the use of these terminations presents great difficulties, foreigners should always employ Adjectives instead. The following are the principal :

181. **on, azo, acho, ote** express LARGENESS, the three latter also implying some degree of DISPROPORTION and AWKWARDNESS.

hombrón, a big man ; **hombrazo,** a tall, badly built man ; **mujerona,*** a big woman.

182. **ito, ico, illo, uelo** express SMALLNESS, **ito** implying in addition NICENESS, FONDNESS, and **uelo** CONTEMPT. Examples :

señorita,* an unmarried lady ; **Pedrillo,** little Peter ;
perrillo, a little dog ; **perruelo,** a cur.

* All these terminations have a Feminine Form.

THE PLURAL OF NOUNS (see also par. 4).

183. Nouns of more than one syllable which end in **s**, and do not take the stress on the last syllable, are alike in the Singular and Plural, thus :

the umbrella, **el paraguas ;** the umbrellas, **los paraguas.**

184. Nouns ending in **í** (accented) add **es,** thus :

the ruby, **el rubí ;** the rubies, **los rubíes.**

FURTHER RULES ON THE SUBJUNCTIVE MOOD.
FOR REFERENCE ONLY.

185. The Subjunctive is generally used after **quienquiera que** (whoever), **cualquiera que** (whatever), and **donde quiera que** (wherever).

I shall not believe it, whoever says so.   **No lo creeré, quienquiera que lo diga.**

186. The Subjunctive is also used in a wish or imprecation.

Long live the King !   ¡ **Viva el rey !**
Thy Kingdom come !   ¡ **Venga Tu reino !**
May he arrive in time !   ¡ **Qué llegue á tiempo !**

A preceding Verb is understood in such sentences, thus :
Quiero que viva el rey, Deseo que llegue á tiempo.

187. The Subjunctive is used after a Superlative, and words equivalent to Superlatives, such as **primero** (first) and **último** (last).

Give it to the first man that comes.   **Déselo Vd al primer hombre que venga.**

188. The Verb is put in the Indicative if it expresses a CERTAIN FACT instead of a doubtful contingency. Compare the following :

although (= even if) he writes to me   **aunque me escriba**
although it is late, I shall not go away   **aunque es tarde, no me iré**

189. The following are the principal Verbs expressing a MENTAL EMOTION which are followed by the Subjunctive (unless the Infinitive can be substituted,—see page 86).

aconsejar, to advise
alegrarse, to be glad
avisar, to advise
consentir, to consent
decir, to tell (only when meaning ' to order ')
dejar, to allow
desear, to want
dudar, to doubt

esperar, to hope
evitar, to prevent
impedir, to prevent
insistir, to insist
intentar, to intend
negar, to deny
pedir, to request
permitir, to permit
preferir, to prefer

prohibir, to prohibit
querer, to wish
regocijarse, to rejoice
rogar, to entreat
sentir, to regret
sorprenderse, to be surprised
suplicar, to entreat
temer, to fear

190. The Subjunctive is used after the following Conjunctions, in addition to those given on page 88.

although, **aunque**
except, **salvo que, excepto que**
for fear that, **por miedo que**
however, **por mas que**
in such a way that, **de modo que, de manera que**

in case, **en caso que**
notwithstanding, **no obstante que**
provided that, **con tal que**
supposing that, **(su)puesto que**
whether, **sea que**
without, **sin que**

VOCABULARY.

The Numbers indicate the Paragraphs in which the Conjugations of IRREGULAR VERBS, and the various ways of translating PRONOUNS, etc., are given.

The Cardinal and Ordinal NUMBERS, and the names of the DAYS and MONTHS, will be found in Lessons 14 and 15.

The Gender of Nouns is only given when it is not in accordance with the Rule in Paragraph 5.

A, AN, un, una, 6
to be able to, 139
accident, accidente
to address, dirigir
to admire, admirar
after, después de
afternoon, tarde, FEM.
against, contra
ago, 133
to agree, 165
to alight, apearse, 102
all, todo, 92
to allow, dejar
almost, casi
already, ya
also, también
altar, altar
always, siempre
among, entre
amusing, divertido
anchor, ancla
and, y, 113
answer, contestación
to answer, contestar
any, 6, 92, 97 to 99, 132
anybody, anyone, 93, 99
to appear, parecer, 168
to applaud, aplaudir
apple, manzana
to approve, 110
are there ? hay ?
to arrive, llegar
as, 49, 136
as many, as much, 49
as soon as, luego que
to ask (enquire), preguntar
to ask (request), 159

asleep, dormido, durmiat, á ; at the, 8 [endo
at home, en casa
at once, ahora
to attain, alcanzar
attentive, atento
aunt, tía
author, escritor

BAD, malo, 19, 94
badly, mal
bank, banco
banker, banquero
battle, batalla
to be, 17
beautiful, hermoso
because, porque
been, estado
beer, cerveza
before, antes de
to begin, 109 [portarse
to behave one's self, como believe, creer
better, best, mejor
bill, cuenta
bird, pájaro
black, negro
blue, azul
boat, buque, bote
book, libro
to be born, nacer, 168
both, ambos, ambas
bottle, botella
bought, comprado
box, caja
boy, muchacho
brave, valiente
bread, pan

to break, romper
breakfast, almuerzo
to bring, 151
broken, roto
brother, hermano
brought, traído
but, pero, 115
to buy, comprar
by, por, 104

CAB, coche
to call, llamar
can, 140, 141
capacious, capaz
captain, capitán
careful, cuidadoso
careless, descuidado
carpenter, carpintero
carriage, coche
to carry, llevar
cat, gato
cause, causa
celebrated, célebre
certain, seguro
chair, silla
to change, cambiar
chapter, capítulo
cheap, barato
cheese, queso
child, niño
child=son, hijo
to choose, 160
church, iglesia
cigar, cigarro
city, ciudad
class, clase, FEM.
clear, claro
clerk, dependiente

clever, hábil
to close, cerrar, 108
coffee, café
cold, frío, 130
collection, colección
to come, 147
to come back, 110
to commence, 109
to complain, quejarse
concert, concierto
to congratulate, felicitar
to conquer, vencer
to consent, 162   [cia
consequence, consecuen-
to be able to be con-
  tained, 153
to continue, continuar
to contradict, 165
on the contrary, al con-
  trario
convenient, conveniente
to cook, cocer, 108
to copy, copiar
corner, rincón
to correct, 160
to cost, 108
could, 141
to count, contar, 110
country, campo
cousin, primo
to cover, 155
cup, taza
customer, parroquiano

DARK, obscuro
daughter, hija
day, día, MASC.
the day after to-morrow
  pasado mañana
dear, caro
to defer, 162
delicious, delicioso
to deny, 109
to destroy, 170
to die, 163
difficult, difícil
difficulty, dificultad
diligent, diligente
to dine, comer
dinner, comida
to direct, dirigir

directly, al instante
to discover, descubrir,
distinct, distinto   [155
to divert, 162
to divide, dividir
to do, 126
doctor, médico
document, documento
dog, perro
dollar, duro, peso
done, hecho
door, puerta
double, doble
doubt, duda
to doubt, dudar
downstairs, abajo
dozen, docena
drawer, cajón
to dream, 110
dress, vestido
to drink, beber
dry, seco

EACH, cada
ear, oreja
early, temprano
easily, fácilmente
easy, fácil
to eat, comer
English, inglés
to enjoy, gozar
enough, bastante
envelope, sobre
to escape, escaparse
to esteem, estimar
evening, tarde, FEM. ;
  noche (night), FEM.
every, cada
every day, todos los días
everything, todo
to examine, examinar
exercise, tema, MASC.
to expect, esperar
experience, experiencia
to explain, explicar
explanation, explicación
eye, ojo

FACT, hecho
faithful, fiel
to fall, 152

father, padre
to fatigue, fatigar
fault, culpa, falta
favor, favor
to fear, temer
to feel, 161
to fight, pelear
to fill, llenar
to find, hallar
to finish, acabar, termi-
fire, fuego   [nar
firm, firme
floor, suelo
flower, flor, FEM.
fog, niebla
to follow, 160
for, para, 112
foreign, extranjero
to forget, olvidar
fork, tenedor
France, Francia
to freeze, 109
French, francés
friend, amigo
from, de ;   from the, 8
fruit, fruta
full, lleno
furniture, muebles, PLU.
future, futuro

GARDEN, jardín
general, general
gentleman, señor, caba-
German, alemán [llero
to get up, levantarse
girl, muchacha
to give, 118
given, dado
glass, vaso
glove, guante
to go, go away, 120
to go out, 148
gold, oro
good, bueno, 19, 94
goods, géneros, PLUR.
grammar, gramática
great, grande, 95
greater, 46
to grow, crecer, 168
growing, creciendo
to guess, adivinar

HALF, medio
hand, mano, FEM.
happy, feliz
hardly, apenas
hat, sombrero
to have, 2, 11
to have to, 145
he, él
head, cabeza
to hear, 150
heavy, pesado
her, to her, 14, 15, 66
here, aquí
hers, 38 to 42
herself, 65, 100
high, alto
him, to him, 66
himself, 65, 100
his, 14, 15, 38 to 42
home, á casa
at home, en casa
to hope, esperar
horse, caballo
hot, cálido, 130
hotel, hotel
hour, hora
house, casa
how ? como ?
how much ? cuánto ?
how many, 92
to hurt, lastimar
husband, esposo

I, yo
idle, holgazán
if, si
ill, enfermo   [tamente
immediately, inmedia-
important, importante
impossible, imposible
in, en   [aplicado
industrious, laborioso,
inhabitant, habitante
ink, tinta
inkstand, tintero
to intend, intentar
to interfere, meterse
to invite, convidar
is there ? hay ?
Italian, italiano
it, 66 ; its, 14, 15

itself, 65, 100

JOURNEY, viaje
jug, jarro

to **KEEP**, guardar
key, llave, FEM.
kindness, bondad
king, rey
knife, cuchillo
to know, 119, 168

LADY, señora
lamp, lámpara
large, grande, 95
last, último
late, tarde
to laugh, 160
lawyer, abogado
lazy, holgazán
to learn, aprender
to leave=start, salir, 148
on the left, á la izquierda
to lend, prestar
less, menos
lesson, lección
to let, dejar, 59
letter, carta
to (tell a) lie, 162
to lie down, acostarse,
light (NOUN), luz   [110
light (ADJECT.), claro
to light, 109
to like, 138
list, lista
to listen, escuchar
listening, escuchando
little, pequeño
a little, un poco
to live, vivir
London, Londres
to look at, mirar
to look for, buscar
looking for, buscando
to lose, 108
to love, amar
low, bajo
luggage, equipajes

MADE, hecho
to make, 126

to make a mistake, equi-
man, hombre   [vocarse
many, 92
to get married, casarse
master, amo
may, 140
me, 65, 66
meat, carne, FEM.
to meet, encontrar, 110
merchant, comerciante
message, parte
met, encontrado
milk, leche, FEM.
mine, 38 to 40
minute, minuto
mistake, error, 102
money, dinero
month, mes
more, más
morning, mañana
most, 47, 48, 157
mother, madre
to move, 108
much, 92, 134, 135
music, música
must, 145
mustard, mostaza
my, 14, 15 ; myself, me

NAME, nombre
near, cerca de
nearly, casi
necessary, necesario
neighbour, vecino
neither, ni
nephew, sobrino
never, jamás, nunca, 77
new, nuevo
newspaper, periódico
niece, sobrina
night, noche, FEM.
no, no
no, none, 92, 132
nobody, nadie
noise, ruido
nor, ni
not, no
nothing, nada
now, ahora
number, número
nut, nuez

to OBEY, obedecer, 168
o'clock, 83
of, de
of the, 8
officer, oficial
often, amenudo
on, sobre
at once, enseguida
one's self, se, 100
only, solamente
open, abierto
to open, abrir, 155
opinion, opinión
or, ó, 114
orange, naranja
order, pedido
to order, mandar
other, otro
ought, 146
our, 14, 15
ours, 38 to 40
ourselves, nos
to overtake, alcanzar
to owe, deber

PAGE, página
painter, pintor
paper, papel
parcel, paquete
part, parte, FEM.
partner, socio
patience, paciencia
to pay, pagar
pear, pera
pen, pluma
pencil, lápiz, MASC.
penny, penique
pepper, pimienta
perhaps, tal vez
to permit, permitir
person, persona
to pick up, recoger
picture, cuadro
pin, alfiler
pipe, pipa
pity, lástima
plate, plato
to play, 154
please, sirva(n)se, see
pleasure, gusto [page 84
pocket, bolsillo

to possess, poseer
possible, posible
postman, cartero
pound, libra
to prefer, 162
present, regalo
to prevent, 160
price, precio
prince, príncipe
principal, principal
to print, 155
professor, profesor
to promise, prometer
proof, prueba
to prove, 110
pupil, discípulo
to put, 127

QUARTER, cuarto
queen, reina
question, pregunta
quickly, deprisa

RAIL, barandilla
rail(way), ferrocarril
to rain, llover
rare, raro
to read, leer
ready, listo
to receive, recibir
to recommend, 109
red, rojo
to refuse, rehusar
regiment, regimiento
to rejoice, alegrarse
to relate, 110
to repeat, 160
to repent, 162
reply, respuesta
to reply, contestar
to resolve, 155
to respect, respetar
to return, 110
rich, rico
on the right, á la derecha
ring, sortija
ripe, maduro
room, cuarto, habitación
room (space), sitio, 153
to rule, regir, 160
to run, correr

SAFE, seguro
said, dicho
sailor, marinero
saint, 96
salt, sal, FEM.
same, mismo, 92
sample, muestra
to satisfy, 165
to say, 123
scarcely, apenas
school, escuela
to see, 124
to seek, buscar
to seem, parecer, 168
seen, visto
to sell, vender
to send, enviar, mandar
serious, grave
servant, criado
to serve, 160
several, varios
she, ella
shilling, chelín
ship, buque
shoe, zapato
shop, tienda
shopkeeper, tendero
short, bajo
to show, enseñar, 110
to shut, 108
silver, plata
to sing, cantar
sir, señor, caballero
sister, hermana
to sit down, 109
to sleep, 164
slowly, despacio
small, pequeño, 46
to smile, 160
to smoke, fumar
smoking, fumando
to snow, 109
so, 49, 136
soldier, soldado
some, 6, 92, 97, 98, 132
something, algo
sometimes, á veces
son, hijo
soon, pronto
as soon as, luego que
to be sorry, 161

Spain, España
Spanish, español
to speak, hablar
speaking, hablando
to spend, gastar
spoken, hablado
spoon, cuchara
to start, salir, 148
station, estación
stick, bastón
still, aún
stone, piedra
street, calle, FEM.
strong, fuerte
to study, estudiar
studying, estudiando
sugar, azúcar
to suggest, 162
to supply, surtir
to suppose, 165
sure, seguro

TABLE, mesa
to take, tomar
taken, tomado
tall, alto
tea, té
to teach, enseñar
to tell, 123
than, que
thank you, gracias
that (CONJ. & REL.) que
that (DEMONST.), 29, 30
the, 6, 7
theatre, teatro
thee, 65, 66
their, 14, 15
theirs, 38 to 42
them, to them, 66, 69
themselves, 65, 100
then, entonces
there, allí, 131
there is, are, etc., 131
these, 29
they, ellos, ellas
thing, cosa
think, creer, 109
this, 29, 30 ; those, 29
thou, tú
to throw, tirar
to thunder, 110

thy, 14, 15
thyself, te
ticket, billete
time, tiempo
time = occasion, vez
time (of day), hora
to tire, cansar
tired, cansado
to get tired, cansarse
to, á (and page 74)
to the, 8
to-day, hoy
to-morrow, mañana
to-night, esta noche
tobacco, tabaco
told, dicho
too, demasiado
too much, too many, 92
tool, herramienta
to touch, tocar
towards, hacia
town, ciudad
train, tren
to travel, viajar
traveller, viajero
truth, verdad

UGLY, feo
umbrella, paraguas
uncle, tío
to understand, com-
    prender
until, hasta
upstairs, arriba
us, to us, 66
useful, útil

VERY, muy, 134, 137
vessel, buque
village, aldea
voyage, viaje

to **WAIT** (for), aguar-
    dar, esperar
waiter, mozo, criado
waiting, aguardando,
    esperando
to walk, 149
to want, desear, 138
to warm, 109
to wash, lavar

watch, reloj
water, agua
way, camino
we, nosotros
week, semana
well, bien
what ? ¿ qué ?
what (RELATIVE) lo que
when, cuando
where, donde
whether, si
which, 34, 53, 55
white, blanco
who, 33, 53, 54, 55
whole, todo
whom ? 33, 54
whose, 33
why ? ¿ por qué ?
wife, esposa, señora
to be willing to, 138
to win, ganar
wind, viento
window, ventana
windy, 130
wine, vino
wing, ala
wish, deseo
to wish, 138
with, con
without, sin
woman, mujer
word, palabra
work, trabajo
to work, trabajar
workman, obrero
worse, peor, 46
to be worth, 128
to wound, 162
to write, escribir, 155
writing, escribiendo
written, escrito

YEAR, año
last year, el año pasado
yes, sí
yesterday, ayer
yet, todavía
you, to you, 1, 66
your, 14, 15, 16
yours, 41, 42
yourself, -ves, 65, 100

SPANISH READING SIMPLIFIED.

A COLLECTION OF
AMUSING ANECDOTES, etc.,
with
COPIOUS FOOT-NOTES on EVERY PAGE,
rendering a
DICTIONARY UNNECESSARY.

THE ONLY FULLY ANNOTATED READER IN EXISTENCE.

PUBLISHED BY

Hugo's Institute for Teaching Foreign Languages,
33 GRACECHURCH STREET, LONDON, E.C. ; and Branches.

INSTRUCTIONS TO STUDENTS.

The Student is assumed to know the ARTICLES and NOMINATIVE PERSONAL PRONOUNS (Lesson 1 in "Spanish Simplified"), the POSSESSIVE ADJECTIVES (Lesson 3) and PRONOUNS (Lesson 8), the DEMONSTRATIVE ADJECTIVES and PRONOUNS (Lesson 6), the INTERROGATIVE ADJECTIVES and PRONOUNS (Lesson 7), the RELATIVE PRONOUNS (Lesson 10), the NUMBERS (Lessons 14 and 15), the PRESENT TENSES of 'tener, haber, ser, estar,' and of the REGULAR VERBS (Lessons 1 to 5), and a few words of very frèquent occurrence. He should also know the ordinary way of forming the FEMININE and PLURAL; and it would be advisable to read carefully through Lesson 12 in our Grammar, before beginning this Reader.

A number after a word refers to the English translation at the foot, which bears the same number. If several words are translated together, the number is given after the first word and the last. The literal translations are followed by a translation in good English, preceded by the sign =

Nouns are translated in the SINGULAR, and Regular Verbs in the INFINITIVE.

PREFACE.

In the study of Languages, the importance of READING the Foreign Idiom as soon as possible is universally admitted.

Unfortunately, every year thousands of students give up the attempt in despair. Very few have the time and perseverance required to search for every word in a Dictionary. A beginner takes three or four hours to go through an ordinary page under these circumstances; and even then it is doubtful whether he has translated correctly.

"HUGO'S SIMPLIFIED READERS" have been compiled to prevent this great waste of time. By their aid, a beginner —after a few weeks' study of our Grammar—can easily translate a page in less than half an hour, WITH THE CERTAINTY THAT HE HAS NOT MISTAKEN THE MEANING OF A SINGLE PHRASE. This is ensured by the copious foot-notes, every word being translated until it has occurred several times. An extensive Vocabulary is thus acquired without effort.

The contents consist of interesting Anecdotes, etc., which amuse the student, as well as instructing him. In selecting, dry extracts from classical authors have been carefully avoided, it being of far more practical use to acquire the language as spoken and written at the present time.

Compilers of Reading Books usually explain the absence of notes by the statement that looking out words in a Dictionary impresses them better on the memory. This is a very poor excuse. The real reason is that ONE PAGE WITH CAREFULLY PREPARED NOTES INVOLVES AS MUCH LABOR AS A DOZEN UNANNOTATED PAGES, and therefore cannot be produced without much trouble and expense.

Most Reading Books are of no more use to the average student than a newspaper or an ordinary book, as it is nearly as much trouble to refer to a Dictionary as to a Vocabulary on a different page; whereas the copious notes in Hugo's Readers, being always at hand for instantaneous reference, make these books invaluable to the learner.

LIST of WORDS
not translated in the Foot-Notes.

Á, to, at
akora, now
al, to the, at the
aili, there
amigo, friend
aquel. that
aquellos, those
aqui, here
ayer, yesterday

Bien, well
buen(o), good

Caballero, sir, gentleman
caballo, horse
calle, street
carta, letter
casa, house
catorce, fourteen
cien(to), hundred
cinco, five
cincuenta, fifty
ciudad, town, city
como, as, how, like, what
con, with
cosa, thing
criado, servant
cual, which
cuando, when
cuarenta, forty
cuarto, room, fourth
cuatro, four
cuchillo, knife
cuyo, whose

De, of, from, to, with
deber, (to) owe
décimo, tenth
del, of the, from the
dia, day
diez, ten

dijo, (he) said *or* told
dinero, money
Dios, God
doce, twelve
donde, where
dos, two

El, the
él, he, him, it
ella, she, her, it
ellos, they, them
en, in, on
entre, between, among
ese, that
esos, those
español, Spanish
este, this
estos, these

Gran(de), great, large

Hablar, (to) speak
hermano, brother
hijo, son
hombre, man
hora, hour, time
hoy, to-day

La, las, the
lección, lesson
libro, book
lo, los, the

Madre, mother
mal(o), bad, ill
mañana, morning, to-morrow
más, more, most
menos, less, least
mi, my
mí, me
mil, thousand
mío, mine

mismo, same
muchacho, boy
mucho, much
muchos, many
mujer, woman
muy, very

Niño, child
no, no, not
noche, night
nono, ninth
nosotros, we, us
noventa, ninety
nuestro, our(s)
nueve, nine
nuevo, new

ó, ú, or
ochenta, eighty
ocho, eight
octavo, eighth
once, eleven
otro, other

Padre, father
papel, paper
para, for, (in order) to
pequeño, small, little
pero, but
pluma, pen
poco, little, a few
por, by, for
porque, because
por qué, why
primer(o), first
puerta, door

Que, which, what, who, that, than
quien, who, whom
quince, fifteen
quinto, fifth

Reloj, watch, clock
rey, king

Segundo, second
seis, six
señor, gentleman, sir, Mr.
señora, lady, madam, Mrs.
sesenta, sixty
sesto, sixth
setenta, seventy
sétimo, seventh
si, if, whether
sí, yes
siete, seven
sin, without
sobre, on, upon
soldado, soldier
sombrero, hat
su, his, her, its, your, their
suyo, his, her(s), your(s), their(s)

Tercer(o), third
tiempo, time
tinta, ink
todo, all
trabajar, to work
trabajo, work
trece, thirteen
treinta, thirty
tres, three
tu, thy
tú, thou, thee
tuyo, thine

Un(o), a, an, one
unos, some, any
usted, Vd., you

Veinte, twenty
vez, time
vivir, (to) live
vosotros, you
vuestro, your(s)

Y, é, and
yo, I

La Hospitalidad.*

Un soldado preguntó[2] á[0] uno de sus camaradas,[3] que volvía[4] de una campaña,[5] si había[6] hallado[7] mucha[1] hospitalidad[1] en Holanda.[1]—¡Oh! sí, mucha,[1] respondió[1]; todo el tiempo que he estado[8] allí lo[0] he pasado[9] en el hospital.

---

0 not to be translated ; 1 the same, or nearly the same, as in English.

2 asked ; 3 comrade ; 4 was returning ; 5 campaign ; 6 (he) had ; 7 found ; 8 been ; 9 passed.

La Cuna.[2]

Una pobre[3] mujer pidió[4] un día limosna[5] á un caballero muy alto[6] con unos piés[7] desmesurados,[8] y le[9] dijo, viendo[10] que no la[13] quería[11] socorrer,[12] que por el amor[14] de Dios le[16] diese[15] al menos[17] uno de sus zapatos.[18]

¡Cómo[19]! ¿ uno de mis zapatos[18] ?   ¿ Y qué quiere[20] Vd. hacer[21] con él ?

Haré[22] una cuna[2] para mi niño.

---

2 cradle ; 3 poor ; 4 asked ; 5 alms ; 6 tall ; 7 foot ; 8 huge ; 9 (to) him ; 10 seeing ; 11 (he) would ; 12 succour ; 13 her ; 14 love ; 15 he should give ; 16 her ; 17 least ; 18 shoe ; 19 what ; 20 will ; 21 do ; 22 (I) shall make.

El Charlatán.

Un charlatán[1] de los[2] que venden[3] específicos[1] universales,[1] mandó[4] á buscar[5] á[0] un médico[6] porque[7] estaba[8] malo.[9] Llegó[10] el médico,[6] y luego[11] que[11] le[13] vió[12] le[13] dijo[14] que no[15] tenía nada,[15] y que podía[16] haberse excusado[16] de llamarle[17] por una cosa tan[18] frívola.[1]

¿ Cómo[19] frívola[1] ? respondió[1] el charlatán,[1] ¿ sabe[20] Vd.[20] que por descuido[21] he tomado[22] una de mis píldoras[23] ?

---

2 those ; 3 sell ; 4 sent ; 5 seek ; 6 physician ; 7 because ; 8 (he) was ; 9 ill ; 10 arrived ; 11 as soon as ; 12 (he) saw ; 13 (to) him ; 14 (he) said ; 15 (he) had nothing=nothing was the matter with him ;   16 (he) might have excused himself (=avoided) ; 17 call(ing) him ; 18 so ; 19 how ; 20 do you know ; 21 carelessness ; 22 taken ; 23 pill.

* English words ending in *ty* usually end in *dad* in Spanish.

El Valor.

Un hombre, que se[2] había vanagloriado[2] de su valor,[1] huyó[3] en cierta[4] ocasión[1] de su contrario,[5] y uno de los testigos[6] de sus fanfarronadas,[7] que le[8] vió[8] correr,[9] le[11] gritó[10] : ¿ Dónde está ese valor[1] ? y él, sin dejar[12] de correr,[9] le[11] replicó[13] : *En las piernas.*[14]

---

0 not to be translated ; 1 the same, or nearly the same, as in English.

2 had bragged ; 3 fled ; 4 (a) certain ; 5 opponent ; 6 witness ; 7 boast ; 8 saw him ; 9 run ; 10 called out ; 11 to him ; 12 =ceasing ; 13 replied ; 14 leg.

El Aldeano[2] y los Monos.[3]

Un aldeano[2] que llevaba[4] de[5] parte[5] de su amo[6] al señor[7] del pueblo[8] de[9] regalo[10] un canasto[11] de peras,[12] encontró[13] en la escalera[14] dos grandes monos[3] con vestidos[16] azules[15] bordados[17] de oro[18] y espada[19] ceñida,[20] que se[21] arrojaron[21] á la fruta[1] en[22] cuanto[22] la[24] vieron.[23] Como[25] el aldeano[2] no[0] había[26] visto[28] nunca[27] esta especie[1] de animales,[1] se[29] quitó la montera[29] con mucha[1] cortesía,[1] y les[31] dejó[30] hacer[32] lo[33] que quisieron.[33]

Apénas[34] agarraron[35] los monos[3] algunas[36] peras[12] cuando se[37] marcharon[37] á comerlas,[38] y tomando[39] entonces[40] su canasto,[11] se[41] presentó[41] al señor.[7] Este[42] notó[43] la falta[44] y preguntóle[45] en qué consistía,[46] á lo[0] que contestó[48] el labriego[47] :

" Señor, lleno[50] venía,[49] pero los señoritos,[51] vuestros hijos, han tomado[52] las[53] que faltan,[54] y quedan[55] comiéndolas[56] en la escalera.[14]—Algunos[36] criados que habían[26] sido[57] testigos[58] del lance,[59] descubrieron[60] la sencillez[61] del aldeano,[2] que fué[62] muy celebrada[1] en la casa, y todo el pueblo[8] se[63] rió[63] de ella.

---

2 villager ; 3 monkey ; 4 was taking ; 5=on the part ; 6 master ; 7 squire ; 8 village ; 9=as a ; 10 present ; 11 basket ; 12 pear ; 13 encountered ; 14 stair-case ; 15 blue ; 16 dress ; 17 embroidered ; 18 gold ; 19 sword ; 20 girded ; 21 flung themselves=darted ; 22 immediately ; 23 they saw ; 24 it ; 25 as ; 26 had ; 27 never ; 28 seen ; 29 he took off his cap ; 30 let ; 31 them ; 32 do ; 33 what they liked ; 34 hardly ; 35 seized ; 36 some ; 37 they marched off ; 38 eat them ; 39 taking ; 40 then ; 41 he presented himself ; 42 =the latter ; 43 noticed ; 44 deficiency ; 45 asked him ; 46 it consisted ; 47 peasant ; 48 answered ; 49 it came ; 50 full ; 51 young gentlemen ; 52 taken ; 53 those ; 54 are missing ; 55 remain=are now ; 56 eating them ; 57 been ; 58 witness ; 59 incident ; 60 discovered=made known ; 61 simplicity ; 62 was ; 63 made merry.

From this point the Student is assumed to understand the formation of the Participles and the Future Tense (*see Lessons 6 and 8 in* "SPANISH SIMPLIFIED.")

Disputa[1] de dos Reos.[2]

Un salteador[3] de caminos[3] y un deshollinador,[4] convencidos[5] de un robo[6] doméstico,[1] fueron[7] condenados[1] á muerte[8] á un mismo tiempo. El salteador,[3] ricamente[9] vestido,[10] subió[11] al patíbulo[12] con mucha[1] arrogancia[1] y descaro,[13] pero pareció[14] que ponía[15] la mayor[16] atención[1] en las exhortaciones[1] del religioso,[17] y el deshollinador[4] se[18] acercó[18] á él para escuchar[19] sus palabras[21] edificantes.[20]—Retírate,[22] le[24] dice[23] el salteador[3] de caminos,[3] y trata[25] de resignarte.[26]— No quiero,[27] le[24] responde,[1] pues[28] yo tengo tanto[29] derecho[30] como[31] tú á estar aquí.

2 criminal ; 3 highwayman ; 4 chimney-sweep ; 5 convicted ; 6 robbery ; 7 were ; 8 death ; 9 richly* ; 10 dressed ; 11 mounted ; 12 gallows ; 13 impudence ; 14 it appeared ; 15 was placing ; 16 greatest ; 17 clergyman ; 18 approached ; 19 listen to ; 20 edifying ; 21 word ; 22 go back ; 23 says ; 24 (to) him ; 25 try ; 26 resign thyself ; 27 I will ; 28 since ; 29 as much ; 30 right ; 31 as.

Un Hijo obediente.

Un padre anciano[2] y rico[3] pero bastante[4] avaro,[5] envió[6] á[0] su hijo á estudiar[1] á Salamanca, encargándole[7] sobre[8] todo que viviese[9] con la más estricta[1] economía.[1] El joven,[10] á[11] fuer de[11] hijo obediente, se[12] informó[12] del precio[13] de los principales[1] artículos[1] de consumo[1] luego[14] que[14] llegó[15] á la ciudad.

Preguntó[16] cuanto[17] costaba[19] una vaca[18] y le dijeron[20] que[0] de trescientos á cuatrocientos francos[1] ; informóse[12] luego[21] del precio[13] de las perdices[22] y le respondieron[1] que[0] de dos á tres francos[1] cada[23] una.

Entonces,[24] dijo para sí[25] el mozuelo,[26] será bueno comer[27] perdices[22] todos los días para obedecer[28] y dar[29] gusto[30] á mi padre.

2 old ; 3 rich ; 4 enough—rather ; 5 stingy ; 6 sent ; 7 charging him ; 8 above ; 9 he should live ; 10 youth ; 11 like ; 12 informed himself=enquired ; 13 price ; 14 as soon as ; 15 he arrived ; 16 he asked ; 17 how much ; 18 cow ; 19 cost ; 20 they told ; 21 afterwards, next ; 22 partridge ; 23 each ; 24 then ; 25 himself ; 26 youth ; 27 to eat ; 28 obey ; 29 give ; 30 pleasure.

* English Adverbs ending in *ly* usually end in *mente* in Spanish.

Estratagema singular de Cristobal Colón.

Cristobal[2] Colón[2] hizo[3] un desembarco[4] en Jamaica en 1504, y trató[5] de formar[1] un establecimiento.[6] Los insulares[7] se[8] apartaron[8] de la costa[9] dejando[10] á[0] los Españoles[11] sin viveres.[12] Una estratagema[1] singular[1] se[13] puso[13] en ejecución[1] en vista[14] de tal[15] apuro.[16]

Debía[17] haber muy en breve[17] un eclipse[1] de luna.[18] Colón mandó[19] llamar[20] á[0] los jefes[21] de los pueblos[23] vecinos,[22] y les[24] dijo con tono[1] firme[1] : Muy pronto[25] seréis[26] castigados[26] ; el dios todopoderoso[27] de los Españoles,[11] que yo adoro,[1] va[28] á daros[28] sus más terribles[1] golpes,[29] y en prueba[30] de lo[0] que os[32] digo,[31] veréis,[33] desde[34]esta[34] noche, encenderse[35] la luna,[18] después[36] oscurecerse,[37] y negaros[38] su luz.[39] Este será[40] el preludio[1] de vuestras desgracias,[41] si no os[42] aprovecháis[42] de mi aviso.[43]

Comienza[44] en efecto[1] á[45] pocas[45] horas el eclipse.[1] La desolación[1] entre[46] los salvajes[47] es tan[48] grande que van[49] todos á postrarse[50] á los piés[51] de Colón, jurando[52] que nada[53] le[55] faltaría.[54] Este hombre hábil[56] aparenta[57] dejarse conmover[57] ; se[58] encierra[58] como[59] para desarmar[1] la cólera[60] celeste,[1] y muéstrase[61] poco después,[56] anunciando[1] que Dios se[62] ha apiadado[62] y que la luna[18] volvería[63] á aparecer.[63] Los Indios,[1] que quedaron[64]persuadidos[1]de[0]que este estranjero[1]disponía[65]de la[0]naturaleza[66] á su arbitrio,[67] no le[69] dejaron[68]carecer[70]de cosa alguna.[71]

2 Christopher Columbus ; 3 made ; 4 landing ; 5 tried ; 6 settlement ; 7 islander ; 8 withdrew ; 9 coast ; 10 leaving ; 11 Spaniard ; 12 provisions ; 13 =was put ; 14 view ; 15 such ; 16 want ; 17=there was very soon to take place ; 18 moon ; 19 ordered ; 20 to call ; 21 chief ; 22 neighbouring ; 23 village ; 24 to them ; 25 soon ; 26 you will be punished ; 27 almighty ; 28 is going to give you ; 29 blow ; 30 proof ; 31 I say ; 32 to you ; 33 you will see ; 34 from this=this very ; 35=show its light ; 36 afterwards ; 37 disappear ; 38 deny you ; 39 light ; 40 will be ; 41 misfortune ; 42 you avail yourselves ; 43 warning ; 44 begins ; 45=in a few ; 46 among ; 47 savages ; 48 so ; 49 they go ; 50 prostrate themselves ; 51 foot ; 52 swearing ; 53 nothing ; 54 should be wanting ; 55 to him ; 56 clever ; 57 pretends to allow himself to be affected ; 58=withdraws ; 59 as if ; 60 anger ; 61 shows himself ; 62 has been appeased ; 63 would appear again ; 64 remained ; 65 disposed ; 66 nature ; 67 will ; 68 let ; 69 him ; 70 be in want ; 71 any

From this point the Student is assumed to understand the formation of the **Imperative** and **Past Definite** (*see Lessons 9 and 10 in* "SPANISH SIMPLIFIED").

Un niño positivo.

Un niño lloraba[2] mucho porque había[3] perdido[4] dos francos[1] que tenía.[3] Un tío[5] suyo[6] le regaló[7] igual[8] cantidad[9] para consolarle,[10] pero el niño lloraba[11]aún[12] más y decía[13]: "Si no hubiese[14] perdido[4] mis dos francos,[1] ahora tendría[15] cuatro."

2 wept ; 3 he had ; 4 lost ; 5 uncle ; 6 (of) his ; 7 *regalar,* to present ; 8 equal ; 9 quantity ; 10 console him ; 11 wept ; 12 still ; 13 said ; 14 I had ; 15 I should have.

La Forma de la Tierra.

Un maestro[2] de escuela,[3] queriendo[4] un día explicar[5] á sus discípulos[6] la forma[1] de la Tierra,[7] la[9] comparó[8] con su tabaquera,[10] la[0] cual era[11] redonda.[12] Pocos días después,[13] presentóse[14] en la escuela[3] un inspector,[1] y según[15] costumbre,[16] dirigió[17] algunas[18] preguntas[19] á los escolares.[1] Después[20] de examinarlos[20] de gramática[1] y aritmética,[1] pasó[21] á geografía,[1] y les[23] preguntó[22] cual era[11] la forma[1] de la Tierra.[7]

Todos permanecieron[24] callados.[25] El maestro,[2] á[26] fin de[26] refrescar[27] la memoria[1] de los muchachos, sacó[28] la tabaquera[10] del bolsillo[29]; pero desgraciadamente,[30] para hacer[31] honor[1] al inspector,[1] había[32] aquel día traído[33] una tabaquera[10] de plata[34] que no[35] usaba más que[35]los[36] domingos,[36]y que era cuadrada.[37]

Inmediatamente,[1] un discípulo[6] levantó[38] la mano[39] para indicar[1] que él sabía[40] la respuesta,[41] y dijo :

" Señor, la Tierra[7] es cuadrada[37] los[36] domingos,[36] y redonda[12] los demás[42] días de la semana.[43] "

2 master ; 3 school ; 4 wishing ; 5 to explain ; 6 pupil ; 7 earth ; 8 *comparar,* to compare ; 9 it ; 10 snuff-box ; 11 was ; 12 round ; 13 after ; 14 presented himself ; 15 according to ; 16 custom ; 17 *dirigir,* to address ; 18 some ; 19 question ; 20 after examining them ; 21 *pasar,* to pass ; 22 *preguntar,* to ask ; 23 them ; 24=remained ; 25 silent ; 26 in order to ; 27 refresh ; 28 *sacar,* to draw out ; 29 pocket ; 30 unfortunately ; 31 do ; 32 had ; 33 brought ; 34 silver ; 35 he only used ; 36 on Sundays ; 37 square ; 38 *levantar,* to raise ; 39 hand ; 40 knew ; 41 answer ; 42 other ; 43 week.

Los cinco Toros.

El Marqués[1] de Villa Hermosa[2] tenía[3] intención[1] de pasar[4] á un lugar[5] vecino[6] á sus estados[7] donde se[10] celebraba[10] una corrida[8] de toros.[9] Sabiendo[12] los alcaldes[11] la intención[1] del marqués,[1] fueron[13] á Cuenca, donde estaba,[2] y con expresivas[1] súplicas[14] le[16] rogaron[15] se[17] dignase[17] ir[18] á tiempo que pudiese[19] ver[20] la función.[1] Alegróse[21] el marqués del convite,[22] y con grande alborozo[23] les[25] preguntó[24] : ¿ y qué toros[9] tenéis[26] ?

Uno de los alcaldes[11] respondió[1] : Cuatro, excelentísimo[1] señor ; y si vuestra Excelencia[1] viene,[27] serán cinco.

---

0 not to be translated ; 1 the same, or nearly the same, as in English.

2 beautiful ; 3 had ; 4 pass ; 5 place ; 6=near ; 7 state ; 8=fight ; 9 bull ; 10 was taking place ; 11 magistrates, authorities ; 12 knowing ; 13 went ; 14 request ; 15 *rogar*, to entreat ; 16 him ; , 17=to condescend ; 18 to go ; 19 he could ; 20 see ; 21 was pleased ; 22 invitation ; 23 joy ; 24 *preguntar*, to ask ; 25 them ; 26 have you ; 27 comes.

La Habladora.

Para vengarse[2] de una habladora[3] insufrible[4] y perjudicial,[1] la[5] presentaron[1] un día un sujeto[6] que la[8] dijeron[7] era[9] un literato[10] de una conversación[1] interesante.[11] Como[12] su flaco[13] era[9] el[14] de hablar mucho y de creerse[15] con talento,[1] le[16] recibió[16] con mucho placer[17]; pero ansiosa[18] por lucir[19] su pico[20] se[21] puso[21] á hablar al momento[1] haciéndole[22] mil preguntas[23] diferentes[1] sin lograr[24] la menor[25] respuesta.[26]

Hecha[27] la visita,[1] ¿ está Vd. contenta[1] de su[28] presentado[28] ? la[8] preguntaron.

¡ Oh ! si[29] estoy encantada[29]: es hombre de gran talento.[1]

A esta exclamación[1] todos se[30] echaron á reir,[30] pues[31] este gran talento era[9] un mudo.[32]

---

2 avenge themselves ; 3 chatterbox ; 4 insufferable ; 5 to her ; 6 subject =person ; 7 they told ; 8 her ; 9 was ; 10 literary man ; 11 interesting ; 12 as ; 13 weakness ; 14=that ; 15 believ(ing) herself ; 16 she received him ; 17 pleasure ; 18 anxious ; 19 to show off ; 20 loquacity ; 21 she put herself =she began ; 22 makıng to him=putting to him ; 23 question ; 24 obtain- (ing) ; 25 least ; 26 reply ; 27 done=over ; 28=the person presented to you ; 29=I am indeed enchanted ; 30 burst out laughing ; 31 for ; 32 dumb.

From this point the Student is assumed to understand the formation of the **Imperfect Indicative** and **Conditional Indicative** (*see Lesson 11 in* "SPANISH SIMPLIFIED").

~~~~~~~~~~~~~~~~~~~~~~~~~~~~~~~~~~~~~~~

El Cura y sus Visitas.

Cuando los curas[3] párrocos[2] visitan[1] sus feligreses,[4] algunas[5] veces[6] hállanse[7] en varios[1] incidentes,[1] unos[5] agradables[8] y otros tristes.[9]   Hallóse[10] en uno de los primeros casos[11] el cura[3] de una parroquia[12] no lejos[13] de Londres.

Había visitado[1] algunos[5] de sus feligreses[4] cuando llegó[14] á la casa de uno que se[15] hallaba[15] en las delicias[16] del día[17] de lavado.[17]   La buena mujer no queriendo[18] presentarse[19] delante[20] del señor[0] cura[3] con el vestido[21] de lavar,[21] escondióse[22] detrás[23] del enjugador,[24] y dijo á su muchacho[25] que cuando abriera[26] la puerta al cura, le[28] dijera[27] que había salido[29] de casa.

Entró[30] el cura, y el muchacho cumpliendo[31] su encargo[32] empezó[33] á decirle[34] que su madre había salido[29] á dar[35] un paseo.[36]   Pero la mujer, sin advertirlo,[37] dejaba[38] ver[38] la punta[39] del pié[40] por[0] debajo[41] del enjugador.[24]

El cura apercibiéndolo[42] dijo al muchacho : Cuando tu madre vuelva[43] le[45] dirás[44] que la próxima[46] vez[6] que salga[47] á paseo,[48] no[49] olvide[49] de llevarse[50] los piés,[50] porque son cosas[51] muy útiles[52] para las personas[1] aficionadas[53] á andar.[53]

---

0 not to be translated ; 1 the same, or nearly the same, as in English.

2 parochial ; 3 parson ; 4 parishioner ; 5 some ; 6 time ; 7 they find themselves ; 8 agreeable ; 9 sad ; 10 found himself ; 11 case ; 12 parish ; 13 far ; 14 *llegar*, to arrive ; 15 found herself=was ; 16 delight ; 17 washing-day ; 18 wishing ; 19 to present herself ; 20 before ; 21 washing-dress ; 22 hid herself ; 23 behind ; 24 clothes-horse ; 25 boy=son ; 26 he should open ; 27 he should tell ; 28 him ; 29 gone out ; 30 *entrar*, to enter ; 31 *cumplir*, to fulfil ; 32 instruction ; 33 began ; 34 tell him ; 35 give=take ; 36 walk ; 37 noticing it ; 38=allowed to be seen ; 39 point ; 40 foot ; 41 underneath ; 42 perceiving it ; 43 comes back ; 44 thou wilt tell ; 45 her ; 46 next ; 47 she goes out ; 48 walk ; 49= she is not to forget ; 50 take her feet with her ; 51 thing ; 52 useful ; 53=fond of walking.

El Lacayo inocente.

Un caballero mandó[2] á[0] su lacayo[3] que viese[4] la hora que era en el reloj[5] de sol[5] que había[6] sobre una piedra[7] en el jardín[8]; y después[9] de haber[9] tardado[10] más de[11] una hora, le[13] llevó[12] el reloj[5] de sol[5] y le[13] dijo : Ahí[14] está, busque[15] Vd. la hora,[15] pues[16] yo no he podido[17] hallarla.[18]

---

2 *mandar*, to send ; 3 footman ; 4 he might see ; 5 sun-dial ; 6=(there) was ; 7 stone ; 8 garden ; 9 after having ; 10 *tardar*, to delay ; 11=than ; 12 *llevar*, to carry ; 13 to him ; 14 here ; 15 look for the time yourself ; 16 for ; 17 been able ; 18 to find it.

La Tetera.

Un marinero[1] á[2] bordo[2] de una fragata[3] mercante,[1] tuvo la desgracia[4] de dejar[5] caer[6] al mar[7] una tetera[8] de plata,[9] y lleno[10] de temor[11] se[12] fué[12] al camarote[13] del comandante,[1] y le[15] dijo[14] : Mi[0] capitán,[1] ¿ se[16] puede decir[16] de una cosa[17] que se[18] sabe[18] donde está, que está perdida[19] ?

No, puesto[20] que se[18] sabe[18] su paradero.[21]

En ese caso,[1] nada[22] tenéis que temer[22] por vuestra tetera,[8] porque yo sé[23] que está en el fondo[24] del mar.[7]

---

2 on board ; 3 frigate ; 4 misfortune ; 5 let ; 6 fall ; 7 sea ; 8 tea-pot ; 9 silver ; 10 full; 11 fear ; 12 he went ; 13 cabin ; 14 said ; 15 to him ; 16 can it be said ; 17 thing ; 18 (it) is known ; 19 lost ; 20 supposing ; 21 position ; 22 you have nothing to fear ; 23 know ; 24 bottom.

Una Orden.

El ilustre[1] caballero Taylor refería[2] un día los honores[1] que había recibido[3] de las diferentes[1] cortes[1] de Europa,[1] y las órdenes[4] con que había sido condecorado[1] por un gran número[1] de soberanos.[5]

Un caballero que se[6] hallaba[6] cerca[7] de[7] él le dijo que no había nombrado[8] al rey de Prusia[1] : Presumo[1] (añadió[9]) que éste[10] no[0] os[12] dió[11] ninguna[13] orden.

Perdone[14] Vd.,[14] repuso[15] Taylor, pues[16] me ha dado[17] la orden[4] perentoria[1] de salir[18] de[18] sus Estados.[19]

---

2 was relating ; 3 received ; 4 order ; 5 sovereign ; 6 found himself= was ; 7 near ; 8 *nombrar*, to name ; 9 *añadir*, to add ; 10=this one ; 11 gave ; 12 you ; 13 no ; 14 (I beg your) pardon ; 15 replied ; 16 since ; 17 given ; 18 go out of=quit ; 19 states.

From this point the Student is assumed to know the **Conjunctive Personal Pronouns**, and the Rules on their position (*see Lesson 12 in* "SPANISH SIMPLIFIED ").

El Condenado.

Un hombre condenado[2] á las llamas[3] se[0] escapó[1] de las manos[4] de la[0] justicia.[1] No pudiendo[5] hacer[6] otra cosa,[7] le quemaron[8] en efigie.[1] Aquel mismo día atravesó[10] cabalmente[11] el reo[9] una de las más altas[12] montañas[13] de los Pirineos,[1] y decía[14] después[15]: Nunca[16] he tenido[17] más frío[18] que el día que me quemaron.[8]

---

2 *condenar*, to condemn ; 3 flame ; 4 hand ; 5 being able ; 6 to do ; 7 thing; 8 *quemar*, to burn ; 9 criminal ; 10 passed over ; 11 exactly ; 12 high ; 13 mountain ; 14 he used to say ; 15 afterwards ; 16 never ; 17=been ; 18 cold.

El Juez, el Abogado y el Burro.

En un distrito[1] judicial[1] de Luisiana,[1] estaba el tribunal[1] ocupado[1] con la vista[2] de una causa,[3] cuyo abogado[4] no gozaba[5] de[0] gran favor[1] con el juez.[6] Resumía[7] el magistrado[1] los hechos[8] de la causa,[3] cuando rebuznó[10] descompasadamente[11] un burro,[9] allí[12] cerca.[12]

¿ Qué es eso ? preguntó[13] el juez[6] con enojo.[14]

Nada,[15] señor, contestó[16] el abogado,[4] es el eco[1] de la voz[17] de vuestra señoría.[18]

Callóse[19] el juez,[6] aunque[20] hubiera[21] podido mandar[21] á la cárcel[23] al insolente,[22] pero la casualidad[24] vino[25] en su ayuda.[26]

Cuando el abogado[4] refutaba[1] con gran calor[27] ciertas[28] observaciones[1] del juez,[6] volvió[29] el burro á rebuznar[29] con tanta[30] fuerza,[31] que no se[32] oía[32] la voz[17] del abogado.   Entonces[33] el juez dijo con mucha gravedad[1]:

" Calle[34] uno de Vds. si quieren[35] ser oídos,[36] porque hablando los dos á un tiempo es imposible.[1] "

---

2 =trial; 3 lawsuit ; 4 lawyer ; 5 *gozar*, to enjoy ; 6 judge ; 7 was summing up ; 8 fact ; 9 donkey ; 10 *rebuznar*, to bray ; 11 excessively ; 12 there near=close by ; 13 *preguntar*, to ask ; 14 anger ; 15 nothing ; 16 *contestar*, to reply ; 17 voice ; 18 lordship ; 19 kept silent ; 20 although ; 21 he could have sent ; 22 insolent (fellow*) ; 23 prison ; 24 chance ; 25 came ; 26 aid ; 27 heat ; 28 certain ; 29 the donkey brayed again ; 30 so much ; 31 force ; 32 was heard ; 33 then ; 34 be silent ; 35 you wish ; 36 heard.

* *Adjectives* are very frequently used as *Nouns* in Spanish.

Disputa entre un Viajero Español y un Indiano.

Un viajero[2] español encontró[3] á[0] un indiano[1] en cierto[4] bosque.[5] Ambos[6] iban[7] á[8] caballo.[8] El español, que temía[9] que el[0] suyo no pudiese[10] hacer[11] el viaje,[12] porque era muy malo, quiso[13] cambiar[14] con el[15] del indiano,[1] que era joven[16] y vigoroso.[1] El indiano se[17] negó á ello,[17] y el español entonces[18] le[19] movió[19] una disputa.[1] Vinieron[20] á las manos,[21] y el español, que estaba bien armado,[1] se[22] apoderó[22] del caballo del indiano, en[23] el que[23] siguió[24] su camino.[25]

El infeliz[26] indiano le siguió[24] á[27] lo lejos,[27] y fué[28] á dar[29] queja[30] al juez[31] del primer pueblo[32]; obligado[1] el español á comparecer[33] con el caballo, sostuvo[34] que éste era suyo, y muy suyo como que[0] lo había criado[35] él mismo[36] desde[37] chico.[38]

No habiendo pruebas[39] de lo contrario,[1] el juez[31] iba[40] á declarar[1] absuelto[41] de la demanda[1] al español, cuando quitándose[42] su capa[43] el indiano y cubriendo[44] con ella repentinamente[45] la cabeza[46] del caballo, dijo al mismo tiempo al juez[31]:

Yo probaré[47] de un modo[48] incontestable[1] mi aserción[1]; que[49] diga[49] ahora mi contrario,[50] ¿ de qué ojo[51] es tuerto[52] el caballo ?

Del derecho,[53] contestó[54] el español sin detenerse.[55]

Pues[56] no[57] lo es de ninguno,[57] repuso[58] el americano,[1] destapando[59] la cabeza[46] del animal.[1]

Convencido[60] el juez[31] con una prueba[39] tan ingeniosa[1] y fuerte,[61] adjudicó[1] el caballo al indiano, y se terminó[1] la disputa.[1]

---

2 traveller ; 3 *encontrar*, to meet ; 4 certain ; 5 wood ; 6 both ; 7 were going ; 8 on horseback ; 9 *temer*, to fear ; 10 could ; 11 do ; 12 journey ; 13 wanted ; 14 to change ; 15 the (one) ; 16 young ; 17 refused it ; 18 then ; 19 moved him to ; 20 they came ; 21 hands=blows ; 22 took possession ; 23 upon which ; 24 followed ; 25 way ; 26 unhappy ; 27 at a distance ; 28 went ; 29 give=make ; 30 complaint ; 31 judge ; 32 village ; 33 to appear ; 34 he maintained ; 35 brought up ; 36 himself ; 37 from ; 38 (its) youth ; 39 proof ; 40 was going ; 41 absolved ; 42 taking off ; 43 cloak ; 44 covering ; 45 suddenly ; 46 head ; 47 *probar*, to prove ; 48 manner ; 49 let ... say ; 50 opponent ; 51 eye ; 52 one-eyed ; 53 right ; 54 *contestar*, to answer ; 55=hesitating ; 56 then ; 57 not it is of none=he is not so in either ; 58 replied ; 59 uncovering ; 60 convinced ; 61 strong.

El Subalterno Escocés.

Se[2] refiere[2] una anécdota[1] de un Escocés[3] que era oficial[4] del Ejército[5] Británico[6] y fué mandado[7] con su regimiento[1] á Gibraltar. En aquél entonces[8] era subalterno[1] y hallábase[9] un día de[10] guardia[10] con otro compañero[11] oficial[4] que tuvo la desgracia[12] de caer[13] en un precipicio[1] de cuatrocientos piés[14] de profundidad[15] y quedó[16] muerto.[16]

Era deber[17] del subalterno[1] dar[18] cuenta[19] de lo[20] ocurrido[20] en[10] la guardia[10] y habiéndolo[21] hecho así,[21] añadió[22] la fórmula[1] de costumbre[23] ; "nada[24] de[0] particular[1] ha ocurrido[1] en la guardia."

El fatal[1] accidente[1] de la caída[25] en el precipicio[1] del otro oficial[4] vino[26] á oídos[27] del comandante,[1] y naturalmente[1] la frase[28] de "nada[24] de particular[1] ocurrido,[1]" le causó[1] extrañeza.[29]

"¡ Cómo[30] !" exclamó[1] el Mayor[31] de la Brigada,[1] "¿Vd. llama[32] á[0] esto nada[24] de particular, cuando su compañero[11] oficial[4] ha[16] muerto[16] cayendo[33] de una altura[34] de cuatrocientos piés[14] ?"

"Bien, Señor," replicó[1] el joven[35] oficial, "no[0] he creído[36] que hubiera[37] en ello nada de extraordinario[1] ; si el pobre[38] amigo hubiese[39] caído[40] en un precipicio[1] de cuatrocientos piés y no hubiera[39] muerto,[41] lo hubiera[42] hallado[43] muy extraordinario[1] en[44] efecto,[44] y lo hubiera[42] puesto[45] en el parte.[46] "

---

2 is related ;   3 Scotchman ;   4 officer ;   5 army ;   6 British ;   7 *mandar*, to send ;   8 then ;   9 found himself=was ;   10 on guard ;   11 companion=fellow ;   12 misfortune ;   13 (to) fall ;   14 foot ;   15 depth ; 16=was killed ;   17 duty ;   18 to give ;   19 account ;   20 what occurred ; 21 having done so ;   22 *añadir*, to add ;   23 custom ;   24 nothing ;   25 fall ; 26 came ;   27=ears ;   28 phrase ;   29 astonishment ;   30 what ;   31 major ; 32 *llamar*, to call ;   33 falling ;   34 height ;   35 young ;   36 *creer*, to believe ;   37 there was ;   38 poor ;   39 had ;   40 fallen ;   41 died ;   42 I should have ;   43 *hallar*, to find ;   44 indeed ;   45 put ;   46 report.

Un predicador[2] dijo en un sermón[1] que san[3] Francisco[1] Xavier había convertido[1] en un día diez mil[4] hombres en una isla[1] desierta.[1]

---

2 preacher ;   3 saint ;   4 thousand.

El Enfermo invisible.

Un filósofo,[1] poco[2] amigo de los médicos, tuvo una[3] vez[3] que[4] guardar cama[4] por una grave[1] enfermedad,[1] y un amigo envió[5] al[6] momento[6] á[7] buscar[7] un facultativo.[8] Luego[9] que llegó[9] se[0] lo anunciaron[1] al enfermo,[10] quien respondió[1] : Decidle[11] que estoy malo, y que no[0] recibo[1] á[0] nadie.[12]

0 not to be translated ; 1 the same, or nearly the same, as in English.

2 little ; 3=once ; 4 to keep [his bed] ; 5 sent ; 6 at once ; 7 to seek=for ; 8 physician ; 9 as soon as he arrived ; 10 invalid ; 11 tell him ; 12 nobody.

El Negro.

Carlos[2] y dos amigos suyos llegaron[3] á un hotel[1] de Nueva[4] York, donde debían[5] pasar[1] la noche.[6] No había[7] vacía[8] más que una habitación[9] con una cama,[10] en la[0] cual se[11] acomodaron[11] sus dos amigos, y Carlos[2] se[0] resolvió[1] á dormir[12] en un sofá.[1]

Un negro[1] que estaba parando[13] en el mismo hotel, ofreció[14] dividir[1] su cama[10] con él, cuya oferta[1] fué inmediatamente[1] aceptada.[1] Carlos fué[15] á acostarse,[16] encargando[18] antes[17] al mozo[19] que[20] le despertase[20] á las cinco de la mañana ; pero apénas[21] cayó[22] dormido,[22] cuando sus amigos deseando[23] divertirse[24] á su costa,[1] vinieron[25] á la habitación,[9] y le[26] ennegrecieron la cara[26] con hollín,[27] de[28] tal[28] manera[1] que parecía[29] que en la cama[10] había[30] dos negros.[1]

El mozo[19] le despertó[31] á la hora que había indicado[1]; pero, ¡ cual no[0] sería su sorpresa[1] cuando al[32] mirarse[32] al espejo[33] con objeto[1] de peinarse,[34] vió[35] una cara[37] negra[36] en[38] vez[38] de una blanca[39] !—" ¡ Oh ! " exclamó[1] ; " este imbécil[1] de mozo[19] ha despertado[31] al negro[1] en[38] vez[38] de despertarme[31] á[0] mí[0] "; y diciendo[40] esto, volvió[41] á acostarse[41] tranquilamente.[1]

2 Charles ; 3 *llegar*, to arrive ; 4 new ; 5 they had to ; 6 night ; 7 there was ; 8 empty ; 9 room ; 10 bed ; 11 accommodated themselves ; 12 sleep ; 13 *parar*, to stop ; 14 offered ; 15 went ; 16 lie down ; 17 before=first ; 18 instructing ; 19 waiter ; 20 that he should wake him ; 21 hardly ; 22 he fell asleep ; 23 *desear*, to wish ; 24 to divert themselves ; 25 came ; 26 blacked his face ; 27 soot ; 28 in such ; 29 it seemed ; 30 there were ; 31 *despertar*, to wake ; 32 on looking at himself ; 33 mirror ; 34 comb(ing) his hair ; 35 he saw ; 36 black ; 37 face ; 38 instead ; 39 white ; 40 saying ; 41 he went back to bed.

From this point the Student is assumed to be acquainted with the Rules in "SPANISH SIMPLIFIED," as far as the commencement of the **Irregular Verbs** *(Lesson 19).*

El Sermón.

En el último[2] sermón[1] de una misión,[1] que se[3] predicaba[3] en cierta[4] parroquia,[5] lloraron[6] todos los oyentes[7] menos uno, á[0] quien preguntó[9] su vecino[8] : ¿ Por qué no lloras[6] ? y él respondió[1] : Porque no soy de esta parroquia.[5]

---

2 last ; 3 was preached ; 4 certain ; 5 parish ; 6 *llorar*, to weep ; 7 hearer ; 8 neighbour ; 9 asked.

Los Hijos de Noé.

Se[3] presentó[3] un tonto[2] al obispo[4] para[5] que le ordenase,[5] y el padre había ya[6] suplicado[7] que no se[8] le pusiesen[8] cuestiones[1] difíciles[1] en[9] atención á[9] su escaso[10] talento.[1]   El obispo[4] para servirle[11] le hizo[12] sólo[13] esta pregunta[14]: Sem,[1] Cham[1] y Japhet,[1] hijos de Noé,[1] ¿ quién fué su padre ?

No supo[15] responder,[1] y no fué aprobado.[16]

Fuese[17] á su casa y dijo á su padre lo[18] que[18] se[19] le había preguntado,[19] y que no había podido[20] responder,[1] porque esas cosas tan difíciles[1] eran sólo[13] para hombres muy sabios.[21]

Su padre se[22] echó á reir,[22] y le dijo que no había[23] cosa más fácil.[24]—Si el obispo[4] te hubiera[25] preguntado[26]: ¿ el hijo del gobernador[27] de quién es hijo ? hubieras[28] respondido[1] " del gobernador[27]": ¿ no es verdad[29] ?

En[30]efecto,[30]dijo el necio[2]á su padre, no hay[31]cosa más fácil.[24]

En[32] seguida[32] se[17] fué[17] al obispo,[4] y le dijo que ya[6] sabía[33] la respuesta[34] que debía[35] darse[35] á su pregunta.[14]

Volvió[36] á hacérsela[36] el obispo con su santa[37] paciencia[1] : Sem, Cham y Japhet, hijos de Noé, ¿ quién fué su padre ?

Y respondió[1] muy satisfecho[38] : El gobernador.[27]

---

2 fool ; 3 *presentarse*, to present one's self ; 4 bishop ; 5 in order that he might ordain him ; 6 already ; 7 *suplicar*, to request ; 8=should be put to him ; 9 in view of ; 10 scanty ; 11 serve him ; 12 made=put ; 13 only ; 14 question ; 15 he knew=could ; 16 *aprobar*, to approve ; 17 he went ; 18 what ; 19=he had been asked ; 20 been able to ; 21 learned ; 22 burst out laughing ; 23 there was ; 24 easy ; 25 had ; 26 *preguntar*, to ask ; 27 governor ; 28 thou wouldst have ; 29 truth ; 30 in effect=indeed ; 31 there is ; 32=then ; 33 he knew ; 34 answer ; 35=ought to be given ; 36=put it to him again ; 37 holy ; 38 satisfied.

La Venganza heroica.

Tuvieron[3] un altercado[1] bastante[4] acalorado[5] en un café[1] dos particulares,[2] y uno de ellos, para vengarse,[6] tuvo[3] la bajeza[7] de escribir[8] al amanecer[9] en la puerta del otro, INFAME.[10]

Este último[11] fué[12] á buscarle[12]; pero un criado le dijo que no estaba en su casa, y le suplicó[13] dejase[14] por[15] escrito[15] lo[16] que[16] tuviese[3] que comunicarle.[1]

No, respondió,[1] puede[17] Vd.[17] solamente[18] decirle[19] que he venido[20] á volverle[21] su visita,[1] porque esta mañana me[0] ha dejado[22] escrito[23] su nombre[24] en mi puerta.

---

2 certain persons ; 3 had ; 4 enough=rather ; 5 heated ; 6 revenge himself ; 7 meanness ; 8 write ; 9 dawn ; 10 rascal ; 11 latter ; 12 went to seek him=called on him ; 13 *suplicar*, to request ; 14 (that) he should leave; 15=in writing ; 16 what ; 17 you may ; 18 only ; 19 tell him ; 20 come ; 21 return him ; 22 *dejar*, to leave ; 23 written ; 24 name.

Los cuatro Caballeros de Industria.

Cuatro caballeros[2] de industria[2] habiendo comido[3] en una taberna,[1] hicieron[4] subir al criado[4] y acordaron[5] el escote[6] por el gasto[7] hecho.[8]   El primero hizo[9] como que ponía[9] la mano[10] en el bolsillo.[11]   El otro se[12] la cogió[12] deteniéndola,[13] diciendo[14] que quería[15] pagar.[16]   El tercero hizo[17] la misma rúbrica,[18] y el cuarto mandó[19] al criado que no tomase[20] dinero[21] alguno[21] de ellos.

Como ninguno[22] quería[15] ceder,[23] uno de ellos dijo : vendemos[24] los ojos[25] al criado, como en el juego[26] de la gallina[27] ciega,[27] y aquél[28] que coja[29] pagará.[16]

Ponen[30] en obra[31] su proyecto[1]: y mientras[32] que el muchacho iba[33] palpando[34] en el cuarto, ellos descamparon lindamente.[35]

Sube[37] el amo[36] y nuestro muchacho le coge,[29] y teniéndolo[38] firme[1] le decía[39]: Vd. será el que pagará la cuenta.[40]

---

2 swindler ; 3 *comer*, to dine ; 4 they made the servant mount=called the servant upstairs ; 5 *acordar*, to agree on ; 6=settlement ; 7 expense ; 8 made ; 9 did as though he put=pretended to put ; 10 hand ; 11 pocket ; 12 took hold of it ; 13 detaining it ; 14 saying ; 15 would ; 16 *pagar*, to pay ; 17 did ; 18=performance ; 19 *mandar*, to order ; 20 he should take ; 21 any money ; 22 no one ; 23 give way ; 24 *vendar*, to blindfold ; 25 eye ; 26 game ; 27 blind hen=blind man's buff ; 28=the one ; 29 (he) catches hold of ; 30 they put ; 31 work=execution ; 32 while ; 33 was going ; 34 *palpar*, to grope about ; 35 neatly=softly ; 36 master ; 37 *subir*, to go up ; 38 holding him ; 39 said ; 40 bill.

Luis XIV. y el Cortesano.

Luís[1] catorce preguntó un día á[0] uno de sus cortesanos[2] : ¿ Sabe[3] Vd. el castellano[4] ?

No, Señor, respondió[1] el cortesano,[2] pero lo aprenderé.[5]

Se[6] aplicó[6] mucho para aprender[5] aquel idioma,[7] y después[8] de haber[8] tomado muchísimo trabajo,[9] porque le parecía[10] que el rey tenía intención[1] de nombrarle[11] embajador[1] en la corte[1] de España,[12] dijo un día á Luís catorce

Señor, ahora ya[13] sé[14] el[0] castellano.[4]

Muy bien, respondió[1] el rey, en ese caso[1] puede[15] Vd. leer[15] el[0] Don Quijote en su original.[1]

2 courtier ; 3 know ; 4 Castilian=Spanish ; 5 *aprender*, to learn ; 6 *aplicarse*, to apply one's self ; 7 language ; 8 after having ; 9 work ; 10 it appeared ; 11 appoint him ; 12 Spain ; 13 already ; 14 I know ; 15 you can read.

El Estudiante sagaz.[2]

Estando en la clase[1] un escolar[1] travieso[3] y chistoso,[4] pidió[5] licencia[6] á su maestro para salir,[7] pero éste[8] se[9] la negó[9] con enfado.[10] Finjió[11] el estudiante[1] que no le había oído,[12] repitió[1] la súplica,[13] y se[14] le volvió á decir[14] que[0] no ; pero entonces[15] salió,[16] y el maestro no le detuvo.[17]

Entró[1] una hora después,[18] y el maestro encolerizado[19] le dijo : ¿ Cómo te has atrevido[20] á salir[7] sin mi licencia[6] ?

Respondióle[1] muy humildemente[21] el discípulo[1] :

Le[0] pedí[5] á[0] Vd. licencia[6] dos veces y ambas[22] me dijo que[0] no ; como dos negaciones[1] afirman,[1] creí[23] que consentía[1] Vd. y salí[16] sin aguardar[24] más respuesta.[25]

Quedó[26] desenojado[27] el maestro, y se[28] rió[28] de la agudeza.[29]

2 sagacious ; 3 turbulent ; 4 humorous ; 5 asked ; 6 permission ; 7 go(ing) out ; 8=the latter ; 9 denied it to him ; 10 vexation ; 11 *finjir*, to pretend ; 12 heard ; 13 request ; 14=was again told ; 15 then ; 16 went out ; 17 detained ; 18 afterwards ; 19 angry ; 20 *atreverse*, to dare ; 21 humbly ; 22 both ; 23 I thought ; 24 wait(ing) ; 25 reply ; 26 *quedar*, to remain ; 27 appeased ; 28 he laughed ; 29 acuteness.

¿ Ha visto Vd. " el Barbero[1] de Sevilla[1] ?

No, señor, me[2] afeito[2] solo.[3]

2 I shave myself ; 3 alone.

El Barbero de José II.

Un día, habiendo llegado el emperador[1] José[1] á una ciudad antes[2] que[2] su acompañamiento,[3] le preguntó el ama[4] de la posada,[5] si pertenecía[6] al séquito[3] del emperador.[1]

No, respondió[1] el príncipe.[7]

Sin[8] embargo,[8] con tan lacónica[1] respuesta[9] no quedó[10] satisfecha[1] la curiosidad[1] de la buena mujer.   Buscó[11] un pretesto[1] para entrar[1] en su cuarto, y viéndole[12] ocupado[1] en afeitarse,[13] le preguntó si tenía algún[14] cargo[15] cerca[16] del emperador.[1]

Sí, respondió[1] el monarca[1]; algunas[14] veces le afeito.[13]

---

2 before ; 3 suite ; 4 mistress ; 5 inn ; 6 he belonged ; 7 prince ; 8 nevertheless ; 9 reply ; 10 *quedar*, to remain ; 11 *buscar*, to seek ; 12 seeing him ; 13 *afeitar*, to shave ; 14 any, some ; 15 office ; 16 near.

Los dos Marineros.

Dos marineros,[2] el uno inglés[3] y el otro irlandés,[4] convinieron[5] en[6] socorrerse[6] mutuamente[1] en el caso[1] de sucederles[7] algún accidente[1] en el combate.[1]   Tuvo el inglés la desgracia[8] de perder[9] una pierna,[10] y su compañero[11] le cargó[12] al momento sobre sus espaldas[13] para llevarle[14] á curar.[1]

En el camino[15] vino[16] otra bala[1] de cañón,[1] y le[17] llevó[17] la cabeza[18] al herido,[19] pero el irlandés[4] no lo advirtió[20] y siguió[21] con el cuerpo[22] sin detenerse.[23]

Un oficial[24] que le vió[25]pasar[1] con el tronco[26] de un hombre sobre las espaldas,[13] le preguntó á donde iba.[27]

A[28] buscar,[28] al cirujano,[29] responde.[1]—Pero, majadero,[30] ¿ no ves[31] que llevas[14] un cuerpo[22] sin cabeza[18] ?

A estas palabras[32] puso[33] en tierra[34] su carga,[35] y exclamó[1] mirando[36] atentamente[1] el cadáver[37] :

¡ Si él mismo[38] me ha dicho[39] que era una pierna[10] la[0] que había perdido[9] ! ! !

---

2 sailor ; 3 English(man) ; 4 Irish(man) ; 5 agreed ; 6 to help each other ; 7 happen(ing) to them ; 8 misfortune ; 9 *perder*, to lose ; 10 leg ; 11 companion ;   12 loaded=took ; 13 shoulder ;   14 *llevar*, to carry ; 15 way ; 16 came ;   17=took off ; 18 head ;   19 wounded (man) ;   20 noticed ; 21 followed=went on ;   22 body ;   23 stop(ping) ;   24 officer ;   25 saw ; 26 trunk ; 27 he was going ; 28 to seek=for ; 29 surgeon ; 30 blockhead ; 31 seest thou ; 32 word ; 33 he put ; 34 ground ; 35 burden ; 36 looking at ; 37 corpse ; 38 himself ; 39 told.

El nuevo Hércules.

Un artesano[1] que pasaba[2] en el país[3] por muy diestro[4] en los ejercicios[5] de fuerzas,[6] y al mismo tiempo muy robusto,[1] se[7] veía[7] frecuentemente[1] obligado[1] á medirlas[8] con algunos.[9] Vino[10] uno de muy lejos[11] á luchar[12] con nuestro campeón,[13] y le dijeron[14] que estaba en el cercado[15] de la casa trabajando.[16] Echa[17] pié[18] á tierra[19] y va[20] á buscarle al momento con el caballo de la brida,[21] que ató[22] á una estaca[23] del cercado.[15]

Camarada,[1] le dice,[24] he oído[25] hablar mucho de vuestras fuerzas,[6] y vengo[26] de cuarenta millas[27] á veros[28] y ensayar[29] cuál de los dos puede[30] tumbar[31] al otro.

No había hecho[32] más que concluir[1] estas palabras,[33] cuando nuestro hércules soltó[34] al momento el azadón,[35] le cogió[36] por las piernas,[37] le arrojó[38] al prado[40] inmediato[39] por[41] encima de[41] la tapia,[42] y volviendo[43] á tomar[43] con mucha serenidad[1] el azadón,[35] continuó su trabajo.[44]

Luego[45] que[45] el pobre[46] diablo[46] se[47] levantó[47] como pudo[48] después[49] de[49] tan fuerte[50] porrazo[51] : Y[0] bien, le dice[24] el otro, ¿ tiene Vd. alguna cosa más que[52] mandarme[52] ?

No, señor, gracias,[53] le responde[1] espantado[54] del vuelo[55] ; écheme[56] Vd.[0] acá[57] por el mismo camino[58] mi caballo, pues[59] he concluido[1] mi comisión,[1] y me quiero[60] marchar.[61]

---

2 *pasar*, to pass ; 3 country ; 4 dexterous ; 5 exercise ; 6 strength(s) ; 7 saw(=found) himself ; 8 *medir*, to measure ; 9=others ; 10 came ; 11 far ; 12 to wrestle ; 13 champion ; 14 they told ; 15 enclosure ; 16 *trabajar*, to work ; 17 he throws=puts ; 18 foot ; 19 ground ; 20 goes ; 21 bridle ; 22 *atar*, to tie ; 23 stake ; 24 (he) says ; 25 heard ; 26 I come ; 27 mile ; 28 (to) see you ; 29=to try ; 30 can ; 31 overthrow ; 32 done ; 33 word ; 34 loosened=threw down ; 35 pick-axe ; 36 took hold of ; 37 legs ; 38 *arrojar*, to fling ; 39 adjoining ; 40 meadow ; 41 over ; 42 mud-wall ; 43 again taking ; 44 work ; 45 as soon as ; 46 poor devil=fellow ; 47 got up ; 48 (best) he could ; 49 after ; 50 strong ; 51 blow ; 52 to command me ; 53 thanks ; 54 *espantar*, to frighten ; 55 flight ; 56 *echar*, to throw ; 57 (over) here ; 58 way ; 59 since ; 60 I want ; 61 *marcharse*, to go away.

¿ En qué mes[2] hablan menos[3] las[0] mujeres ?
En Febrero,[1] porque sólo[4] tiene veinte y ocho días.

2 month ; 3 least ; 4 only.

Dos Borrachos.

Un borracho[2] de setenta años[3] iba[4] una vez buscando por[5] todas partes[5] un cuervo[7] joven.[6]

¿ Para qué lo quiere[8] Vd. ? preguntó un campesino.[9]

He oído[10] decir,[11] respondió el beodo,[2] que estas aves[12] viven trescientos años,[3] y quiero[8]saber[13]por mí[14]mismo[14]si es cierto.[15]

Otro borracho[2] se[16] hallaba[16] una noche á deshora[17] sentado[18] en la esquina[19] de una calle, cuando acertó[20] á pasar[1] por[21] allí[21] una patrulla.[1]

¿ Qué hacéis[22] ahí[23] ? le pregunta el sargento.[1]

Veo[24] que la tierra[25] anda,[26] y estoy esperando[27] que[28] pase mi casa[28] por[29] aquí[29] para meterme[30] en ella.

---

2 drunkard ; 3 year ; 4 went ; 5=everywhere ; 6 young ; 7 raven ; 8 want ; 9 countryman ; 10 heard ; 11 say ; 12 bird ; 13 (to) know ; 14 myself ; 15 certain=true ; 16=was ; 17=an untimely hour ; 18 seated ; 19 corner ; 20=happened ; 21=that way ; 22 are you doing ; 23 here ; 24 I see ; 25 earth ; 26 goes round ; 27 *esperar*, to wait ; 28=for my house to pass ; 29=this way ; 30 put myself=go.

El Quitamanchas.

Un bribón[2] se introdujo[1] en casa de un caballero, entró[1] hasta[3] la antesala[4] del primer piso,[5] y no viendo[6] cosa de[0] que pudiese[7] sacar[8] partido[8] sino[9] es[0] de[0] dos libreas[10] de los criados, se[0] decidió[1] á apropiárselas[11] por no salirse[12] con las manos[14] vacías.[13]

Al[15] bajar[15] la escalera[16] halló al amo,[17] quien le preguntó de quién eran aquellos vestidos,[18] y adónde los llevaba.[19]

¿ Pues[20] que,[20] señor, responde[1] con mucha serenidad,[1] no me conocéis[21] ? Yo trabajo[22] para vuestros criados ; soy el quitamanchas,[23] y limpio[24] los vestidos[18] de vuestros lacayos.[1]

En ese caso,[1] dijo el dueño[25] de la casa, voy[26] á darte[27] mi bata,[28] pues[29] la he llenado[30] de aceite.[31]

Y al mismo tiempo se la dió.[32]

---

2 rascal ; 3 as far as ; 4 ante-chamber ; 5 floor ; 6 seeing ; 7 he could ; 8= make off with ; 9 except ; 10 livery ; 11 appropriate them to himself ; 12 go away ; 13 empty ; 14 hand ; 15 on descending ; 16 staircase ; 17 master ; 18 suits ; 19 *llevar*, to carry ; 20=why ; 21 do you know ; 22 *trabajar*, to work ; 23 scourer ; 24 *limpiar*, to clean ; 25 owner ; 26 I am going ; 27 give thee ; 28 dressing-gown ; 29 since ; 30 *llenar*, to fill ; 31 oil ; 32 he gave.

El Representante del Pueblo.[2]

Un candidato[1] de un arrabal[3] de una ciudad dijo á sus constituyentes que si querían[4] nombrarle[5] diputado,[6] les haría[7] gozar[8] en todas estaciones[9] del[0] tiempo[10] que quisiesen.[11] Este ofrecimiento[12] fué tan seductor,[13] que no pudieron[14]menos de[15] nombrar[5] á[0] este hombre que parecía[16] tener un don[17] celestial.[1]

Algún tiempo después[18] de[18] la elección,[1] fué[19] á buscarle uno de sus constituyentes,[1] y le pidió[20] un poco de[0] lluvia.[21]

Bueno, amigo mío, le dijo el diputado[6]: pero ¿ por qué pides[22] la[0] lluvia[21] ? ¿ no hará[23] daño[24] á vuestros prados[25] ?

Yo la necesito[26] para mis trigos,[27] pues la yerba[28] ó el heno[29] ya[30] está en casa.

¿ Pero vuestro vecino[31] ha encerrado[32] el[0] suyo ? Yo estoy persuadido[1] de[0] que ahora la lluvia[21] le perjudicaría[33] mucho.

Eso[0] sí, es verdad,[34] no le vendría[35] muy bien.

Pues[36] en ese caso,[1] amigo mío, ya[30] sabéis[37] lo[38] que[38] os he dicho.[39] Yo os he prometido[40] proporcionaros[41] el tiempo[10] que queráis[42] ; pero si yo os doy[43] la lluvia,[21] perjudicaré[33] á[0] vuestro vecino[31]: así[44] pues,[44] el partido[45] más prudente[1] será el[0] de oíros[46] juntos,[47] y que os[48] concertéis[48] sobre la especie[49] de tiempo[10] que os convenga[50] á[0] todos, y entonces[51] os prometo[40] complaceros[52] ; porque mi intención[1] no es de suscitar[53] querellas[1] entre mis conciudadanos[54] dando[55] la preferencia[1] á los unos sobre los otros.

---

2 village ; 3 suburb ; 4 they would ; 5 *nombrar*, to appoint ; 6 deputy ; 7 he would make=cause ; 8 (to) enjoy ; 9 season ; 10 weather ; 11 they wanted ; 12 offer ; 13 attractive ; 14 they could (do) ; 15=than ; 16 appeared ; 17 gift ; 18 after ; 19 went ; 20 requested ; 21 rain ; 22 dost thou ask ; 23 will it do ; 24 damage ; 25 meadow ; 26 want ; 27 wheat ; 28 herb =grass ; 29 hay ; 30 already ; 31 neighbour ; 32 shut up=housed ; 33 *perjudicar*, to injure ; 34 truth=true ; 35 it would come ; 36 then ; 37 you know ; 38 what ; 39 told ; 40 *prometer*, to promise ; 41 to portion to you ; 42 you want ; 43 give ; 44 therefore ; 45 course ; 46 hear you ; 47 together ; 48 you agree ; 49 kind ; 50 suits ; 51 then ; 52 (to) please you ; 53 to stir up ; 54 fellow-citizens ; 55 (by) giving.

Más[2] vale[2] acostarse[3] sin cenar[4] que levantarse[5] con deudas.[6]

---

2 it is worth more=it is better ; 3 to go to bed ; 4 sup[ping] ; 5 to get up ; 6 debt.

El Corregidor y el Mayorazgo.

Un caballerito[2] mayorazgo[3] muy loco[4] y muy gastador[5] estaba disgustado[6] con el corregidor[7] del pueblo,[8] que era hijo de un carnicero.[9] El mayorazgo[3] vendió[10] unas tierras[11] para sostener[12] su lujo[13] y sus caprichos,[1] sin pensar[14] en sus acreedores[15]; y un día que se presentó[1] muy elegante[1] en un onvite[16] se[17] puso[17] á referir[18] las modas[19] y los trajes[20] que se[21] había hecho,[21] cuando repentinamente,[22] por abochornarle[23] le dijo el corregidor[7] :

Mejor[25] hiciera[24] si tratase[26] Vd.[26] de pagar[27] sus deudas.[28]

En[29] efecto,[29] tiene[30] Vd. razón,[30] y mañana voy[31] á satisfacerlas[32]; hágame[33] su recibo[34] por una cabeza[35] de ternera[36] y unas lenguas[37] que debo á su padre de Vd.

---

2 young gentleman ; 3 first-born=heir ; 4 silly ; 5 spendthrift ; 6 displeased ; 7 magistrate ; 8 village ; 9 butcher ; 10 *vender*, to sell ; 11 land ; 12 support ; 13 luxury ; 14 think(ing) ; 15 creditor ; 16 feast ; 17 he put himself=he began ; 18 relate ; 19 fashion ; 20 costume ; 21=he had had made ; 22 suddenly ; 23 (to) irritate him ; 24 you would do ; 25 better ; 26 you tried ; 27 pay ; 28 debt ; 29 indeed ; 30 you are right ; 31 I am going ; 32 satisfy them ; 33 make me (out) ; 34 receipt ; 35 head ; 36 calf ; 37 tongue.

Padre é Hijo.

El mariscal[2] Lefèvre era hijo de un pobre molinero[3] de la[0] Alsacia. Siendo aún[4] joven[5] entró en las Guardias[1] Francesas,[1] y era sargento[1] cuando estalló[6] la Revolución,[1] que hizo[7] sucesivamente[1] de él un oficial, un general, y por[8] último,[8] bajo[9] el Imperia,[10] un mariscal[2] de Francia.[1]

Estaba muy descontento[1] de su hijo, cuya conducta[1] dejaba[11] mucho que[12] desear.[12] Un día estando dirigiéndole[13] amargos[14] reproches,[1] le dijo entre otras cosas :

Tú no haces[15] caso[15] de mis consejos[16] ni reconvenciones,[17] mal sujeto[18] : diríase[19] que te crees[20] superior[1] á tu padre.

Es muy posible,[1] respondió desdeñosamente[21] su hijo ; porque después[22] de[22] todo, mi padre era hijo de un pobre molinero,[3] y yo soy hijo de un rico[23] mariscal de Francia.

---

2 marshal ; 3 miller ; 4 still ; 5 young ; 6 *estallar*, to break out ; 7 made ; 8 finally ; 9 under ; 10 empire ; 11 *dejar*, to leave ; 12 to desire ; 13 addressing to him ; 14 bitter ; 15=payest attention ; 16 advice ; 17 recrimination ; 18=fellow ; 19=one would say ; 20 *creer*, to believe ; 21 disdainfully ; 22 after ; 23 rich.

El Juramento.

Un escribano[2] tomó un coche[1] de[3] alquiler[3] para ir[4] á un pueblo[5] cerca[6] de[6] Sevilla,[1] y el cochero[7] le pidió[8] catorce pesetas.

¿ Afirmarás[1] tú bajo[9] juramento[10] que ese es el precio[11] que se[12] paga[12] por este viaje[13] ?—Sí, señor.

El escribano[2] sacó[14] entonces[15] y puso[16] sobre la mesa un crucifijo,[1] le hizo[17] jurar[18] y le dió[19] seis pesetas, diciéndole[20] que retenía[21] lo restante[22] por el acta[1] de la prestación[23] del juramento.[10]

2 notary ;   3 on hire ;   4 go ;   5 village ;   6 near ;   7 driver ;
8 asked ; 9 under ; 10 oath ; 11 price ; 12 is paid ; 13 journey ; 14 *sacar*,
to draw out ; 15 then ; 16 put ; 17 made ; 18 swear ; 19 gave ; 20 telling
him ;   21 retained ;   22 remainder ;   23 administration.

El Caballo y las Ostras.

Un viajero[2] llegó á una posada[3] en una[4] noche de ʌas más frías[4] de Diciembre,[1] y al[5] pasar[5] por[6] la cocina[7] vió[8] que todos los asientos[9] estaban ocupados[1] por la mucha gente[10] que había[11] alrededor[12] del fuego,[13] causándole[1] la mayor[14] pena[16] el no poder[16] acercarse[17] á calentarse[18] las manos.[18]

Mozo,[19] dijo en alta[20] voz[21] al criado, lleva[22] dos docenas[1] de ostras[23] á mi caballo.

El mozo[19] obedeció,[24] y las personas[1] que estaban calentándose[25] alrededor[12] de la lumbre,[13] no pudiendo[16] resistir[1] al deseo[26] de ver[27] un animal[1] tan extraordinario,[1] se[28] levantaron[28] y marcharon[1] en tropel[29] á la caballeriza.[30]

Entretanto,[31] el viajero[2] tomó el mejor[32] asiento[9] en frente[33] del fuego,[13] y pocos momentos[1] después[34] volvió[35] el mozo[19] á decirle,[36] seguido[37] de los curiosos,[1] que el caballo no quería[38] comer[39] las ostras.[23]

¡ Cómo ! ¿ no las quiere[40] ? pregunta muy serio[1] el viajero[2] ; pues[41] entonces,[41] ponme[42] aquí la mesa, y yo me[0] las comeré á su salud.[43]

2 traveller ; 3 inn ; 4 one of the coldest nights ; 5 in passing ; 6 through ;
7 kitchen ; 8 he saw ; 9 seat ; 10 people ; 11 there were ; 12 round ; 13 fire ;
14 greatest ;   15 pain ;   16 be(ing) able ;   17 (to) draw near ;   18 warm his
hands ; 19 waiter ; 20 high ; 21 voice ; 22 take ; 23 oyster ; 24 obeyed ;
25 *calentar*, to warm ; 26 desire ; 27 see ; 28 got up ; 29 crowd ; 30 stable ;
31 meanwhile ; 32 best ; 33 front ; 34 after ; 35 came back ; 36 tell him ; 37
followed ; 38 would ; 39 eat ; 40 he likes ; 41 well then ; 42 put me ; 43 health.

Otra, otra.

Un capitán de buque[2] que no[0] había estado nunca[3] en el teatro,[1] ni tenía voto[4] ni aún[5] oído[6] para la música,[1] fué[7] una noche á la ópera en compañía[1] de un amigo.   Cuando se[9] acabó[9] la función,[8] se[7] fué[7] á su posada,[10] donde le preguntaron cómo habían desempeñado[11] las actrices[1] sus papeles.[12]

No me han gustado,[13] respondió ; allí había[14] una mujer que lo ha hecho[15] tan mal, que la han hecho[16] volver[17] á empezar[17] dos ó tres veces gritando[18] : " otra,[19] otra."

---

2 ship ; 3 never ; 4=authority ; 5 yet ; 6 ear ; 7 went ; 8 performance ; 9 finished itself=was over ; 10 inn ; 11 *desempeñar*, to fulfil ; 12=parts ; 13 *gustar*, to please ; 14 there was ; 15 done ; 16 made ; 17 return to begin =begin again ; 18 *gritar*, to call out ; 19=encore.

Las Estatuas.

Un tendero[2] que en poco tiempo se[3] hizo[3] rico,[4] compró[5] las haciendas[6] de un caballero, y un día quiso[7] hacer[8] ver[8] á[0] uno de sus amigos su nueva adquisición.[1]

Llegaron al jardín[9] y le mostró[10] diferentes[1] estatuas[11] de bronce[1] que adornaban[1] las avenidas.[12]

¿ Qué figura[1] es esta ? le dice[13] su amigo, mostrándole[14] un busto.[1]

¿ Esa figura ? ... espere[15] Vd. ... no me[16] acuerdo[16] ...ah, sí, esa debe[17] ser la de Venus ó Vulcano, pero no sé[18] positiva-mente[1] cuál de las dos; lo[0] preguntaremos al jardinero[19] ; como son del mismo metal,[1] es muy difícil[1] distinguirlas.[1]

---

2 shopkeeper ; 3 made himself ; 4 rich ; 5 *comprar*, to buy ; 6 estate ; 7 wished ; 8 to make see=to show ; 9 garden ; 10 *mostrar*, to show ; 11 statue ; 12 avenue ; 13 says ; 14 showing him ; 15 *esperar*, to wait ; 16 I remember ; 17 must ; 18 I know ; 19 gardener.

Un caballero que tenía una grande antipatía[1] por la música[1] fué preguntado ¿ por qué no se[0] suscribía[1] á una serie de conciertos[1] ? y para decidirle[1] á ello le dijeron[2] que su hermano se[0] había suscrito.[1]—Bien, dijo él, si yo fuera[3] tan sordo[4] como mi hermano, entonces me[0] suscribiría.

---

2 they told ; 3 were ; 4 deaf.

La Apuesta.

Cierto[2] caballero tenía,[3] como á punto[4] de honra,[5] no[6] servirse jamás[6] de afirmativa.[1] Otro, á quien contaron[7] esta rareza,[8] apostó[9] que le haría[10] responder[1] SI, ó NO, la primera vez que le encontrase.[11]

Verificada[1] la apuesta,[12] sucedió[13] que un día vió[15] el apostador[14] al caballero que se[16] dirigía[16] derechamente[17] á entrar[1] en una iglesia.[18]   Salióle[19] al encuentro,[19] saludóle,[20] y le preguntó : Con[21] que[21] ¿ va[22] Vd. á la iglesia[18] ?

Este es el camino,[23] respondió el caballero.

2 certain ; 3 held ; 4 point ; 5 honor ; 6=never to make use ; 7 *contar*, to relate ; 8 originality ; 9 *apostar*, to bet ; 10 he would make ; 11 he met ; 12 bet ; 13 *suceder*, to happen ; 14 wagerer ; 15 saw ; 16 was directing himself ; 17 straight ; 18 church ; 19=he went to meet him ; 20 *saludar*, to bow ; 21 well ; 22 go ; 23 way.

Las dos Orejas.

Un ratero[2] á quien ya[3] habían cortado[4] una oreja[5] en Bristol por castigo,[6] entró[1] en una tienda,[7] y dijo quería[8] una pieza[9] del mejor[10] encaje[11] que hubiese.[12]   Mostráronle[13] varias,[1] y después[14] de haber[14] elegido[15] la que le agradó,[16] preguntó al comerciante[17] cuánto[18] le llevaría[19] por medirle[20] el largo[21] igual[1] al espacio[1] que separaba[1] sus orejas.[5]

El comerciante[17] dijo que[0] dos reales.[1]

Bueno, dijo el ratero[2] pagándole[22] ; pero como yo tengo una oreja[5] aquí, y la otra está clavada[23] en la picota[24] de Bristol, creo no tendrá Vd. hoy bastante[25] encaje[11] para medirme[20] lo concertado,[26] y voy[27] á tomar la pieza[9] á[28] buena cuenta,[28] sin[29] perjuicio de que procure[29] completarme[1] el resto[1] lo más pronto[30] posible.

2 rogue ; 3 already ; 4 *cortar*, to cut (off) ; 5 ear ; 6 punishment ; 7 shop ; 8 he wanted ; 9 piece ; 10 best ; 11 lace ; 12 there was ; 13 they showed him ; 14 after having ; 15 chosen ; 16 *agradar*, to please ; 17 merchant ; 18 how much ; 19=he would charge ; 20 *medir*, to measure ; 21 length ; 22 *pagar*, to pay ; 23 *clavar*, to nail ; 24 gibbet ; 25 enough ; 26 agreed on (quantity) ; 27 I am going; 28 on account; 29=without prejudice to your trying; 30 soon.

¿ Qué es lo[2] que[2] se[3] nos aparece[3] una vez en un minuto,[1] dos veces[4] en un momento,[1] y nunca[5] en un siglo[6] ?—La letra[1] M.

2 what ; 3 appears to us ; 4 time ; 5 never ; 6 century.

El gran Rey.

Uno de los últimos[2] reyes de España,[3] á[0] quien la suerte[4] de las armas[1] había privado[5] de varias[1] plazas[6] considerables,[1] recibía[7] sin[8] embargo[8] de la mayor[9] parte[1] de sus cortesanos[10] et título[1] de Grande.

Su Grandeza,[11] dijo un español, se[12] parece[12] á[0] la de los fosos,[13] que se[14] hacen[14] mayores[9] en proporción á la tierra[15] que les[16] quitan.[16]

---

2 last ;   3 Spain ;   4 chance=fortune ;   5 *privar*, to deprive ;   6 place ; 7 *recibir*, to receive ;   8 nevertheless ;   9 greater ;   10 courtier ;   11 greatness ;   12 resembles ;   13 ditch ;   14 make themselves=become ;   15 land, earth ;   16 they take away from them.

El Aldeano y el Mercader.

Pasando un aldeano[2] por una tienda[3] que tenía la anaquelería[4] casi[5] vacía[6] de géneros,[7] entró en ella, y con ironía[1] preguntó al mercader[8] qué era lo[0] que allí se vendía.[9]   Este quiso[10] también[11] burlarse[12] y le contestó[13] con enfado[14] : Aquí se venden[9] cabezas[15] de asnos.[16]

Grande es la venta[17]de esta casa, según[18]veo,[19]le dice[20]riendo[21] á carcajadas[21] el aldeano,[2] pues no queda[22] más que la tuya.

---

2 villager ;   3 shop ;   4=shelves ;   5 almost ;   6 empty ;   7 goods ;   8 dealer ;   9 *venderse*, to be sold ;   10 wanted ;   11 also ;   12 to jest ;   13 *contestar*, to answer ;   14 vexation ;   15 head ;   16 ass ; 17 sale ;   18 according as ;   19 I see ;   20 says ;   21 laughing boisterously ;   22 *quedar*, to remain.

El Vice-Cónsul flemático.

Un soberano[2] mandó[3] suspender[1] un día su arenga[4] á un orador[1] diciéndole[5]: ¿ Quién es Vd. ?—Señor, le respondió,[1] soy el segundo cónsul de mi pueblo.[6]—¿ Y por qué no ha venido[7] el primero ?—Tened,[8] señor, la bondad[9] de perdonarie,[10] pues tiene una razón[13] bastante[11] poderosa.[12]—Yo no veo, repone[14] el príncipe[15] irritado,[1] que es lo que puede[16] alegar.[17] —Señor, contesta el orador[1] con su natural[1] flema,[18] es que murió[19] ayer.—Entonces el rey le mandó[3] continuar.[1]

---

2 sovereign ;   3 *mandar*, to order ;   4 harangue ;   5 saying to him ; 6 town ;   7 come ;   8 have ;   9 kindness ;   10 *perdonar*, to pardon ;   11 sufficiently ;   12 powerful ;   13 reason ;   14 replies ;   15 prince ; 16 **he can** ;   17 allege ;   18 phlegm ;   19 he died.

La Pronunciación Inglesa.

Para leer[2] el[0] inglés no basta[3] saber[4] pronunciar[1] el alfabeto,[1] pues no hay[5] acaso[6] ninguna lengua[7] en Europa,[1] que presente[1] sonidos[8] tan varios[1] y excepciones[1] tan numerosas[1] á la regla[9] general[1]; de[10] modo que[10] sólo[11] por medio[12] de una lectura[13] asidua[1] y constante,[1] bajo[14] la dirección[1] de un profesor[1] ó practicando[1] con ingleses, se[15] puede[15] conseguir[16] tener una pronunciación[1] más[17] ó menos[17] perfecta.[1]

Hay[5] también[18] otra irregularidad[1] en la ortografía[1] del inglés, francés[19] y otras lenguas,[7] á[20] saber[20]: una misma letra[1] se pronuncia[1] de varias[1] maneras,[1] ó por[21] mejor decir,[21] representa sonidos[8] enteramente[1] distintos,[1] en diferentes palabras[22]; y esta irregularidad[1] es muy extensa.[1] En Español sucede[23] lo mismo con la " Y," la cual se pronuncia á veces como " I " vocal,[24] y á veces como consonante.[1]

Consideradas[1] todas estas irregularidades[1] que ocurren[1] tan frecuentemente,[1] de una manera[1] ú ótra, en la mayor parte[1] de las palabras,[22] casi[25] se[26] puede decir,[26] que las letras[1] inglesas de ninguna manera[1] representan[1] los sonidos[8] del lenguaje,[1] y por[27] consiguiente[27] es en cierto modo[28] imposible[1] hallar la pronunciación de las palabras[22] por la mera[1] vista[29] de las letras manuscritas[1] ó impresas[30] del modo[28] ordinario.[1]   Una cosa es aprender[31] á escribir[32] una palabra,[22] y otra enteramente[1] diferente[1] el saber[33] pronunciarla después[34] de[34] escrita.[35]

(*se continuará en la página*[37] *siguiente.*[36])

---

0 not to be translated ; 1 the same, or nearly the same, as in English.

2 read ; 3 *bastar*, to suffice ; 4 to know (how) ; 5 there is ; 6=perhaps ; 7 tongue ; 8 sound ; 9 rule ; 10 so that ; 11 only ; 12 means ; 13 reading ; 14 under ; 15=it is possible ; 16 to attain ; 17=approaching ; 18 also ; 19 French ; 20=*viz.* ; 21=it should rather be said ; 22 word ; 23 *suceder*, to happen ; 24 vowel ; 25 almost ; 26 it may be said ; 27 consequently ; 28 way ; 29 sight ; 30 printed ; 31 to learn ; 32 (to) write ; 33 know(ing how to) ; 34 after ; 35 written ; 36 following ; 37 page.

El gato[2] escaldado[3] del agua[6] fría[5] huye.[4]

---

2 cat ; 3 *escaldar*, to scald ; 4 flees ; 5 cold ; 6 water.

La Pronunciación Inglesa *(continuación)*.

La Pronunciación Inglesa es tan difícil,[1] que tanto[2] los Americanos como[2] los Ingleses están obligados[1] á tener para su uso[1] "Diccionarios[1] de Pronunciación," con su clave[3] correspondiente[1]; esto es, diccionarios en que las palabras[4] están impresas,[5] tal[6] cual[6] deben[7] escribirse,[8] y á continuación las mismas palabras[4] con ciertos signos,[1] que muestran[9] como deben[7] pronunciarse; el método[1] ó sistema[1] con que esto se[10] hace[10] se[11] denomina[11] "clave,[3]" la cual no es siempre[12] la misma. Estos son los que se llaman[13] "Diccionarios de Pronunciación." No los hay en castellano,[14] porque no se[15] necesitan.[15]

La diferencia[1] entre la manera[1] de escribir[16] y la de pronunciar las palabras[4] en inglés, trae[17] su orígen[1] parte[18] de que la lengua[19] inglesa se ha formado[1] de la mezcla[20] de un gran número[1] de diferentes[1] idiomas,[19] parte[18] de los grandes cambios[21] que han ocurrido[1] en el método[1] de pronunciar muchas palabras[4] durante[22] muchos siglos,[23] mientras[24] que[0] el método de escribirlas no ha cambiado[25] á proporción[1]; pero principalmente[1] á[26] causa de[26] haber adoptado[1] el alfabeto[1] romano[1] para representar[1] el inglés, que tiene muchos más sonidos[27] que el latino,[1] y aún[28] más que el castellano,[14] y que por[29] tanto[29] no puede[30] representarlos[1] por el alfabeto romano.

2 *tanto ... como*, both ... and; 3 key; 4 word; 5 printed; 6 like; 7 they must; 8 be written; 9 *mostrar*, to show; 10 does itself=is done; 11=is entitled; 12 always; 13 *llamar*, to call; 14 Castilian=Spanish; 15=are wanted; 16 writing; 17 draws=owes; 18 part(ly); 19 language; 20 mixture; 21 change; 22 during; 23 century; 24 while; 25 *cambiar*, to change; 26 on account of; 27 sound; 28 yet; 29 therefore; 30 can.

El Libro prestado.

Preguntando un amigo á otro ¿por qué causa[1] no solían[2] volverse[2] á sus dueños[3] los libros prestados[4]? respondió: Porque es más fácil[5] retener[6] los libros que lo[7] que[7] contienen.[8]

2 were usually returned; 3 owner; 4 *prestar*, to lend; 5 easy; 6 (to) retain; 7 what; 8 they contain.

Se[2] cuenta[2] una buena y auténtica[1] historia[1] de la mujer[3] de un manufacturero[1] de encajes[4] de Nottingham, que hallándose con su marido[5] en París y ocupada[1] en mirar[6] los mostradores[7] como sucede[8] á los que visitan[1] París, se[9] enamoró[9] de un pañuelo[10] de encaje[4] de una finura[11] y delicadeza[1] extrema,[1] por el cual el tendero le pidió[12] la moderada[1] suma[1] de cuatro cientos cuarenta francos.[1]

Ella inmediatamente[1] lo hubiese[13] comprado[14] á[15] no impedírselo[15] los diferentes[1] signos[1] de disuasión[1] que le hizo[16] su marido,[5] los cuales le sorprendieron[17] no poco, tanto[18] más, cuanto[19] sabía[20] que su marido[5] era un buen juez en la materia[1]; no podía[21] por[22] consiguiente[22] explicarse[23] esta falta[24] de apreciación[1] sobre tan hermoso[25] trabajo.[26]

Ella examinó[1] el pañuelo[10] otra vez medio[27] dudando,[28] pero el pañuelo era suave[29] en tejido[30] y de hermoso[25] dibujo[31]; lanzó[32] otra mirada[33] á su esposo[5] y no le hallaba otro defecto[1] que el ser[34] caro[35]; de[36] suerte que[36] con cierta pena[37] se[38] fué[38] de allí.

Apenas[39] había[40] salido[41] de la tienda,[42] cuando interpelando[43] á su marido[5] le dijo: Juan,[44] ¿por qué no has querido[45] comprar[14] una cosa tan hermosa[25] como esa?

Tienes[46] razón,[46] querida[47] mía,[47] fué la respuesta[48] de Juan. Efectivamente[49] es un artículo[1] hermoso[25]: pero no he querido[45] comprártelo,[14] pues viene[50] de mi fábrica,[51] y puedo[52] darte[53] otro igual[54] por veinte francos!

---

2 is related ; 3 wife ; 4 lace ; 5 husband ; 6 look(ing) at ; 7 shop-counters; 8 *suceder*, to happen ; 9 *enamorarse*, to fall in love ; 10 handkerchief ; 11 fineness ; 12 asked ; 13 would have ; 14 *comprar*, to buy ; 15=but was prevented by ; 16 made ; 17 *sorprender*, to surprise ; 18=all the ; 19 as ; 20 she knew ; 21 she could ; 22 therefore ; 23 *explicar*, to explain ; 24 want ; 25 beautiful ; 26 work ; 27 half ; 28 *dudar*, to doubt ; 29 soft ; 30 texture ; 31 design ; 32 *lanzar*, to dart ; 33 glance ; 34 be(ing) ; 35 dear ; 36 so that ; 37 pain=regret ; 38 she went away ; 39 hardly ; 40 she had ; 41 gone out ; 42 shop ; 43 *interpelar*, to appeal ; 44 John ; 45 been willing ; 46 hast reason=art right ; 47 my dear ; 48 reply ; 49 certainly, indeed ; 50 it comes ; 51 manufactory ; 52 I can ; 53 give thee ; 54 equal=like it.

¿ En qué se[2] parece[2] un esqueleto[3] á una comida[4] de viernes[5]? En que le[6] falta[6] la carne.[7]

---

2 resembles ; 3 skeleton ; 4 dinner ; 5 Friday ; 6 it lacks ; 7 flesh.

El Misisipí.

Paseábase[2] un europeo[1] por las orillas[3] del Misisipí,[1] río[4] de curso[5] muy veloz,[6] y preguntó á[0] un labriego[7] : ¿ Cómo se[8] llama[8] este río[4] ?—No hay necesidad[1] de llamarle, señor, porque él se[0] viene[9] espontáneamente[10] solo.[11]

---

2 was passing ; 3 bank ; 4 river ; 5 current ; 6 rapid ; 7 peasant ; 8 *llamarse,* to be called ; 9 comes ; 10 voluntarily ; 11 alone=of its own accord.

La Generosidad.

Presentaron[1] á un caballero la cuenta[2] de gastos[3] del entierro[4] de su mujer,[5] y al[6] ver[6] á lo[7] que[7] ascendía, ¡ cómo, señores ! exclamó,[1] ¡ tanto[8] dinero por un convoy[9] fúnebre[9] !

Pues[10] qué[10] ¿ cree Vd. que unos[0] funerales tan magníficos[1] se[11] hacen[11] por nada[12] ? no podemos[13] rebajar[14] un cuarto.[15]

Vamos,[10] vamos,[10] les contesta, hacedme[16] el recibo,[17] pues ahora ya[0] me[18] hago cargo[18] de[0] que[0] mi pobre mujer[5] hubiera[19] pagado[20] muy gustosa[21] el doble[1] por mi entierro,[4] y no quiero[22] cederla[23] en generosidad.[1]

---

2 account ; 3 expense ; 4 burial ; 5 wife ; 6 on seeing ; 7 what ; 8 so much ; 9 funeral ; 10 well ; 11=are done ; 12 nothing ; 13 we can ; 14 to bate ; 15 (a small copper coin) ; 16 make me (out) ; 17 receipt ; 18 I think of it ; 19 would have ; 20 paid ; 21 cheerfully ; 22 I am willing ; 23 (to) give way to her.

Nueva Aritmética.

Un abogado[2] hizo[3] la defensa[1] de un litigante[1] ante[4] un tribunal[1] compuesto[5] de tres jueces,[6] el uno muy sabio,[7] y los otros dos bastante[8] ignorantes.[1]

Perdió[9] el pleito,[10] y queriendo[12] uno de sus compañeros[11] burlarse[13] de él, con este motivo[1] dijo : ¿ Pero, esperaban[14] Vds.[14] otra cosa ?   Era preciso[15] sucediese[16] así[17] con un tribunal[1] de cien jueces.[6]

¡ Cien jueces ! repuso[18] uno de ellos ; ¿ pues[19] no eran tres ?

Uno y dos ceros[20] ¿ cuánto[21] hacen[22] según[23] vuestra cuenta[24]? respondió el abogado.[2]

---

2 lawyer ; 3 made ; 4 before ; 5 composed ; 6 judge ; 7 learned ; 8=rather; 9 he lost ; 10 law-suit ; 11 colleague ; 12 wishing ; 13 to make fun ; 14 did you expect ; 15 necessary ; 16 it should happen ; 17 thus ; 18 replied ; 19 then =but ; 20 zero ; 21 how many ; 22 do they make ; 23 according to ; 24 count.

From this point the Student is assumed to be acquainted with all the Rules in "SPANISH SIMPLIFIED," including the principal Irregular Verbs (*see Lessons 19 to 24*).

El Campanario.

Una señora vió[2] entrar[1] en su cuarto á[0] un hombre de una estatura[1] gigantesca,[1] y preguntó quién era. Es un hombre que viene[3] destinado[1] para la iglesia,[4] respondió el criado.

Mejor[5] diría Vd.,[5] repuso[6] la señora, para el campanario.[7]

---

2 saw ; 3 comes=is ; 4 church ; 5 you would better say ; 6 replied ; 7 steeple.

El Criado fiel.

Un señor, necesitando[2] madrugar,[3] dice á su criado : Juan, mañana debes[4] despertarme[5] á las cuatro en[6] punto.[6]

Será[7] Vd. servido.[7]

Mira[8] que[0] no te[0] olvides.[9]—No tenga Vd. cuidado.[10]

Y Juan, fiel[11] á su promesa,[1] resuelve[1] no echarse[12] en la cama[12] aquella noche ; enciende[13] una vela,[14] y se sienta[15] en una silla.

Pero el sueño,[16] que no hace diferencia[1] entre el desnudo[17] y el vestido,[18] acaba[19] por rendir[20] á Juan, que empieza[21] á dormir[22] como un bendito.[23] De[24] súbito[24] se despierta,[5] consulta azorado[25] el reloj, que marca[1] las dos, y sin darse[26] cuenta[26] de lo que hace, corre[27] á la cámara[28] de su amo, y empieza[21] á gritar[29] desaforadamente[30] :

¡ Señor, señor ! — ¿ Qué[31] hay[31] ? ¿ son ya las cuatro ? responde[1] el amo sobresaltado.[32]

No, señor, replica[1] Juan, no son más que las dos : vengo á decirle que aún[33] le quedan[34] dos horas más para dormir[22]; aprovéchelas[35] Vd.

---

2 wanting ; 3 to rise early ; 4 you must ; 5 *despertar*, to wake ; 6 precisely ; 7=it shall be done ; 8 look ; 9 *olvidar*, to forget ; 10 care= anxiety ; 11 faithful ; 12=to go to bed ; 13 *encender*, to light ; 14 candle ; 15 *sentarse*, to seat one's self ; 16 sleep ; 17 undressed ; 18 dressed ; 19 *acabar*, to finish ; 20 to overcome ; 21 *empezar*, to begin ; 22 to sleep ; 23 blessed ; 24 suddenly ; 25 terrified ; 26=thinking ; 27 *correr*, to run ; 28 chamber ; 29 to call out ; 30 excessively ; 31 what is the matter ; 32 startled; 33 still ; 34 *quedar*, to remain ; 35 *aprovechar*, to take advantage of.

La Base fundamental de la Justicia.

Un abogado[2] que iba á establecer[1] á[0] su escribiente[3] le dijo : Mire[4] Vd.[4] ; antes[5] de[5] ausentarme[6] voy á comunicarle[1] una cosa muy importante.[1] Ya sabe Vd. los favores[1] que me debe, pues yo le he enseñado[7] el oficio,[8] y gracias[9] á mis cuidados[10] no puede dejar[11] de hacer fortuna[1] en este mundo[12]; pero he reservado[1] para el último[13] un servicio[1] interesante.[1]

¿ Y cuál es ?

Es el de indicarle[1] la base[1] fundamental[1] de la justicia.[1]

¿ Y cuál es esa base ?—No puedo decirla mientras[14] no me pague[15] un buen almuerzo.[16]

Consiento[1] en ello, ordene[17] Vd. lo que quiera.[18]

El abogado[2] pidió[19] dos docenas[20] de ostras,[21] jamón,[22] un pavo,[23] langostas,[24] en[25] fin[25] un almuerzo[16] suculento,[1] y después[26] le dijo :

Sepa[27] Vd., pues, que la base de toda la justicia es la prueba,[28] la prueba, amigo mío, la prueba.

Comen,[29] beben,[30] se divierten[31] ; pero todo placer[32] tiene su fin[33] ; viene la cuenta,[34] y el abogado manda[35] se[0] la den[36] al escribiente,[3] que es quien ha hecho aquel obsequio.[37]

¿ Yo ? no, señor.—¿ Cómo que[0] no ? amiguito,[38] ya sabe Vd. lo que hemos convenido.[39]

¿ Pues qué convenio[40] he hecho yo ?

Que se ha comprometido[41] Vd. á pagarlo[15] todo.

¿ Y dónde está la prueba[28] ?

El abogado[2] fué[42] quien pagó[15] por no poder darla,[43] siendo como él mismo[44] le había dicho, la base[1] fundamental[1] de la justicia.[1]

---

2 lawyer ; 3 clerk ; 4 look (here) ; 5 before ; 6 *ausentarse*, to absent one's self ; 7 *enseñar*, to teach ; 8 business ; 9 thanks ; 10 care ; 11 leave=fail ; 12 world ; 13 last ; 14 as long as ; 15 *pagar*, to pay ; 16 breakfast ; 17 *ordenar*, to order ; 18 you like ; 19 requested ; 20 dozen ; 21 oyster ; 22 ham ; 23 turkey ; 24 lobster ; 25 in fact ; 26 afterwards ; 27 know ; 28 proof ; 29 *comer*, to eat ; 30 *beber*, to drink ; 31 *divertirse*, to enjoy one's self ; 32 pleasure ; 33 end ; 34 bill ; 35 *mandar*, to order ; 36 (that) they give ; 37 civility ; 38 young friend ; 39 *convenir*, to agree ; 40 agreement ; 41 *comprometerse*, to undertake ; 42 (it) was ; 43 give it ; 44 himself.

La Puerta cerrada.[2]

Un caballero de una conversación fastidiosa[3] y eterna,[1] dió[4] en la costumbre[5] de ir frecuentemente[1] á una casa donde no gustaban[6] mucho sus visitas[1]; fingía[7] no hacer[8] caso[8] de las respuestas[9] de la criada, que le decía siempre[10] que los amos no estaban en[11] casa,[11] y se introducía[1] sin cumplimiento[12] todos los días con estos pretextos[1]: Bien, bien; mientras[13] vuelven[14] voy á hablar con los niños…Haré[15] rabiar[15] un rato[17] al loro[16] … Aprovecharé[18] esta ocasión[1] para arreglar[19] mi reloj por el del salón, etc.

Una mañana que la criada tenía ya su contestación[9] pensada,[20] le vió venir de lejos[21] desde[22] una ventana,[23] fué corriendo[24] á la puerta, y sin abrirla[25] le dijo desde[22] la rejilla[26]: Señor don Ramón, mi amo y mi ama han salido, los niños están en la escuela,[27] el loro[16] ha muerto,[28] y el reloj está parado.[29]

Cerró la rejilla[26] y no le dió lugar[30] á más conversación.[1]

---

0 not to be translated ; 1 the same, or nearly the same, as in English. 2 *cerrar*, to shut ; 3 tedious ; 4=was ; 5 habit ; 6 *gustar*, to please ; 7 *fingir*, to pretend ; 8=to take notice ; 9 answer ; 10 always ; 11 at home ; 12=ceremony ; 13 while=until ; 14 *volver*, to return ; 15 I will tease ; 16 parrot ; 17 short time ; 18 *aprovechar*, to take advantage of ; 19 (to) regulate ; 20 *pensar*, to consider ; 21 afar ; 22 from ; 23 window ; 24 *correr*, to run ; 25 *abrir*, to open ; 26 lattice ; 27 school ; 28 died ; 29 *parar*, to stop ; 30 place=opportunity.

Un particular[2] que ajustaba[3] un borrico,[4] dijo al molinero[5] que lo tomaría, con la garantía[1] de que no tuviese ningún defecto.[1]

Convengo[6] en ello, respondió el dueño.[7]

Pasados[8] algunos días el comprador[9] advirtió[10] que el borrico[4] era tuerto,[11] y quiso devolvérselo[12] diciéndole :

Amigo mío, su borrico[4] de Vd. no ve más que de un lado,[13] porque sólo[14] abre[14] una ventana.

Toma,[15] responde, eso no es un defecto,[1] sino una desgracia.[16]

---

2 certain man ; 3 was bargaining ; 4 donkey ; 5 miller ; 6 *convenir*, to agree; 7 owner ; 8 passed=after ; 9 buyer ; 10 *advertir*, to notice ; 11 one-eyed ; 12 to return it to him ; 13 side ; 14 only opens ; 15…well ; 16 misfortune.

Cádiz.

Pocos panoramas[1] hay más bellos[2] en el mundo,[3] y casi[4] ningún cuadro[5] en la naturaleza[6] que cautive[7] más los ojos[8] del espectador[9] por su diafanidad[10] y hermosura,[11] que el que ofrece[13] la vista[12] de la ciudad de Cádiz, desde[14] uno de los vapores[15] que hacen la travesía[16] de Sevilla[1] á este puerto,[17] cuando toca[18] al término[19] de su espedición,[1] á los viajeros[20] que contemplan[1] la linda[21] ciudad que se levanta[22] sobre el mar,[23] á[24] la manera[1] de[24] un palacio[1] de plata[25] primorosamente[26] afiligranado.[27] La blancura[28] de sus torres[29] y de las azoteas[30] de sus casas, las cúpulas[1] y los torreones[31] de sus templos, y la belleza[11] armónica[32] de su conjunto,[33] ceñido[34] por la ancha[35] faja[36] de piedra[37] que la circuye,[38] le dan por otro lado[39] el aspecto[1] de un gran buque[40] de alabastro,[1] flotante[1] en medio[41] de los mares.[23]

A[42] medida que[42] el vapor[15] va adelantando[43] rápido[1] hacia[44] el muelle,[45] el viajero[20] menos reflexivo[1] se convence[1] de[0] que se[46] aproxima[46] á una población[1] importante[1] por su movimiento[1] mercantil[1] ; y los numerosos[1] buques[40] de todos portes[47] y con banderas[48] de todas las naciones[1] de Europa, que están anclados[49] en su bahía,[50] y por[51] entre[51] los cuales cruza[52] el vapor,[15] le indican[1] claramente[53] que la bella[2] ciudad aún[54] conserva[1] restos[56] honrosos[55] de su antiguo[57] poderío[58] y de su pristina grandeza.[59]

2 beautiful ; 3 world ; 4 almost ; 5 picture ; 6 nature ; 7 *cautivar*, to captivate ; 8 eye ; 9 spectator ; 10 transparency ; 11 beauty ; 12 view ; 13 offers ; 14 from ; 15 steamer ; 16 passage across ; 17 port ; 18 *tocar*, to touch ; 19 end ; 20 traveller ; 21 pretty ; 22 *levantar*, to raise ; 23 sea ; 24=like ; 25 silver ; 26 elegantly ; 27 filigreed ; 28 whiteness ; 29 tower ; 30 flat roof ; 31 turret ; 32 harmonious ; 33=grouping ; 34 *ceñir*, to gird ; 35 broad ; 36 band ; 37 stone ; 38 *circuir*, to surround ; 39 side ; 40 ship ; 41 middle ; 42 in proportion as ; 43 moving forward ; 44 towards ; 45 quay ; 46 he is approaching ; 47 tonnage ; 48 flag ; 49 *anclar*, to anchor ; 50 bay ; 51 through ; 52 *cruzar*, to cruise ; 53 clearly ; 54 still ; 55 honorable ; 56 remains ; 57 ancient ; 58 power ; 59 greatness.

¿ Quién es el que sin ceremonia[1] y con sombrero puesto,[2] se[3] sienta[3] delante[4] del rey, del papa,[5] ó del emperador[1] ?

El cochero.[6]

2 put=on ; 3 sits down ; 4 before ; 5 pope ; 6 coachman.

La Disputa de Cocina.

Tramaron[2] una disputa[1] la criada y el cochero[3] de un banquero[1] de Murcia, sobre quien de los dos había de ir al desayuno[4] del amo ; y éste, oyendo[5] los gritos,[6] les llamó[7] para resolver[8] sobre esta diferencia.[1] La cocinera[9] se quejaba[10] de[0] que el cochero[3] pasaba toda la mañana rodando[11] por[11] la cocina[12] como un zángano,[13] y que ella tenía tanto[14] que hacer que no podía separarse[1] del fogón[15] un solo[16] instante.[1]

El cochero[3] dijo que la crema[17] no era de[0] su obligación.[1]

Veamos,[18] pues, ¿ cuál es tu obligación ? le preguntó el amo.

Mi oficio,[19] señor, es el[0] de cuidar[20] los caballos, limpiar[21] el coche[22] y llevarlo[23] á donde su merced[24] me mande.[25]

Es verdad,[26] tienes[27] razón,[27] y no exijo[28] más de tí, pues sólo[29] para eso te tengo ; y en este supuesto[30] todas las mañanas te levantarás[31] al amanecer,[32] limpiarás[21] muy bien el coche[22] y los caballos, y antes[33] de[33] almorzar[4] engancharás[34] y llevarás[23] en él á[0] la cocinera[9] al mercado[35] para[36] que compre[36] la crema.[17]

El cochero se[37] rascó las orejas,[37] y se[0] retiró.[1]

---

2 weaved=had ; 3 coachman ; 4 breakfast ; 5 hearing ; 6 cry ; 7 *llamar*, to call ; 8=decide ; 9 cook ; 10 *quejarse*, to complain ; 11 wandering about ; 12 kitchen ; 13 idler ; 14 so much ; 15 hearth ; 16 single ; 17 cream ; 18 let us see ; 19 business ; 20 to look after ; 21 to clean ; 22 coach ; 23 *llevar*=to take ; 24 honor ; 25 orders ; 26 truth ; 27 thou art right ; 28 *exigir*, to require ; 29 only ; 30 supposition ; 31 *levantarse*, to get up ; 32 dawn ; 33 before ; 34 *enganchar*, to harness ; 35 market ; 36 that she (may) buy ; 37 scratched his ears.

Entre un hombre pobre y un hombre rico hay todo un hombre de diferencia.[1]

Un bufón[1] preguntó á[0] uno que tenía las piernas[2] torcidas[3] y la cadera[5] derecha[4] derrengada,[6] ¿ qué camino había tomado[?] para ir á Cádiz ?

He venido todo[7] derecho,[8] respondió.

Pues, señor, en ese caso,[1] repuso[9] el bufón, se ha transformado[1] Vd. enteramente[10] en el camino.

---

2 leg ; 3 distorted ; 4 right ; 5 hip ; 6 crooked ; 7=quite ; 8 straight ; 9 replied ; 10 entirely.

Esopo y el Viajero.

Esopo,[1] el célebre[1] fabulista,[1] era muy pobre, y muchas veces tenía que[2] ir á[3] pié de una ciudad á otra. En una de sus excursiones[1] encontró[4] en el camino á[0] un viajero, el cual deteniéndose[5] le preguntó :

¿ Puede[6] Vd. decirme á qué hora llegaré á aquel pueblo que está sobre la colina[7] ?

En llegando lo sabrá[8] Vd.,[8] contestó[9] Esopo.[1]

Ya lo sé, dijo el viajero ; pero lo que deseo[10] saber, es cuanto[11] tiempo tardaré.[12]

Esopo pareció[13]ofenderse,[1]y repitió[1]la misma contestación.[14]

El viajero continuó[1] su camino diciendo para[15] sí[15] : Este hombre me parece[13] un ignorante[1] y no me dirá[16] lo que necesito[17] saber.

Algunos minutos después[18] oyó[19] que le llamaban,[20] y volviendo[21] la vista,[21] vió á[0] Esopo que le seguía.[22]

¿ Qué quiere Vd. ? le preguntó.

Dentro[23] de hora y media[24] llegará Vd. al pueblo, respondió Esopo.

¿ Y por qué no me lo dijo Vd. cuando se[25] lo pregunté[25] ? Antes[26] necesitaba[17] ver lo[27] ligero[27] que Vd. andaba.[28]

2=to ; 3 on foot ; 4 *encontrar*, to meet ; 5 *detenerse*, to stop ; 6 can ; 7 hill ; 8 you will know ; 9 *contestar*, to answer ; 10 *desear*, to desire ; 11 how much ; 12 *tardar*, to delay ; 13 *parecer*, to seem ; 14 answer ; 15 to himself ; 16 will tell ; 17 *necesitar*, to want ; 18 after ; 19 *oir*, to hear ; 20 *llamar*, to call ; 21=turning round ; 22 *seguir*, to follow ; 23 within ; 24 half ; 25 I asked you ; 26 before=first ; 27=the rate ; 28 *andar*, to walk.

Un pobre zapatero[2] remendón[2] se vió un día apurado[3] para encender[4] la lumbre,[5] y envió á[0] un chiquillo,[6] hijo suyo, á[7] buscar un fuelle prestado,[7] por un momento, á casa de un avaro[8] que vivía en la vecindad[9] ; pero éste dijo al niño : Mira,[10] dile[11] á tu padre, que yo no dejo[12] salir el fuelle[13] de mi casa ; pero que puede venir cuando quiera[14] á soplar[15] todo el día en mi cocina.[16]

---

2 cobbler ; 3=unable ; 4 (to) light ; 5 fire ; 6 little boy ; 7 to seek a pair of bellows lent=to borrow a pair of bellows ; 8 miser ; 9 neighbourhood ; 10 look (here) ; 11 tell ; 12 *dejar*, to let ; 13 bellows ; 14 he likes ; 15 (to) blow ; 16 kitchen.

Foote y el Alcalde.

Viajando[2] una vez el actor Foote por el oeste[3] de Inglaterra[4] se detuvo[5] en una posada[6] para comer.[7]   Al arreglar[8] las cuentas[9] el posadero[10] le preguntó si estaba satisfecho.[1]

Perfectamente,[1] dijo Foote, he comido[7] mejor[11] que nadie[12] en Inglaterra.[4]

Excepto[1] el alcalde,[13] replicó el posadero.[10]

Yo no hago excepción[1] alguna.

Pero debe[14] Vd. exceptuar[1] al alcalde.[13]

Y Foote, encolerizado,[15] volvió[16] á replicar[16] recalcando[17] la voz[18]en cada sílaba[1]que ni aun[19]exceptuaba[1] al mismo[20]alcalde.

Y tomó tales[21] proporciones[1] la pendencia,[22] que el posadero[10] condujo[23] á[0] Foote en presencia[1] del alcalde[13] del lugar.[24]

Sr. Foote, le dijo este venerable[1] magistrado,[1] ha de saber Vd. que desde[25] tiempo inmemorial[1] se[26] conserva[26] aquí la costumbre[1] de hacer siempre[27] una excepción[1] para el alcalde,[13] y con objeto[1] de[0] que lo tenga Vd. presente[1] le condeno[1] á cinco reales[1] de multa,[28] ó á cinco horas de arresto[1] si así[29] lo prefiere.[1]

Foote se vió precisado[30]á pagar la multa.[28] A su salida[31]dijo :

En toda la cristiandad[32] no conozco[33] un hombre más tonto[34] que ese posadero,[10] ... excepto[1] el señor[35] Alcalde — é hizo una solemne[1] reverencia[1] á Su Señoría.[36]

---

0 not to be translated ; 1 the same, or nearly the same, as in English. 2 *viajar*, to travel ; 3 west ; 4 England ; 5 *detenerse*, to stop ; 6 inn ; 7 to dine ; 8 settling ; 9 account ; 10 innkeeper ; 11 better ; 12 nobody= anybody ; 13 mayor ; 14 must ; 15 angered ; 16 returned to reply=replied again ; 17=emphasizing ; 18 voice ; 19 even ; 20 himself ; 21 such ; 22 dispute ;   23 *conducir*, to conduct ;   24 place ;   25 from ;   26 is preserved ; 27 always ; 28 fine ; 29 thus, so ; 30 *precisar*, to compel ; 31 going out ; 32 Christendom ; 33 *conocer*, to know ; 34 foolish ; 35 Lord ; 36 lordship.

La mayor parte de los hombres pasan la mitad[2] de su vida[3] estropeando[4] su salud,[5] y la otra mitad[6] haciendo ensayos[7] para remendarla.[8]

---

2 half ; 3 life ; 4 *estropear*, to cripple, injure ; 5 health ; 6 half ;   7 endeavour ;   8 *remendar*, to mend.

Habiendo una bala[2] enemiga[1] dejado[3] sin brazos[4] á[0] un soldado francés en la batalla de Hastembeck, su coronel[1] le regaló[5] un escudo.[6]—Mi coronel, dijo el soldado, tal[7] vez[7] V.[8] S.[8] cree que he perdido[9] un par[10] de guantes.[11]

---

2 ball ; 3 *dejar*, to leave ; 4 arm ; 5 *regalar*, to present ; 6 crown ; 7 perhaps ; 8 *vuestra señoría*=your honor ; 9 *perder*, to lose ; 10 pair ; 11 glove.

Mostraba[2] un rico sus joyas[3] á un filósofo,[1] y éste le dijo : Gracias, señor, por esas brillantes[1] joyas[3] de que tan cariñosamente[4] me hace Vd. participe.[1]— ¿ Cómo[5] se entiende Vd. participe[5] ?— Sí, señor, Vd. permite[1] que yo las contemple[1] ; y ¿ hace Vd. con ellas otra cosa diferente[1] ?

---

2 *mostrar*, to show ; 3 jewel ; 4 kindly ; 5=how do you mean share ?

Como en los antiguos[1] teatros[1] londonenses[2] no representaban[1] las mujeres, tenían que desempeñar[3] el papel[4] de estas hombres disfrazados.[5] Impacientado[1] una vez Carlos II. esperando[6] el comienzo[7] de la función,[8] el director compareció[9] ante el rey y le dijo :

S.[10] M.[10]dispense,[11]pero la reína[12]no se ha afeitado[13]todavía.[14]

---

2 London ; 3 fulfil ; 4 part ; 5 *disfrazar*, to disguise ; 6 *esperar*, to expect; 7 commencement ; 8 performance ; 9 *comparecer*, to appear; 10 *Su Majestad*, Your Majesty ; 11 *dispensar*, to excuse ; 12 queen ; 13 to shave ; 14 yet.

Cayóse[2] en un río[3] una señorita romántica[1] y poco[4] le faltó para ahogarse.[4]   Pasaba por casualidad[5] un nadador,[6] y lanzándose[7] al río[3] la sacó[8] desmayada,[9] en cuyo estado[10] fué llevada á su casa.—Cuando volvió[21] en sí,[21] declaró[1] á sus padres[12] que quería casarse[13] con el que le había salvado[14] la vida.[15]—Es imposible, dice su padre. — ¿ Es que está ya casado[13] ?—No.—Pues diga Vd. ¿ no es aquel joven[16] vecino[17] nuestro ?—Oh, no : es un perro[18] de Terra-Nova.[19]

---

2 fell ; 3 river ; 4 little was wanting to her to drown herself=was nearly drowned ; 5 chance ; 6 swimmer ; 7 *lanzar*, to fling ; 8 *sacar*, to draw out ; 9 insensible ; 10 state ; 11=came to herself again ; 12 parents ; 13 *casar*, to marry ; 14 *salvar*, to save ; 15 life ; 16 young (man) ; 17 neighbour ; 18 dog ; 19 Newfoundland.

Un caballerito que iba á casarse[2] después de haber confesado,[1] entró[1] en un escrúpulo,[1] y se volvió[3] al confesor.

Padre, le dice, no sé si me he confesado bien, pues veo que no me habéis impuesto[4] ninguna penitencia.[1]

El confesor, que era entendido,[5] le respondió : ¿ Pues no me ha dicho Vd., hijo, que iba á casarse[2] ?

2 *casarse*, to get married ; 3 *volverse*, to go back ; 4 *imponer*, to impose ; 5 knowing.

En la representación[1] de una nueva comedia[1] casera[2] hubo[3] tanta demanda[1] de[4] billetes[5] de entrada,[6] que no fueron suficientes[1] los que había[3] según[7] la capacidad[1] del salón,[1] y algunos de los aficionados[8] que hacían la comedia, introdujeron[1] por el escenario,[9] que tenía una puerta falsa,[1] muchas personas antes de abrir[10] la entrada[6] principal. Al[11] ver[11] esto el director dijo muy enojado[12] : Es una vergüenza[13] dejar llenar[14] el salón antes de entrar[1] la gente.[15]

2 domestic ; 3 there was *or* were ; 4═for ; 5 ticket ; 6 entrance ; 7 according to ; 8 amateur ; 9 scene ; 10 open(ing) ; 11 on seeing ; 12 annoyed ; 13 shame ; 14 (to) fill ; 15 people.

El gracioso[2] de un teatro[1] de París,[1] se[3] metió[3] una mañana en una fonda,[4] la primera que halló á mano, y pidiendo[5] de almorzar,[6] suplicó[7] al fondista[8] le hiciese[9] compañía[1] á la meza. Este, para mostrarle[10] sin duda[11] su aprecio,[12] empezó,[13] sin hablar palabra,[14] á tirar[15] debajo[16] de[16] la mesa las cosas que veía sucias.[17]

El gracioso,[2] que vió arrojar[18] las servilletas,[19] los cubiertos[20] y los cuchillos,[21] no queriendo contrariarle,[22] le imitó tirando[15] precipitadamente[1] las fuentes,[23] los platos[24] y los vasos.[25]

El fondista,[8] sorprendido[26] al ver esto, le preguntó la causa,[1] y él con mucha serenidad[1] le dijo : Hombre,[27] pensaba[28] que quería Vd. que almorzásemos[29] debajo[16] de[16] la mesa.

2 comic actor ; 3 put himself═went ; 4 inn ; 5 asking ; 6 breakfast ; 7 *suplicar*, to entreat ; 8 innkeeper ; 9 that he should make═keep ; 10 *mostrar*, to show ; 11 doubt ; 12 esteem ; 13 *empezar*, to begin ; 14 word ; 15 *tirar*, to throw ; 16 under ; 17 dirty ; 18 fling ; 19 napkin ; 20 cover ; 21 knife ; 22 to oppose ; 23 dish ; 24 plate ; 25 glass ; 26 *sorprender*, to surprise ; 27═well ; 28 *pensar*, to think ; 29 we should breakfast.

El Barómetro.

Un médico andaluz[1] tenía un día algunos amigos á comer[2] en su casa. Uno de ellos le dijo que deseaba ver su hermoso barómetro[1] que decían le había costado[1] mil francos,[1] y mandó á[0] un criado que fuese[3] á buscarlo[3]; pero éste, al[4] traerlo,[4] lo dejó caer[5] y se[6] hizo pedazos.[6]

Todos los convidados[7] demostraron al doctor su sentimiento[8] por tan desagradable[1] accidente.[1]—No os aflijáis,[9] les dijo el médico : este suceso[10] es de buen agüero,[11] pues hace[12] mucho tiempo que no llueve,[12] y como nunca[13] he visto el barómetro tan bajo,[14] es de presumir[1] que vamos á tener agua.[15]

---

2 dine ; 3=he should go and fetch it ; 4 on bringing it ; 5 fall ; 6 made itself pieces=broke in pieces ; 7 guest ; 8 regret ; 9 *afligirse*, to lament ; 10 event ; 11 omen ; 12=it has not rained for a long time ; 13 never ; 14 low ; 15 water=rain.

Un príncipe,[2] queriendo divertirse[1] á costa[1] de uno de sus cortesanos[3] á[0] quien había empleado[4] en diferentes[1] embajadas,[5] le dijo que se parecía[6] á[0] un buho.[7]

Yo, señor, no sé á[0] quien me parezco,[6] respondió : lo que sé es que he tenido el honor[1] de representar[1] muchas veces á[0] Vuestra Majestad.[1]

---

2 prince ; 3 courtier ; 4 *emplear*, to employ ; 5 embassy ; 6 *parecerse*, to resemble ; 7 owl.

Un hombre naturalmente[1] gracioso[2] fué citado[3] para deponer[4] ante el tribunal[1] criminal[1] sobre una disputa[1] muy seria[1] que habían tenido dos comerciantes.[5] Un abogado,[6] que tenía la reputación[1] de procurar[7] siempre desconcertar[1] á[0] los testigos,[8] le preguntó á qué distancia estaba del sitio[9] de la escena.[1]

A un metro,[1] cinco centímetros[1] y seis milímetros,[1] le respondió.

¿ Cómo puede Vd. ser tan exacto ? repuso[10] el abogado.[6]

Porque suponía[11] que algún curioso[12] me lo preguntaría, y he medido[13] el terreno.[14]

---

2 witty ; 3 *citar*, to summon ; 4 depose ; 5 merchant ; 6 lawyer ; 7 try(ing) ; 8 witness ; 9 place ; 10 replied ; 11 *suponer*, to suppose ; 12 inquisitive (person) ; 13 *medir*, to measure ; 14 ground.

El Cirujano.

Un cirujano[2] muy gracioso[3] fué llamado para curar[1] á[0] un caballero caprichoso[1] que se había hecho una pequeña llaga[4] en una pierna.[5]

El criado había ido volando[6] á buscarle y el pobre llegó casi[7] sin aliento[8] suponiendo[9] que era cosa de la mayor importancia.

Reconoció[10] al herido,[11] y no[0] hallando sino[12] un rasguño[13] que se podía curar[1] con tafetán,[14] por burlarse[15] de él mandó á[0] un criado que fuese[16] sin parar[17] á su casa por un bálsamo[1] que indicó,[1] y que volviese[18] al momento.

Pues[19] que,[19] dice el herido,[11] pálido[1] y tremblando[1] de aprensión,[1] ¿ tanto[20] es el peligro[21] ?

No, señor, dice el cirujano[2] ; sino[12] que si tarda,[22] temo[23] que no llegue á tiempo, porque la llaga[4] se va á curar[1]por sí[24] sola.[25]

---

2 surgeon ; 3 witty ; 4 wound ; 5 leg ; 6 *volar*, to fly ; 7 almost ; 8 breath ; 9 *suponer*, to suppose ; 10 *reconocer*, to examine ; 11 wounded (man) ; 12 only ; 13 scratch ; 14 sticking-plaster ; 15 make game ; 16 he (should) go ; 17 stop(ping) ; 18 he (should) come back ; 19=why then ; 20 so much ; 21 danger ; 22 *tardar*, to delay ; 23 *temer*, to fear ; 24 itself ; 25 alone.

La hija de un alcalde[2] estaba cuidando[3] un canario[1] que tenía, y habiendo dejado abierta[4] la ventanilla[5] de la jaula,[6] se[0] escapó[1] el pajarillo.[7]

La primera precaución[1] que tomó su padre, luego[8] que[8] lo supo,[9] fué mandar cerrar[10] las puertas de la ciudad.

---

2 mayor ; 3 *cuidar*, to take care of ; 4 open ; 5 little window ; 6 cage ; 7 little bird ; 8 as soon as ; 9 he knew ; 10 to (be) shut.

Un pobre artesano[1] que estaba enfermo[2] y sin un cuarto,[3] dijo á un amigo que pensaba consultar[1] su mal[4] con el médico N—, pero que recelaba[5] hacerlo por no poder pagarle, y el amigo le contestó : Creo que harás[6] muy mal en llamarle si no tienes dinero, porque cuando él está enfermo,[2] y se consulta á[0] sí[0] mismo[0] sobre lo que debe[7] tomar, se[0] saca[8] un duro[9] de un bolsillo[10] y se[0] lo mete[11] en otro.

---

2 ill ; 3 a small Spanish coin ; 4 complaint ; 5 *recelar*, to mistrust ; 6 thou wilt do ; 7 he must ; 8 *sacar*, to draw ; 9 dollar ; 10 pocket ; 11 *meter*, to put.

El Hombre sin Sesos.

Dos suizos[2] estaban riñendo[3] con el mayor encarnizamiento[4] en medio[5] de una plaza[6] pública,[1] y un aldeano,[7] que casualmente[1] pasaba por[8] allí,[8] quiso[9] separarlos[1] por compasión[1] ; pero ellos, que estaban ciegos[10] de furor, le echaron[11] á tierra de un sablazo,[12] y le hicieron[13] una herida[14] en la cabeza,[15] por lo que fué preciso[16] le reconociese[18] un cirujano.[17]

Procediendo[1] éste[19] con tiento[20] para saber si tenía lastimados[21] los sesos[22] : No se canse[23] Vd. en buscarlos, le dijo el aldeano,[7] pues cuando me metí[24] en la contienda,[25] ya no los tenía.

---

2 Swiss ; 3 *reñir*, to quarrel ; 4 fury ; 5 middle ; 6 place ; 7 villager ; 8=that way ; 9 wanted ; 10 blind ; 11 *echar*, to throw ; 12 cut from a sabre ; 13 made=gave ; 14 wound ; 15 head ; 16 necessary ; 17 surgeon ; 18 should examine ; 19=the latter ; 20=care ; 21 *lastimar*, to hurt ; 22 brains ; 23 *cansar*, to tire ; 24 *meterse*, to put one's self=to interfere ; 25 quarrel.

¿ Qué hace Vd. ? dijo á un gotoso,[2] que estaba comiendo[3] jamón,[4] un amigo suyo : ¿ no ve Vd. que el jamón[4] es malo para la gota[5] ?

Así[6] es, respondió el doliente[7]; pero es bueno para el gotoso.[2]

---

2 gouty (person) ; 3 *comer*, to eat ; 4 ham ; 5 gout ; 6 so ; 7 invalid.

Habiendo dicho un[2] sugeto[2] á una señora que un boticario[3] amigo suyo había quebrado[4] y se había visto obligado[1] á cerrar[5] la botica,[6] le preguntó la causa.[1]   Respondióla que era un hombre honrado,[7] que en[8] vez[8] de cargar[9] de remedios[1] á[9] sus enfermos,[10] les aconsejaba[11] respirar[1] aire[1] puro,[1] por cuyo consejo[12] perdía[13] todo el beneficio[1] que debía[16] dejarle la venta[14] de sus drogas.[15]

¡ Pobre hombre ! replicó la señora, es lástima[17] que no pueda[18] vivir de aire[1] como sus enfermos.[10]

---

2 a person=some one ; 3 apothecary ; 4 *quebrar*, to become bankrupt ; 5 shut ; 6 apothecary's shop ; 7 honorable ; 8 instead ; 9 load(ing) ; 10 patient ; 11 *aconsejar*, to advise ; 12 advice ; 13 *perder*, to lose ; 14 sale ; 15 drug ; 16 ought ; 17 pity ; 18 can.

El Poeta y el Pastelero.

Un poeta[1] hizo en unos versos[1] el elogio[2] de un pastelero,[3] y éste creyó debía[4] demostrarle[5] su reconocimiento[6] regalándole[7] un pastel,[8] lo que ejecutó[1] inmediatamente[1]; pero habiendo advertido[9] el poeta[1] que el papel que cubría[10] el fondo[11] del pastel[8] era parte[1] de su producción,[1] reconvino[12] amargamente[13] á[0] su protegido[14] por tal desprecio,[15] y éste le respondió:

¿ Pero qué motivo[1] tiene Vd. para quejarse[16] ? Ahora es cuando estamos juego[17] á juego,[17] pues Vd. ha hecho versos[1] sobre mi pasta,[18] y yo he hecho pastas sobre sus versos.[1]

---

2 eulogy ; 3 pastry-cook ; 4 he ought ; 5 *demostrar*, to demonstrate ; 6 gratitude ; 7 *regalar*, to present ; 8 pie ; 9 *advertir*, to notice ; 10 *cubrir*, to cover ; 11 bottom ; 12 *reconvenir*, to reproach ; 13 bitterly ; 14 protected=*protégé* ; 15 contempt ; 16 complain(ing) ; 17 game to game=quits ; 18 pastry.

Más vale[2] un "toma," que dos "te daré."

¿ Me haría Vd. el favor[1] de prestarme diez pesetas[1] ?
Pero, señor, no tengo el honor[1] de conocerle.[3]
Precisamente[1] acudo[4] á Vd. por esta misma[5] razón[5] ; pues los que me conocen[3] nunca[6] quieren prestarme un céntimo.[1]

---

2 is worth ; 3 *conocer*, to know ; 4 *acudir*, to appeal ; 5=very reason ; 6 never.

El jardinero del Jardín Botánico[1] confió[2] á un criado algo[3] tonto[4] dos hermosos higos[5] para Buffón. Por el camino[6] el mensajero,[7] vencido[8] de la tentación,[1] se[0] tragó[9] uno y al presentar[10] el otro al Naturalista,[1] éste, que esperaba[11] recibir dos, dijo al criado : ¿ Qué has hecho con el otro higo[5] ?

He hecho así,[12] le respondió, y tragóse[9] el otro con la mayor tranquilidad[1] del mundo.[13]

---

2 *confiar*, to entrust ; 3 somewhat ; 4 foolish, simple ; 5 fig ; 6 way ; 7 messenger ; 8 *vencer*, to conquer ; 9 *tragar*, to swallow ; 10 present(ing) : 11 *esperar*, to expect ; 12 thus ; 13 world.

El Eclipse suspendido.

El eclipse[1] de sol[2] que fué pronosticado[1] para el año de 1724, asustó[3] tanto á[0] los aldeanos[4] de algunos países,[5] que el cura[6] de un pueblo, no pudiendo confesar[1] á[0] tantos parroquianos[7] como acudían,[8] creyendo llegado el día del juicio,[9] les dijo en el púlpito[1] : Hijos míos, no[10] hay que daros prisa,[10] pues el eclipse[1] ha sido trasladado[11] por orden[1] del señor alcalde[12] para el[13] mes que viene.[13]

2 sun ; 3 terrified ; 4 villager ; 5 country ; 6 clergyman ; 7 parishioner ; 8=went (to him) ; 9 judgment ;   10 there is no occasion to give yourselves hurry=hurry yourselves ; 11 postponed ; 12 mayor ; 13 next month.

Un caballero que comía en un hotel pidió[2] á[0] uno á su lado[3] si le haría el favor[1] de pasarle la mostaza.[4]

¿ Cree[5] Vd. que soy un criado ? le respondió.

Ah, no, señor, le dijo el otro, creía[5] que era Vd. un caballero.

2 *pedir*, to ask ; 3 side ; 4 mustard ; 5 *creer*, to believe.

Estaba una compañía[1] de quintos[2] haciendo el ejercicio[3] cuando uno de ellos, en[4] vez[4] de levantar[5] la pierna[7] derecha,[6] levantó[5] la izquierda.[8]

El oficial, que estaba al extremo[1] de la fila,[1] habiendo observado[1] dos piernas[7] muy próximas[9] gritó[10] : ¿ Quién es ese bruto[1] que levanta[5] las dos piernas[7] á la vez ?

2 conscript ; 3 exercise=drill ; 4 in place ; 5 *levantar*, to raise ; 6 right ; 7 leg ; 8 left ; 9 close together ; 10 shouted out.

Un sujeto[2] muy inocentón[1] aseguraba[3] que no tenía confianza[1] alguna en la vacuna,[4] y fundaba[5] su aserto[6] en la experiencia[1] : Había[7] en una familia,[1] decía, un niño sano[8] y robusto[1] que dos meses después de estar vacunado cayóse[9] de un árbol[10] y se estrelló[11] contra[12] las piedras.[18]—¿ Y aún se quiere prueba[14] más convincente[1] de[0] que la vacuna[4] no sirve[15] para nada[15] ?

2 person ; 3 *asegurar*, to assert ; 4=vaccination ; 5 *fundar*, to base ; 6 assertion ; 7 there was ; 8 healthy ; 9 fell ; 10 tree ; 11 was dashed to pieces ; 12 against ; 13 stone ; 14 proof ; 15 serves for (=is worth) nothing.

El Pordiosero[3] holgazán.[2]

Un muchacho de once á doce años[4] se llegó[5] un día á una señora que iba á[6] pié[6] con una doncella,[7] y la pidió un duro[8] de limosna.[9]

¡ Cómo ! ¿ un duro[8] ? responde admirada[10] : ¿ Qué modo[1] es ese de pedir la caridad[11] ?

Señora, responde[1] el muchacho, pues que Vd. me lo niega,[12] ya no importunaré[1] á[0] ninguna otra persona : esta corta[13] cantidad[14] me hubiera[15] hecho desistir[1] del partido[16] que iba á tomar.—Y al[17] decir[17] esto dió un profundo[1] suspiro[18] y se marchó[19] llorando.[20]

¡ Cómo ! dice la señora á su doncella[7] : ¿ tendrá este desgraciado[21] algún designio[1] que le induzca[22] á ejecutar[1] un disparate[23] ? No quiero que por un duro se[25] pierda[25] ese infeliz.[24] Toma, dice llamándole, ahí[26] tienes tu duro : pero dime,[27] ¿ por qué te afligistes[28] tanto cuando te lo negué[12] ?

Señora, es porque me veía en la precisión[29] de trabajar.

---

2 idle ; 3 beggar ; 4 year ; 5 *llegarse*, to approach ; 6 on foot ; 7 maid ; 8 dollar ; 9 alms ; 10 astonished ; 11 charity ; 12 *negar*, to deny ; 13 short =small ; 14 quantity ; 15 would have ; 16 course ; 17 on saying ; 18 sigh ; 19 *marcharse*, to walk away ; 20 *llorar*, to weep ; 21 unfortunate (one) ; 22 (may) induce ; 23 silly action ; 24 unhappy ; 25 (should) be lost ; 26 here ; 27 tell me ; 28 *afligirse*, to lament ; 29 necessity.

Un hombre muy glotón[2] decía : mi padre comía mucho, mi madre muy aprisa,[3] y yo he heredado[4] ambas[5] cualidades.[1]

---

2 gluttonous ; 3 quickly ; 4 *heredar*, to inherit ; 5 both.

Un ladrón[2] que marchaba[3] al patíbulo,[4] suplicó[5] que detuviesen[6] la comitiva[7] delante[8] de[8] una taberna,[1] y pidió un vaso[9] de aguardiente.[10] Se lo dieron, y después de haberlo bebido[11] : No tengo suelto[12] en este momento, le dijo al tabernero,[13] pero te lo pagaré á la vuelta.[14]

---

2 thief ; 3 *marchar*, to go ; 4 gallows ; 5 *suplicar*, to request ; 6 they (should) stop ; 7 retinue=procession ; 8 before ; 9 glass ; 10 brandy ; 11 *beber*, to drink ; 12 change ; 13 tavern-keeper ; 14 return.

La Interpretación.

Un hombre fué conducido[1] ante[2] el magistrado[1] por la sospecha[3]de haber robado[4]un hermoso[5]carnero[6]á[7]un pastor[8]llamado Bonifacio Conde Sanz Diaz, y le preguntó si sabía[9] leer.[10]

Un poco, señor, respondió.[1]

Pues[0] entonces no podía[9] Vd. ignorar[11] de quién era el carnero[6] que confiesa[1] haber hallado, y que sin[12] embargo[12] dice ser suyo, pues ya ve que tiene la marca[1] de estas cuatro iniciales,[1] B.C.S.D.

Es verdad[13] que las tiene, pero yo creí que decían : " Buen Carnero Sin Dueño.[14] "

---

2 before ;   3 suspicion ;   4 *robar*, to steal ;   5 fine ;   6 sheep ;   7=from ; 8 shepherd ;   9 (he) could ;   10 read ;   11 be ignorant ;   12 nevertheless ; 13 truth=true ;   14 owner.

Viajaban[2] en un coche[1] varios[1] amigos, uno de los cuales empezó[3] á dormir.   Al[4] poco rato[4] le despertó[5] uno de sus compañeros diciéndole : Hemos corrido[6] ya una gran distancia[1] desde[7] que se[8] durmió Vd.[8]

¿ Mucha ? preguntó el que dormía.

Sí, muchísima, le dijo el otro, estamos á[0] más de[9] diez leguas[1] lejos[10] de aquí.

---

2 *viajar*, to travel ;   3 *empezar*, to begin ;   4 after a short time ;   5 *despertar*, to wake ;   6 *correr*, to run ;   7 since ;   8 you fell asleep ;   9=than ; 10 far=distance.

Viajando un caballero, llegó á un sitio[2] donde era preciso[3] pasar[1] un río en una barca.[4]   Entró[1] en ella, y viendo que el agua[5] estaba agitada[1] : Dígame Vd., amigo, dijo al barquero,[6] ¿ le ha sucedido[7] á Vd. alguna vez el perder[8] á[0] los pasajeros[1] estando las aguas[5] enfurecidas[9] ?

Nunca,[10] señor, le respondió,[1] porque los que se han ahogado[11] siempre se[12] han vuelto á hallar[12] al día siguiente.[13]

---

2 place ;   3 necessary ;   4 boat ;   5 water ;   6 boatman ;   7 *suceder*, to happen ;   8 losing ;   9 furious=rough ;   10 never ;   11 *ahogarse*, to be drowned ;   12=have been found again ;   13 following.

La Calabaza y la Bellota.

Un campesino,[2] al regresar[3] á su casa un día de verano[4] se tendió[5] para reposar[1] un ratito,[6] á la sombra[7] de una corpulenta[1] encina,[8] á la contemplación de la cual nuestro campesino[2] se puso[9] á menear[10] la cabeza[11] y á decirse[12] á sí mismo[12] :

Si hubiera[13] yo sido el Criador,[14] hubiera[15] dispuesto[16] las cosas de otra manera[1] ; hubiera[15] hecho que las calabazas[17] creciesen[18] de este árbol,[19] y á[0] las bellotas[20] las hubiera[15] hecho el fruto[1] de tallos[21] delicados.[1]—Y en esto empezó[22] á dormir.

Apenas había cerrado[23] los ojos,[24] cuando habiéndose desprendido[25] una bellota[20] y dándole[26] en la nariz,[27] le despertó.[28]

¡ Imbécil[29] de mí[29] ! exclamó[1] entonces ; suerte[30] he tenido que la fruta[1] de este árbol[19] es la bellota[20] ; pues si hubiese[13] sido una calabaza,[17] me hubiera[15] dejado aquí tendido[5] con la cabeza[11] aplastada.[31]

---

2 countryman ; 3 return ; 4 summer ; 5 *tender*, to stretch out ; 6 short time ; 7 shade ; 8 oak ; 9 *ponerse*=to begin ; 10 shake ; 11 head ; 12 say to himself ; 13 had ; 14 Creator ; 15 I should have ; 16 disposed ; 17 pumpkin ; 18 (should) grow ; 19 tree ; 20 acorn ; 21 stalk ; 22 *empezar*, to begin ; 23 *cerrar*, to shut ; 24 eye ; 25 *desprender*, to loosen ; 26=striking him ; 27 nose ; 28 *despertar*, to wake ; 29=fool that I am ; 30 luck ; 31 crushed.

¿ Por qué en invierno[2] sale[3] tarde[4] el sol[5] ?

Porque como hace[6] frío,[7] no[8] le gusta madrugar.[8]

---

2 winter ; 3 goes out=rises ; 4 late ; 5 sun ; 6 it makes=it is ; 7 cold ; 8 early rising pleases him not=he does not like getting up early.

Estaba un estudiante[1] acompañando[1] á[0] algunas señoras por el museo[1] de Oxford y parándose[2] delante[3] de[3] una espada[4] muy enmohecida[5] les dijo : Ahí[6] tienen Vds. la espada[4] con que Balaam amenazó[7] de muerte[8] á su burra.[9]

Jamás he oído, observó una de la concurrencia,[10] que Balaam tuviese[11] una espada,[4] sino que ese profeta[1] deseaba una, como cuenta[12] su historia.[1]

Tiene[13] Vd. razón,[13] replicó el estudiante, y ésta es precisamente[1] la que el profeta[1] deseaba.

---

2 stopping ; 3 before ; 4 sword ; 5 rusty ; 6 here ; 7 *amenazar*, to threaten ; 8 death ; 9 ass ; 10 company ; 11 had ; 12 *contar*, to relate ; 13 you have reason=you are right.

Los Cometas.

Los cometas[1] son unos astros[2] que por su irregular[1] y sorprendente[3]aparición[1] han despertado[4] el temor[5] de los pueblos,[6] siendo mirados[7] como signos[1] de la cólera[8] celeste[1] y profetas[1] de calamidades[1] y desastres.[1] Pero la ciencia[9] ha conseguido[10] demostrar[1] que son, valiéndonos[11] de una célebre expresión,[1] "astros[2] inocentes,[1]" que se mueven[12] como los planetas[1] alrededor[13] del sol[14] en unas órbitas[1] elípticas,[1] es decir, de forma[1] ovalada,[1] muy largas[15] y muy estrechas.[16]

Se presentan[1] acompañados[1] de una ráfaga[17] luminosa[1] que los rodea[18] completamente[1] ó se extiende[1] hacia[19] un solo lado.[20] Esta ráfaga[17] recibe el nombre de cola,[21] barba[22] ó cabellera.[23] Los cometas, al[24] recorrer[24] su órbita,[1] se[25] encuentran[25] unas veces muy lejanos[26] y otras muy próximos[27] al sol.[14] Cuando están muy lejos,[26] se congelan[1] por falta[28] de calor,[29] y cuando se aproximan[30] al sol, el calor[29] gasifica[31] parte[1] de los líquidos[1] que pueden contener[1] en su superficie,[32] y extiende[1] su atmósfera[1] en el espacio.[1] El sol ilumina[1] esta tenue[33] materia[1] así extendida,[1] y forma esa ráfaga[17] luminosa,[1] causa[1] de tanto temor.[5]

El número[1] de cometas es inmenso.[1] Keplero decía : Más cometas hay en el cielo[34] que peces[35] en el mar.[36]

Sin[37] embargo,[37] son pocos[38] los que se[39] conocen,[39] de[40] tal modo[40] que pueda[41] anunciarse[41] con exactitud[1] su reaparición.

Muchos se alejan[42] á distancias[1] inconcebibles[1] de nuestro sistema[1] planetario,[1] y es probable que atraídos[43] por astros[2] pertenecientes[44] á otro sistema,[1] dejen[45] de pertenecer[44] al nuestro, convirtiéndose[1] en planetas de otro sol.[14]

---

2 star ; 3 surprising ; 4 awaked ; 5 fear ; 6 people=nations ; 7 *mirar*, to look on ; 8 anger ; 9 science ; 10 succeeded ; 11 availing ourselves ; 12 *mover*, to move ; 13 round ; 14 sun ; 15 long ; 16 narrow ; 17 cloud ; 18 *rodear*, to encircle ; 19 towards ; 20 side ; 21 tail ; 22 beard ; 23 hair ; 24=in traversing ; 25=are ; 26 distant ; 27 near ; 28 want ; 29 heat ; 30 they approach ; 31 turns to gas ; 32 surface ; 33 thin ; 34 sky ; 35 fish ; 36 sea ; 37 nevertheless ; 38 few ; 39 are known ; 40 in such a way ; 41 may be foretold ; 42 *alejar*, to move away ; 43 attracted ; 44 *pertenecer*, to belong ; 45 *dejar*, to cease.

Los cometas son los únicos[46] cuerpos[47] celestes[1] que la mayoría[48] de los astrónomos[1] no creen que estén habitados,[1] porque no se[49] concibe[49] que existan[1] habitantes[1] en astros[2] que pasan[1] por tan bruscas[1] transiciones[1] de calor[29] y frío,[50] y que están sujetos[1] á una variación[1] completa de todos sus elementos.[1]

---

46 only ; 47 body ; 48 majority ; 49 it is imagined ; 50 cold.

El Marinero y su Amigo.

Un marinero iba á embarcarse[1] en un navío[2] próximo[3] á darse á la vela[3] para las Indias,[1] y un amigo suyo que trataba[4] de disuadirle[1] de un viaje tan largo[5] y tan peligroso,[6] le preguntó :

Dime,[7] ¿ dónde murió tu padre ?

En un naufragio,[8] respondió el marinero.

¿ Y tu abuelo[9] ?

Un día yendo á la pesca[10] se levantó[11] una tempestad[1] tan furiosa,[1] que la barca[1] se[12] fué á pique,[12] y él se ahogó.[13]

¿ Y tu bisabuelo[14] ?—En un viaje que hizo á América, el navío[2] chocó[15] contra unas peñas,[16] y se hundió.[17]

Y ¿ cómo eres tan temerario[18] que te atreves[19] á embarcarte,[1] sabiendo que tu padre, tu abuelo[9] y tu bisabuelo[14] han muerto en el mar[20] ?

Es posible, respondió el marinero ; pero dime,[7] ¿ dónde murió tu padre ?

Muy tranquilamente[1] en su cama.[21]

¿ Y tu abuelo[9] ? ¿ y tu bisabuelo[14] ?

De la misma manera[1] ; muy dulcemente[22] en sus lechos.[23]

¿ Y cómo pues, repuso el marinero, eres tan temerario,[18] que te atreves[19] á meterte[24] en la cama[21] todos los días, sabiendo que tu padre, tu abuelo y tu bisabuelo han muerto todos en ella ?

---

2 ship ; 3 near to give itself to the sail=about to set sail ; 4 *tratar*, to try ; 5 long ; 6 perilous ; 7 tell me ; 8 shipwreck ; 9 grandfather ; 10 fishing ; 11 *levantar*, to raise ; 12 *irse á pique*, to founder ; 13 *ahogar*, to drown ; 14 great grandfather ; 15 *chocar*, to strike ; 16 rock ; 17 *hundir*, to sink ; 18 rash ; 19 *atreverse*, to dare ; 20 sea ; 21 bed ; 22 quietly ; 23 couch ; 24 put thyself=go.

Fontenelle y los Espárragos.

Fontenelle gustaba[2] mucho de los espárragos,[1] sobre todo arreglados[3] con aceite.[4]

El abate[5] Terrasson, á[6] quien también le gustaban,[6] pero con manteca,[7] vino un día á pedirle[8] de comer,[8] y le suplicó[1] que le hiciera[9] un gran favor dándole la mitad[10] de los espárragos que tenía en su plato,[1] y mandó que se[11] pusiese[11] esta mitad[10] con manteca.[7]

Poco antes de sentarse[12] á la mesa[13] el abate[5] empezó[14] á ponerse[15] mal, y al[16] fin[16] le dió una fuerte[17] apoplejía.[1]

Fontenelle, que tal[18] vió, se levanta[19] de[20] súbito[20] y corre[21] precipitadamente[1] á la cocina[22] gritando[23] : ¡ Todos con aceite,[4] todos con aceite !

2=was fond ;   3=prepared ; 4 oil ; 5 *abbé* ;   6=who also liked them ; 7 butter ; 8 ask him to dine ; 9 would do ;   10 half ;   11=should be put ; 12 *sentarse*, to sit down ; 13 table ; 14 began ; 15=become ; 16 at length ; 17 strong ; 18 as much ; 19 *levantarse*, to get up ; 20 suddenly ; 21 runs ; 22 kitchen ; 23 calling out.

El amigo que no presta,[2] y el cuchillo[3] que no corta,[4]
Cuando se[5] pierden[5] poco importa.[6]

---

2 *prestar*, to lend ; 3 knife ; 4 *cortar*, to cut ; 5 they are lost ; 6 it matters.

Una caravana[1] de cuatrocientos gallegos[2] pasaba de Madrid á Galicia para la celebración de las fiestas[3] de Santiago,[4] y á[5] pesar[5] de ser tantos se[6] dejaron robar[6] por media[7] docena[8] de gitanos.[9]   Al[10] llegar[10] á la villa[11] inmediata[1] se[12] dirigieron[12] los gallegos[2] á ver al alcalde,[13] que se extrañó[14] de lo ocurrido.[15]

¿ Cómo puede explicarse que cuatrocientos hombres permitan[1] á seis pilletes[16] que les roben[1] hasta[17] el último céntimo[1] ?   Vergüenza[20] me daría el ser[18] tan cobarde.[19]

A lo cual respondió uno de ellos, el más cuerdo,[21] por[22] supuesto[22] : ¿ Pero no ve V.[23] S.[23] que íbamos solos[24] ?

---

2 Galician ; 3 festival ; 4 St. James ;   5 in spite ; 6 let themselves be robbed ; 7 half ; 8 dozen ; 9 gipsy ; 10 on arriving ; 11 town ; 12=went ; 13 mayor ; 14 *extrañarse*, to be astonished ; 15 occurrence ; 16 scoundrel ; 17 up to ; 18 be(ing) ; 19 cowardly ; 20 shame ; 21 discreet ; 22=doubtless ; 23 your worship (*señoría*) ; 24 alone.

La falsa Alerta.[2]

Durante el sitio[3] de Gibraltar,[1] en el momento en que los ingleses esperaban[4] de un instante[1] á otro un ataque[1] general, un centinela[1] que habían colocado[5] de noche á la entrada[6] de frente[7] de la torre[8] del Diablo,[9] estaba al extremo[10] de la muralla,[11] silbando[12] y fijando[13] sus miradas[14] sobre las líneas[1] españolas, no soñando[15] más que fuego,[16] bombas,[1] minas,[1] brecha[1] y fuego de fila.[17]   Al lado[18] de su garita[19] tenía un puchero[20] donde había ocultado[21] su comida,[22] que consistía en un potaje[1] de habichuelas.[23]

Una mona[24] muy grande, (sabido es que la cima[25] de esta roca[1] está siempre cubierta[26] de estos animales) alentada[27] por el silencio[1] del centinela,[1] y llevada[28] del olfato,[29] se acercó[30] al puchero[20] y metió[31] su cabeza para regalarse[1] con lo que contenía[1]; pero después que satisfizo[1] su necesidad,[1] cuando quiso escaparse,[1] no pudo sacar[32] la cabeza, y se[33] llevó[33] el puchero[20] por gorro,[34] marchando con las patas[36] traseras.[35]

Esta terrible[1] aparición[1] apenas[37] se presentó á los ojos del centinela, tropezando[38] con cuanto[39] encontraba,[40] convirtió[1] al pobre mono[24] en un granadero[1] español[1] ensangrentado,[41] y herido[42] mortalmente.[1]   Ya exaltada[1] su imaginación[1] con esta idea, y lleno de miedo,[43] disparó[44] su fusil[45] gritando[46] con todas sus fuerzas[47] que el enemigo[1] había escalado[48] la muralla.

La gran guardia[1] tomó al momento las armas[1] con este aviso,[49] el tambor[50] resonó[51] por[52] todas partes,[52] y en diez minutos estuvo toda la guarnición[53] formada para la batalla.[1]

---

0 not to be translated ; 1 the same, or nearly the same, as in English.

2 alarm ; 3 siege ; 4 *esperar*, to expect ; 5 placed ; 6 entrance ; 7 front ; 8 tower ; 9 devil ; 10 end ; 11 rampart ; 12 *silbar*, to whistle ; 13 *fijar*, to fix ; 14 glance ; 15 *soñar*, to dream ; 16 fire ; 17 file ; 18 side ; 19 sentry-box ; 20 pot ; 21 hidden ; 22 meal ; 23 bean ; 24 monkey ; 25 summit ; 26 covered ; 27 encouraged ; 28 attracted ; 29 smell ; 30 *acercarse*, to approach ; 31 *meter*, to put ; 32 draw out ; 33 carried away ; 34 night-cap ; 35 hind ; 36 paws, legs ; 37 hardly ; 38 stumbling ; 39=whatever ; 40 it met ; 41 bloodstained ; 42 wounded ; 43 fear ; 44 *disparar*, to discharge ; 45 gun ; 46 calling out ; 47 force(s) ; 48 scaled ; 49 information ; 50 drum ; 51 *resonar*, to resound ; 52=everywhere ; 53 garrison.

El supuesto[54] granadero,[1] á quien incomodaba[1] mucho el sombrero, y que estaba casi ciego[55] con el peso[56] del puchero, no estuvo mucho tiempo sin ser descubierto, y su prisión[57] restableció[1] la tranquilidad[1] en el campo[1] que se había creído sorprendido.[58]

54 supposed ; 55 blind ; 56 weight ; 57 capture ; 58 surprised.

Destapa[2] un amo de casa un cántaro[3] de vino delicado,[1] cuya[4] vasija[4] conservaba[5] cuidadosamente lacrada[6] y sellada[7] hacía[8] tiempo.[8]   Como encontró[9] que faltaba[11] la mitad[10] del vino, empezó á investigar[1] las causas[1] de aquel fenómeno,[1] hallando en la parte inferior[12] del cántaro[3] un pequeño agujero[13] tapado[14] con cera.[15]

En vista[16] de esto llama á la criada, y le dice : ¿ Quién te ha mandado[17] beber el vino que aquí falta[11] ?

¿ Por dónde quiere[18] Vd. que lo haya[19] sacado[19] ?

Por este agujero[13] que has hecho.

¡ Yo ! ¿ Pero, señor, aunque[20] hubiera[21] hecho el agujero,[13] no ve Vd. que por donde falta[11] el vino es por[22] encima[22] y el agujero[13] está por[23] debajo[23] ?

2 *destapar*, to uncover=open ; 3 pitcher ; 4 which vessel ; 5 *conservar*, to preserve ; 6 waxed ; 7 sealed ; 8=for a long time ; 9 he found ; 10 half ; 11 *faltar*, to be wanting *or* missing ; 12=lower ;   13 hole ;   14 *tapar*, to stop up ; 15 wax ; 16 view ; 17 ordered ; 18=suppose ; 19 have drawn out ; 20 although, even if ; 21 I (should) have ; 22 at the top ; 23 at the bottom.

Una mujer rica calzada[2] por un zapatero[4] á[3] la moda,[3] nota[1] que el mismo día que estrenaba[5] unos zapatos estaban rotos[6] á[7] las[7] cuatro horas.   Hace[8] llamar al zapatero,[8] y le manifiesta[1] su estrañeza[9] por aquel resultado.[1]

El industrial coje[10] el zapato roto,[6] lo examina atentamente,[1] y después de reflexionar[1] sobre las causas de aquel accidente,[1] exclama[1] de[11] pronto[11] : ¡ Ya[12] caigo[12] ! ¿ Ha salido Vd. á[13] pié[13] con ellos ?

2 shod ; 3 fashionable ; 4 shoemaker ; 5 *estrenar*, to use for the first time ; 6 broken ; 7=in ; 8=she has the shoemaker sent for ; 9 surprise ; 10 *cojer*, to pick up ; 11 suddenly ; 12=I have it ; 13 on foot.

El Ciego y su Dinero.

Sabidas son las precauciones[1] que toman los ciegos[2] para ocultar[3] el dinero. Uno que poseía[4] quinientos francos, no considerándolos seguros en el miserable cuarto que habitaba,[1] bajó[5] una noche al corral[6] de la casa y los enterró[1] al pié de un árbol.[7] Un vecino de la misma casa que por casualidad[8] había bajado[5] al patio,[9] notó[1] la acción[1] del ciego, y al[10] retirarse éste,[10] desenterró[1] el dinero y se lo apropió.[1]

Cuando el ciego fué á visitar su tesoro,[11] no lo halló, como era natural ; pero lejos[12] de quejarse[13] y desesperarse,[13] disimuló[1] su dolor[14] y se[15] puso[15] á reflexionar.[1] Informóse de la gente[16] que vivía en la casa y supo que había en ella un vecino desocupado,[17] chismoso[18] y malgastador.[19] No necesitó saber más el ciego para sospechar[20] que el tal[21] vecino era el ladrón,[22] y con aire[1] risueño[23] fué á buscarle y le dijo :

Vecino, sé que sois hombre discreto[1] y amigo de hacer un favor ; vengo á consultaros sobre un punto[24] muy importante para mí. Poseo[4] mil francos, de los cuales tengo escondidos[25] quinientos en paraje[26] seguro. Tengo intención de esconder[25] también la otra mitad[27] y desearía que me dijeseis[28] si debo ocultarlos[3] en el mismo sitio[26] ó en otro diferente, para no perderlo todo en caso de hurto.[29]

Alegróse[30] el vecino con la culpable[1] esperanza[31] de pillar[32] toda la cantidad,[33] é instó[34] al ciego á[0] que los depositara[1] en el mismo escondrijo.[35]

Prometiólo[36] así el robado,[37] y el ladrón[22] se[38] apresuró[38] á volver[39] á poner[39] los quinientos francos al pié del árbol,[7] para coger[40] luego[41] los mil. Pero aquella misma noche fué

---

2 blind ; 3 *ocultar*, to conceal ; 4 *poseer*, to possess ; 5 *bajar*, to descend ; 6 yard ; 7 tree ; 8 chance ; 9 courtyard ; 10 on the latter's retiring ; 11 treasure ; 12 far ; 13 complain(ing) and despair(ing) ; 14 grief ; 15=began ; 16 people ; 17 unoccupied ; 18 slander repeating ; 19 extravagant ; 20 suspect ; 21= said ; 22 thief ; 23 smiling ; 24 point ; 25 *esconder*, to hide ; 26 place ; 27 half ; 28 you (should) tell ; 29 theft ; 30 *alegrarse*, to rejoice ; 31 hope ; 32 plunder(ing) ; 33 quantity ; 34 urged ; 35 hiding-place ; 36 *prometer*, to promise ; 37 robbed ; 38 hastened ; 39 put again ; 40=get ; 41 afterwards.

el ciego al paraje[26] donde enterró su dinero, y habiendo hallado sus quinientos francos, se los metió[42] en el bolsillo[43] y puso[42] en su lugar[44] un papel con estas palabras :

Bien decía yo que era Vd. hombre amigo de hacer un favor ; mil gracias por haberme ayudado[45] á recobrar[46] mi dinero.

---

42 put ;   43 pocket ;   44 place, stead ;   45 helped ;   46 recover

---

Vendíase en pública[1] subasta[2] la colección[1] de cuadros de un aficionado[3] inteligente.[1]   Al[4] presentar el subastador[4] un cuadrito[5] que representaba un burro,[6] y que tenía un mérito[1] real, empezaron á pujarlo[7] dos pintores,[8] pero un ricacho[9] que se[10] la daba de[10] inteligente[1] lo subió[11] en un momento á cuatro mil reales.

Uno de los pintores[8] se dirije[12] al rico, y le dice cortésmente[13] : Cuando tanto interés[1] demuestra[14] Vd., presumo[1] que será un retrato[15] de familia,[1] y me[0] retiro para no perjudicar[1] á Vd.

---

2 auction ; 3 amateur ; 4 on the auctioneer's presenting ; 5 small picture ; 6 donkey ; 7 outbid (for) it ; 8 painter ; 9 very rich man ; 10=boasted of being ; 11 *subir*, to raise ; 12 addresses ; 13 politely ; 14 manifest ; 15 portrait.

Para dar Mahoma[1] más crédito[1] á sus imposturas[1] hizo ocultar[3] en un pozo[5] seco[4] á[0] uno de sus compañeros,[2] con orden[1] de gritar[6] cuando él pasara[1] : Mahoma es el enviado[7] de Dios.

Hízolo así[8] el escondido,[9] quedando[11] todo[10] el mundo[10] admirado[12] de aquella maravilla[13] ; pero el falso apóstol,[1] temiendo que se[14] descubriera[14] su artificio,[1] ordenó[15] inmediatamente[1] á los fanáticos[1] que le seguían[16] que cegaran[17] el pozo[5] para evitar[18] que fuera[19] profanado en el porvenir.[20]

---

2 companion ;   3 hide ;   4 dry ;   5 well ;   6 call out ;   7=messenger ; 8 thus ; 9 hidden (person) ; 10 all the world=everybody ; 11 remaining ; 12 astonished ; 13 marvel ; 14 would be discovered ; 15 ordered ; 16 *seguir*, to follow ; 17 they should blind=stop up ; 18 avoid ; 19 it should be · 20 future.

El Perro hábil.

Es corriente[2] entre los cazadores[3] hablar de los extraordi-
narios sucesos[4]ocurridos[1] en su diversión[1] favorita[1] y ponderar[5]
las excelencias[1] de sus perros. En el descanso[6] de una partida[7]
de caza,[7] á la que asistía[8] Alejandro Dumas, se hablaba de lo[9]
de siempre[9] : de perros. Dumas oyó referir[10] maravillas[11] de
inteligencia[1] realizadas[1] por estos animalitos.[1] Cuando le
llegó su turno,[1] ponderó[5] también la inteligencia de su perro.

¡Oh! decía, mi perro tiene una inteligencia[1] superior.[1] Un
día que yo almorzaba[12] en el jardín con un amigo, Fanor—
que[0] así se[13] llamaba[13] mi perro—esperaba[14] sumiso[15] que,
como de costumbre,[9] le arrojara[16] los restos[17] de mi almuerzo.[18]

Mas[19] viendo que no me acordaba[20] de él, se[21] fué[21] al fondo[22]
del jardín y vino hacia[23] mí, trayendo en la boca[24] una rama[25]
de NO[26] ME OLVIDES.[26]

2=usual ; 3 hunter ; 4 incident ; 5 exaggerate ; 6 halting ; 7 hunting expe-
dition ; 8 was present ; 9=as usual ; 10 related ; 11 marvel ; 12 was break-
fasting ; 13 *llamarse*, to be called ; 14 was waiting ; 15 submissively ; 16
I(should) fling ; 17 remains ; 18 breakfast ; 19 but ; 20 *acordarse de*, to remember ; 21 *irse*, to go away ; 22 bottom ; 23 towards ; 24 mouth ; 25 sprig ;
26 forget me not.

Enrique VIII., rey de Inglaterra, y Carlos V., rey de España,
eran dos príncipes de un carácter[1] muy vivo[2] : el primero resolvió enviar un mensajero[3] al segundo, y nombró[4] al[5] efecto[5]
á sir Tomas More, su canciller.[6] Este al recibir sus instrucciones[1] hizo[7] presente[7] á Enrique el temor[8] que tenía de encar-
garse[9] de semejante[10] mensage que podía costarle la vida[11]: á
lo cual respondió el rey, que si Carlos atentaba[12] á sus días,[12]
haría[13] degollar[13] á todos los españoles que hubiese[24] en sus
estados.[15]—Agradezco[16] mucho á vuestra majestad,[1] dijo el
canciller,[6] el honor que hace á mi persona, pero dudo,[17]
señor, que ninguna de las cabezas de esos caballeros pueda[18]
colocarse[19] sobre mis hombros.[20]

---

2 hasty ; 3 messenger ; 4 appointed ; 5=for the purpose ; 6 chancellor ; 7
=represented ; 8 fear ; 9 taking charge ; 10 (a)like ; 11 life ; 12 attempted his
days=life ; 13=he would have...beheaded ; 14 were ; 15 dominions ; 16 *agra-
decer*, to be grateful ; 17 *dudar*, to doubt ; 18 can ; 19 be put ; 20 shoulders.

El Asedio de Amberes.

Mientras[2] los Españoles mantenían[1] en 1580 el tenaz[3] asedio[4] de Amberes,[5] sucedió[6] una cosa de poca importancia[1] que acarreó[7] un grande acontecimiento.[8] Estaba enferma una señora de la ciudad, y necesitaba para su cura[1] tomar leche[9] de burras.[10] Como no era posible hallarlas en la plaza,[11] un joven[12] se ofreció á ir por una á los arrabales,[13] no[14] obstante[14] hallarse en poder[15] del enemigo[1]; en efecto ya traía[16] una, cuando fué apresado,[17] y conducido al duque[1] de Parma.

Este general trató[18] con bondad[19] al joven[12]; alabó[20] su honradez,[21] é hizo[22] cargar[23] la burra[10] de perdices,[24] capones[1] y de cuanto[25] pudiese[26] ser útil[27] á un enfermo, ordenando que todo se[28] lo llevase[28] á la señora, y diciendo al ayuntamiento[29] y pueblo de Amberes[5] que él les deseaba toda suerte[30] de prosperidades.[1]

Esta generosidad[1] inesperada[31] del duque produjo[1] una revolución general en su favor, sugeriendose[32] enviarle á[33] nombre[33] del público[1] dulces[34] y vinos de la ciudad. Los espíritus[1] se calmaron[1] con estas mutuas[1] atenciones,[1] y empezando á pensar que los Españoles no eran tan fieros[35] como se creía, esta opinión evitó[36] muchos males,[37] é hizo[22] que se rindiese[38] la plaza.[11]

Este suceso[39] causó tanta alegría[40] á Felipe[1] II., que habiéndole llegado la noticia[41] á media[42] noche,[42] á[43] pesar[43] de lo misterioso[1] y austero[1] que era, fué al cuarto de su hija Isabel, dando golpes[44] á la puerta, y gritando[45] : ¡ Amberes[5] es nuestro, Amberes es nuestro !

Quien nació[46] para ahorcado[47] no morirá[48] ahogado.[49]

---

2 while ; 3 tenacious ; 4 siege ; 5 Antwerp ; 6 *suceder*, to happen ; 7 carried=led to ; 8 event ; 9 milk ; 10 ass ; 11 place ; 12 youth ; 13 suburb; 14 notwithstanding ; 15 power ; 16 he was bringing ; 17 captured ; 18 *tratar*, to treat ; 19 kindness ; 20 *alabar*, to praise ; 21 gallantry ; 22= caused ; 23 to (be) load(ed) ; 24 partridge ; 25=whatever ; 26 might ; 27 useful ; 28 should be taken ; 29 corporation ; 30 kind ; 31 unexpected ; 32=it being suggested ; 33=in the name ; 34 sweetmeats ; 35 cruel ; 36 avoided=prevented ; 37 evil ; 38 surrendered (*rendir*) ; 39 event ; 40 joy ; 41 news ; 42 midnight ; 43 in spite ; 44 blow ; 45 calling out; 46 was born ; 47=hanging ; 48 *morir*, to die ; 49 *ahogar*, to drown.

El Negro fingido.[2]

Dos jóvenes hermanos, cerrajeros[3] de oficio,[4] se[0] embarca-ron[1] hace[5] sesenta años para la Jamaica. Luego que llegaron buscaron alguna ocupación,[1] pero no la hallaron en su oficio,[4] porque necesitaban algún dinero para establecerse.[1] Viéndose sin auxilio[6] alguno, apelaron[7] á un recurso[8] bastante[9] extra-ordinario, y fué el siguiente.[10]

Uno de ellos, que tenía los cabellos[11] muy crespos,[12] se disfrazó[13] de negro,[1] se tiñó[14] el rostro[15] y todo el cuerpo,[16] y fué conducido[1] por su hermano á la casa de un banquero,[1] á[0] quien suplicó[17] le prestase[18] cincuenta doblones[1] sobre la venta[19] de aquel negro. Como éste era fuerte[20] y vigoroso,[1] logró[21] el hermano el préstamo[22] que deseaba. Recibido el dinero, se[0] escapó[1] el fingido[2] negro de casa del prestamista,[23] volvió á casa de su hermano, y se lavó[24] de piés á cabeza. En vano[1] ofrecieron los periódicos recompensas al[25] que le presentase,[26] pues era imposible hallarle.

Los dos hermanos formaron[1] su establecimiento[1] de cerra-jeros[3] con los cincuenta doblones, ganaron[27] mucho dinero y volvieron á su país[28] ricos; pero es de advertir,[29] que antes de ausentarse[30] de la Jamaica, restituyeron[1] el préstamo[22] con los intereses[1] al banquero, y le dieron las gracias recordán-dole[31] la anécdota del negro.

---

2 *fingir*, to pretend; 3 locksmith; 4 trade; 5=ago; 6 help; 7 they had recourse; 8=expedient; 9=rather; 10 following; 11 hair; 12 curly; 13 disguised; 14 *teñir*, to dye; 15 face; 16 body; 17 he requested; 18 he (would) lend; 19 sale; 20 strong; 21 obtained; 22 loan; 23 lender; 24 washed; 25 to the (one); 26 (might) present; 27 gained; 28 country; 29 to (be) observe(d); 30 absent(ing) themselves; 31=reminding him of.

Decía un andaluz[2]: Conocí á un hombre tan alto, tan grueso,[3] y que pesaba[4] tanto, que cuando se[0] murió tuvieron los sepul-tureros[5] que hacer dos viajes para llevarlo al cementerio.[1]

UN RICO.—Es tarde y voy á dejar[6] á Vd.
UN POBRE.—¿ Cuánto ?

---

2 Andalusian; 3 corpulent; 4 weighed; 5 grave-diggers; 6 leave.

El Eco singular.

Hablando un día un gracioso[2] con un caballero muy mentiroso[3] que regresaba[4] de un largo[5] viaje, éste le refería[6] los ecos[1] maravillosos[7] que había oído en varios países, particularmente[1] en las ruínas[1] de un templo[1] antiguo[1] que repetía[1] la misma palabra siete veces.

¡Ba ! ba ! eso no tiene nada de admirable,[8] responde nuestro bufón[1] : aquí en este país, sin ir más lejos,[9] hay un eco... ¡pero qué eco ! ! ! un eco en el castillo[10] de un señor cerca del lago[11] Killarney, donde me ha sucedido[12] muy frecuentemente[1] gritar : Buenos días, señor eco ; y nunca ha dejado[13] de responderme : Buenos días, caballerito, ¿ cómo está Vd. ?

2 witty man ; 3 mendacious ; 4 was returning ; 5 long ; 6 was relating ; 7 wonderful ; 8 extraordinary ; 9 far ; 10 castle ; 11 lake ; 12 happened ; 13 left=omitted.

La Nuez.

Dos muchachos que jugaban[2] al pié de un nogal,[3] hallaron en el suelo[4] una nuez[5] que se[0] había caído del árbol.[6]

Es mía, dijo uno de ellos, pues yo he sido el que la he visto el primero.

No, respondió el otro ; es mía, porque yo he sido el que la he recogido[7] del suelo.[4]

No pudiendo ponerse[8] de acuerdo[8] respecto[1] al legítimo[1] dueño[9] de la nuez,[5] ya estaban dispuestos[10] á disputársela[1] á golpes,[11] cuando un joven[12] que pasaba,[1] habiéndose enterado[13] del motivo[1] de la querella,[1] cogió[14] la nuez, la partió,[15] y poniéndose en medio[16] de los muchachos, les dijo :

Yo voy á poneros de[17] acuerdo.[17] La mitad[18] de la cáscara[19] pertenece[20] al[21] que la vió el primero, y la otra mitad[18] al[21] que la recogió[7] del suelo.[4] Respecto á la pepita,[22] yo me la guardo[23] en pago[24] de la decisión[1] que he dado. Este es, añadió[25] riendo,[26] el resultado[1] usual de todos los pleitos.[27]

2 *jugar,* to play ; 3 walnut-tree ; 4 ground ; 5 nut ; 6 tree ; 7 *recoger,* to pick up ; 8=to agree ; 9 owner ; 10 disposed ; 11 blow ; 12 young (man) ; 13 acquainted ; 14 took hold of ; 15 divided=cracked ; 16 middle ; 17 in accord ; 18 hair ; 19 shell ; 20 *pertenecer,* to belong : 21 to the (one) ; 22 kernel ; 23 *guardar,* to keep ; 24 payment ; 25 he added ; 26 laughing ; 27 lawsuit.

El Retrato mal pagado.

Mandóse[2] retratar[2] un caballero, y contrató[1] con el pintor[3] que le pagaría[4] generosamente,[1] si le sacaba[5] el retrato[6] parecido.[7] El pintor[3] lo hizo muy semejante[8] al original[1]; pero el retratado[9] cometió[1] la indignidad[1] de no querer pagarle, imaginando[1] con esta malicia[1] sacar[10] baratísimo[11] el retrato,[6] que el pintor[3] para nada podía aprovechar.[12]

Más diestro[13] el artista,[1] le dijo que, supuesto[14] no quería pagarle, se[15] quedaría[15] con él hasta[16] que tuviese[16] por conveniente cumplir[17] lo[18] contratado.[18]

El pintor hizo[19] poner un marco[19] al retrato,[6] y lo expuso[1] al público[1] sobre la puerta de su casa con esta inscripción[1]: ' Aquí estoy por no pagar mis deudas.[20] '

El original del retrato, que fué conocido de todo[21] el mundo,[21] supo al instante la burla[22] que le había hecho el pintor, y como todos le vituperaban,[1] se vió precisado[23] á pagar al artista cuanto[24] quiso para sacar[10] el retrato de sus manos.

2=ordered his portrait to be painted ; 3 painter ; 4 *pagar*, to pay ; 5 turned out ; 6 portrait ; 7=like (him) ; 8 resembling ; 9 (person) painted ; 10 to draw out=get ; 11 very cheap ; 12=make use of ; 13 skilful ; 14 supposing ; 15 it should remain ; 16=until he found it ; 17 to fulfil ; 18 what was contracted ; 19=had a frame put ; 20 debt ; 21=everybody ; 22 jest, trick ; 23 compelled ; 24 as much as.

Uno que estaba preso[2] en París por deudas, envió á buscar á su acreedor,[3] diciendo que tenía algo[4] que comunicarle.

Presentóse al acreedor,[3] y le dice : Pues, señor, pensando en[o] la vida[5] que paso[1] aquí tan triste[6] y fastidiosa,[7] he creído conveniente decirle á Vd. que estoy con pena[8] por el gasto[9] que le estoy ocasionando[1] diariamente,[10] y no sé cuando se[11] acabará.[11] Escuche Vd. Hágame[12] salir[12] de esta prisión,[1] y en lugar[13] de los dos francos[1] que le cuesto en ella, me dará, estando libre,[14] la mitad,[15] y el resto[1] lo iremos[16] descontando[16] de la deuda.

---

2 imprisoned ; 3 creditor ; 4 something ; 5 life ; 6 dull ; 7 tedious ; 8 trouble ; 9 expense ; 10 daily ; 11 it will end ; 12=release me ; 13 place ; 14 free ; 15 half ; 16=we will gradually deduct.

Las tres Preguntas.

Federico[1] el Grande tenía costumbre,[1] siempre que observaba[1] en su guardia[1] un nuevo soldado, de preguntarle estas tres cosas : ¿ Qué edad[2] tienes ? ¿ Desde[3] cuándo[3] sirves[4] ? ¿ Recibes con regularidad tu sueldo[5] y tus raciones[1] ?

Un joven Francés, que no podía hablar siquiera[6] una palabra en alemán,[7] fué admitido[1] en este cuerpo[8] de guardia.[1] El rey debía[9] pasar revista[10] tres días después, y le hicieron aprender tres respuestas correspondientes[1] á las preguntas que el rey solía[11] hacer y en el mismo orden.

Llegado el día de la revista,[10] Federico observó este soldado, y no dejó[12] de hacerle dichas[13] preguntas, pero empezó por la segunda.

¿ Desde[3] cuándo[3] sirves[4] ?—Veinte y un años, señor.

¡ Como ! ¿ veinte y un años ? ¿ qué edad[2] tienes, pues ? Tres días, señor.

Ah, dijo el rey, uno de los dos habrá perdido el entendimiento.[14]—Precisamente[1] los dos, dijo el joven, que tomaba estas palabras por la tercera pregunta.

¡ Como ! dijo el rey, esta es la primera vez que se[15] me trata de[15] loco.[16]

El Francés, que ya había apurado[17] todo lo que sabía de alemán,[7] guardaba un silencio absoluto. Pero el capitán[1] se apresuró[18] á explicar el enigma al rey, que celebró[19] mucho la chanza.[20]

---

2 age ;   3 since when=how long ;   4 dost thou serve ;   5 pay ; 6 even ; 7 German ; 8 body ; 9 had to ; 10 review ; 11 was in the habit of ;   12= omitted ; 13 said ; 14 understanding ;   15=I have been called ;   16 mad ; 17 exhausted ; 18 made haste ; 19=was amused with ; 20 joke.

Se había dado orden terminante[2] á un suizo[3] de[0] que no dejara[4] entrar[1] á nadie en el jardín de las Tullerias.   Se le presenta[1] un ciudadano.[5]—No se permite[1] la entrada,[6] dijo el suizo.[3]—Pero yo no quiero entrar, dijo el otro, solo[7] quiero salir[8] de Pont-Royal.—Ah, replicó el suizo, eso ya[0] es otra cosa ; si se[9] trata[9] de salir[8] ya[0] puede Vd. pasar.[1]

2=definite, strict ; 3 Swiss ; 4 he (should) allow ; 5 citizen ; 6 entry ; 7 only ; 8 (to) go out ; 9 it is a question.

El Giro[2] del Sol.

Hallábase un caballero, muy rudo,[3] en cierta tertulia[4] donde se hablaba del sol y del modo[1] como gira[5] alrededor[6] de la tierra, que tiene la figura[1] de una bola.[7] Quiso mezclarse[8] en la conversación[1] para sostener[1] que aquello era imposible,[1] supuesto[9] que[9] los mismos[10] ojos convencían[1] de que la tierra era llana.[11]

Diéronle diversas razones para desengañarle[12] de aquel error, y entre otras cosas le dijeron :

Ya ve Vd. cómo el sol sale[13] diariamente[14] en un mismo paraje,[15] y se[16] pone[16] al opuesto.[17] ¿ Cómo es pues posible, que vuelva del Occidente,[18] donde se[16] pone,[16] al Oriente,[19] donde sale,[13] si no pasa por[20] debajo[20] ?

¡ Bonita[21] pregunta ! replicó el porfiado[22] ignorante[1] : viene de[23] noche.

---

2 turning round=revolution ; 3=stupid ; 4 assembly ; 5 it revolves ; 6 round ; 7 ball ; 8 (to) mix ; 9=because ; 10=very, even ; 11 flat ; 12 disabuse him ; 13=rises ; 14 daily ; 15 place ; 16=sets ; 17 opposite ; 18 west ; 19 east ; 20 underneath ; 21 pretty (ironically used)=silly ; 22 obstinate ; 23=at.

En materia[1] de testamentos,[2] no hemos visto otro más notable[1] que el que otorgó[3] en 1793 un caballero[4] de industria[4] de París. Hélo[5] aquí[5] :

Nada tengo, debo mucho, dejo lo demás[6] á los pobres.

? will ; 3 executed=left ; 4 swindler ; 5 here it is ; 6 rest.

Un músico,[2] diestro[3] en su arte,[1] pero muy envanecido[4] de su mérito,[1] tuvo un día la honra[5] de hablar con cierto soberano,[6] el cual reparando[7] que llevaba[8] unas malísimas medias,[9] le preguntó : ¿ si era el músico[2] de quien le habían hablado con tanto elogio [10]?—No lo sé, señor, respondió, pero puedo vanagloriarme[11] de tener una voz que hago[12] de ella cuanto[13] quiero.—Pues si así es, dijo el rey, te aconsejo[14] que te hagas un par[15] de medias,[9] porque las necesitas mucho.

De esta manera[1] se[16] burló[16] el soberano[6] de la ridícula[1] vanidad[1] del músico.[2]

---

2 musician ; 3 skilful ; 4=vain ; 5 honor ; 6 sovereign ; 7 noticing ; 8 *llevar*, to wear ; 9 stocking ; 10 eulogy, praise ; 11 boast ; 12 I make ; 13 whatever ; 14 *aconsejar*, to advise ; 15 pair ; 16 made fun.

El Cochero aturdido.[2]

Un caballero de buen humor[1] tomó una noche con algunos amigos de su mismo humor un coche[1] de[3] alquiler,[3] y mandó al cochero[4] les condujese[5] detrás[6] de[6] una casa donde habían de llamar á[7] otro[8] sujeto.[8]

Llegaron, fingieron[9] subir[10] todos, y después, dando[11] vuelta[11] al coche,[1] empezaron á entrar por una portezuela[12] y salir por la otra, sin que lo notase[13] el cochero,[4] por[14] manera[14] que veía entrar mucha gente[15] y no alcanzaba[16] cómo podían ya caber[17] tantas personas allá[18] dentro,[19] hasta[20] que[20] el pobre diablo,[21] lleno de admiración,[22] abandonó[1] el coche y se fué á la taberna[1] inmediata,[23] donde declaró[1] que conducía[24] una legión[1] de demonios,[1] pues había contado[25] ya diez y ocho, y no sabía donde se metían.[26]

---

2 confused ; 3 on hire ; 4 coachman ; 5 to drive ; 6 behind ; 7=for ; 8=some one else ; 9 pretended ; 10 to ascend ; 11 going round ; 12 little door ; 13 noticed ; 14=so ; 15 people ; 16=understood ; 17 be contained ; 18 there ; 19 within ; 20 until ; 21=fellow ; 22 astonishment ; 23 adjoining ; 24 he was driving ; 25 counted ; 26 *meter*, to put.

Decía un mal pintor[2] que iba á blanquear[3] su casa para pintarla[4] después.[5]—Píntala primero, le dijo otro pintor, y que[6] la blanqueen[6] enseguida.[7]

¡ **Portero**[1] ! — ¿ Qué manda[8] Vd. ? — ¿ No vive aquí un caballero que hace[9] pocos días se[0] ha muerto ?
No, señor, en la casa de[10] al lado.[10]—Gracias.

---

2 painter ; 3 whitewash ; 4 paint it ; 5 afterwards ; 6 let them whitewash it ; 7 directly after ; 8 order=want ; 9 ago ; 10=next door (*lado*, side).

Un particular[2] solicitó[1] una importante plaza.[3]—Pero Vd. es bibliotecario,[4] le dijo su protector, ¿ desea Vd. pues renunciar[5] este empleo[6] ?—Oh, no, de[7] ninguna manera.[7]—Entonces, ¿ cómo podrá Vd. cumplir[8] con[0] su obligación en el otro destino,[9] que reclamará[10] todo su tiempo ?—Con la mayor facilidad[1] del mundo, puesto[11] que[11] nunca voy á mi biblioteca.[12]

---

2 certain person ; 3 place ; 4 librarian ; 5 give up ; 6 employment ; 7 not at all ; 8 fulfil ; 9 situation ; 10 will demand ; 11=because ; 12 library.

SPANISH

CONVERSATION

SIMPLIFIED.

A Collection of frequently occurring

CONVERSATIONAL PHRASES

INTRODUCING

all the IMPORTANT IDIOMS.

PUBLISHED BY

Hugo's Institute for Teaching Foreign Languages,

33 GRACECHURCH STREET, LONDON, E.C. ; and Branches.

CONVERSATIONAL EXERCISES,

based chiefly on the Rules in "SPANISH SIMPLIFIED," and gradually introducing the most IMPORTANT IDIOMS.

Good day (*or* Good morning), sir.	Buenos días, señor (*or* caballero).
Good afternoon (*or* Good evening), miss.	Buenas tardes, señorita.
Good night (*or* Good evening), madam.	Buenas noches, señora.
How are you?	¿ Cómo está Vd. ?
Very well, thank you ; and you ?	Muy bien, gracias ; ¿ y Vd. ?
I am very well now, but I have been ill.	Estoy muy bien ahora, pero he estado enfermo.
What was the matter with you ?	¿ Qué tenía Vd. ?
What is the matter with her ?	¿ Qué tiene ella ?
Nothing is the matter with me.	No tengo nada.
What do you say ?	¿ Qué dice Vd. ?
What do you mean ?	¿ Qué quiere Vd. decir ?
What is this called in Spanish ?	¿ Cómo se llama esto en español ?
How is that said in English ?	¿ Cómo se dice eso en inglés ?
I have heard that he will not do it.	He oído decir que no quiere hacérlo.
Can you speak Spanish or Italian ?	¿ Sabe Vd. hablar español ó italiano ?
I am very sorry for it.	Lo siento mucho.
They were not very sorry.	No lo sintieron mucho.
Are you not sorry for it ?	¿ No lo siente Vd. ? [Vd.
What do you want ?	¿ Qué quiere Vd. ? ¿Qué desea
I am glad to see you.	Me alegro de verle.
Good-bye (till to-morrow).	Hasta mañana.
Good-bye (till Wednesday).	Hasta el Miércoles.
Good-bye (till I see you again).	Hasta la vista.
Good-bye (farewell, adieu).	Adios.

I beg your pardon.	Dispénseme Vd.
They were not very glad to hear that.	No se alegraron mucho de oir eso.
We are very glad to find you at home.	Nos alegramos mucho de encontrarle (á Vd.) en casa.
Please give me your hat and your gloves.	Sírvase darme su sombrero y sus guantes.
Here they are.	Aquí los tiene Vd.
Many thanks.	Muchas gracias.
Do you think it will rain before the evening ?	¿ Cree Vd. que lloverá antes que anochezca ?
It is certain that they have not made a mistake.	Es cierto que no se han equivocado. X
We cannot do anything in this matter.	No podemos hacer nada sobre este asunto.
I am hungry.	Tengo hambre.
Are you not thirsty ?	¿ No tiene Vd. sed ?
They were very hungry.	Tenían mucha hambre.
Will not the child be hungry?	¿ No tendrá hambre el niño ?
He would be very thirsty.	Tendría mucha sed.
What will you do with this letter ?	¿ Qué hará Vd. con esta carta ?
I shall send it by post.	La enviaré por el correo.
Although I have not done my work, I will go with you now.	Aunque no he hecho mi trabajo, iré ahora con Vd. X
With the greatest pleasure.	Con muchísimo gusto.
When did the carriage come back ?	¿ Cuándo volvió el coche ?
It is better to arrive too soon than too late.	Vale más llegar un poco temprano, que demasiado tarde.
There are several mistakes in this exercise.	Hay varias faltas en este tema.
Why will you not come to the theatre to-morrow ?	¿ Por qué no quiere Vd. venir mañana al teatro ?
Who told you so ?	¿ Quién se lo dijo á Vd. ?
That girl is very fond of her brother.	Esa muchacha quiere mucho á su hermano.
Speak louder.	Hable Vd. más alto.

The post has not come in yet.	El correo no ha llegado todavía.
Do not speak (*plur.*) so low.	No hablen Vds. tan bajo.
Wait a little ; I have several things to tell you.	Aguarde Vd. un poco ; tengo varias cosas que decirle.
I cannot do it now.	No puedo hacerlo ahora.
Do us the favor to direct us to the railway station.	Háganos el favor de dirigirnos á la estación del ferrocarril.
I must do something else.	Debo hacer otra cosa.
Listen to me a moment.	Escúcheme un momento.
Please take a seat.	Sírvase tomar asiento.
I believe not.	Creo que no.
We say it is so.	Decimos que sí.
He was afraid not.	Temía que no.
I hope so.	Espero que sí.
Don't you think so ?	¿ No cree Vd. que sí ?
I say it is not.	Digo que no.
I expect not.	Espero que no.
Certainly not.	Ciertamente que no.
What are you looking for ?	¿ Qué busca Vd. ?
Whom are you looking for ?	¿ A quién busca Vd. ?
Do you know where Señor Martinez lives ?	¿ Sabe Vd. donde vive el señor Martinez ?
Will you take anything ?	¿ Quiere Vd. tomar algo ?
Many thanks ; I am not hungry, but I should very much like a glass of wine.	Mil gracias ; no tengo hambre, pero de buena gana bebería un vaso de vino.
I am rather tired.	Estoy algo cansado.
When did your mother return home ?	¿ Cuándo volvió á casa su madre (de Vd.) ?
I do not know why he has not sent the answer.	No sé por qué no ha enviado la respuesta.
How old is your uncle ?	¿ Cuántos años tiene su tío ?
I am twenty-eight years old.	Tengo veintiocho años.
He is more than thirty.	Tiene más de treinta años.
I do not know what to do about this matter.	No sé que hacer en este asunto.
You cannot make a mistake.	Vd. no puede equivocarse.

You must do it some other way. — Vd. debe hacerlo de otro modo.

I want to consult you about this letter. — Deseo consultarle sobre esta carta.

They will doubtless come next week. — Sin duda vendrán la semana que viene.

Could you not hear him ? — ¿ No podían Vds. oirle ?

Yes ; but we could not understand what he meant. — Sí ; pero no podíamos comprender lo que quería decir.

Do you know what time it is ? — ¿ Sabe Vd. que hora es ?

I don't know the exact time ; my watch does not go well. — No sé la hora exacta ; mi reloj no va bien.

His watch always goes badly. — Su reloj va siempre mal.

It is a little fast. — Está un poco adelantado.

It is generally very slow.   [to ten. — Va generalmente muy atrasado.   [punto.

It is exactly twenty minutes — Son las diez menos veinte en

It is about one o'clock. — Es cerca de la una.

It is not late yet. — No es tarde todavía.

My watch is not going. — Mi reloj no anda.

I cannot wind it up ; I have left the key at home. — No puedo darle cuerda ; he dejado la llave en casa.

This is of no importance. — Esto no es de ninguna importancia.

It does not matter. — No importa.

What does it matter ? — ¿ Qué importa ?

Where were you going when we met you yesterday ? — ¿ Adónde iba Vd. cuando le encontramos ayer ?

I am going to read this newspaper. — Voy á leer este periódico.

What is the news ? — ¿ Qué hay de nuevo ? or ¿ Qué se dice de nuevo ?

Nothing is more certain. — Nada es más seguro.

Be quiet directly ! — ¡ Cállese Vd. al instante !

These children will not be silent.   [first. — Estos niños no quieren callarse.   [visto primero.

Please tell me who saw it — Sírvase decirme quien lo ha

Come in ! — ¡ Entre Vd. !

Can you change me this foreign money ?	¿ Puede Vd. cambiarme este dinero extranjero ?
Walk this way.	Pase Vd. adelante.
Is your master at home ?	¿ Está su amo en casa ?
No, madam ; he is out, and will not return before the evening.	No, señora : está fuera, y no volverá antes de la noche.
What a pity ! I should like to see him.	¡ Qué lástima ! desearía verle.
Will you give me your name ?	¿ Quiere Vd. darme su nombre?
You are right.	Vd. tiene razón.
I am not right.	No tengo razón.
We are right this time.	Tenemos razón esta vez.
I am sure they are wrong.	Estoy seguro de que no tienen razón.
His friend was wrong.	Su amigo no tenía razón.
Who is this gentleman who is coming towards us ?	¿ Quién es este señor que viene hacia nosotros ?
He is a friend of my cousin's, but I do not know his name.	Es un amigo de mi primo, pero no sé su nombre.
Can you direct me to — Street ?	¿ Puede Vd. dirigirme á la calle de — ?
With much pleasure.	Con mucho gusto.
You must take this road.	Vd. debe tomar este camino.
Go straight on.	Vaya Vd. derecho.
Take the second street on the right.	Tome Vd. la segunda calle á la derecha.
The street you want is the first on the left.	La calle que Vd. quiere es la primera á la izquierda.
Ask again, when you get to the market.	Pregunte de nuevo, cuando llegue al mercado.
You will see the station in front of you.	Vd. verá la estación en frente.
Whom are you writing to ?	¿ A quién escribe Vd. ?
I am writing to my brother : I have several things to say to him.	Escribo á mi hermano ; tengo varias cosas que decirle.
All that they told you is true.	[verdad. Todo lo que le han dicho es

The windows are not shut.

Las ventanas no están cerradas.   [puerta ?

Shall I shut the door ?

¿ Quiere Vd. que (yo) cierre la

Please give me some bread and cheese.

Hágame el favor de darme un poco de pan y queso.

What will you drink ?

¿ Qué quiere Vd. beber ?

I should like a glass of beer, if there is any.

Quisiera un vaso de cerveza, si la hay.

You cannot do better.

Vd. no puede hacer cosa mejor

Where are you going ?

¿ Adónde va Vd. ?

I am going home ; will you come with me ?

Voy á casa ; ¿ quiere Vd. venir conmigo ?

No, thank you ; I must stay here, because I have a great deal to do.

No, gracias ; debo quedarme aquí, porque tengo mucho que hacer.

I am very sorry, but I cannot do it.

Lo siento mucho, pero no puedo hacerlo.

Is anybody at home ?

¿ Hay alguien en casa ?

What hour is that striking ?

¿ Qué hora está dando ?

It is just striking eleven.

Están dando las once.

The hour is just about to strike.

La hora va á dar.   [media ?

Has it struck half past five yet ?

¿ Han dado ya las cinco y

Not yet ; but I think it will strike soon.

Todavía no ; pero creo que darán pronto.

It has just struck one.

La una acaba de dar.

It had just struck eight.

Las ocho acababan de dar.

It is a beautiful day.

Hace un día hermoso.

It is fine (weather).

Hace buen tiempo.

It is very bad weather.

Hace muy mal tiempo.

It was not fine.

No hacía buen tiempo.

Do you think it will be fine to-morrow ?

¿ Cree Vd. que hará buen tiempo mañana ?

It is not snowing.

No está nevando.

I believe it will rain soon.

Creo que lloverá pronto.

I expect a letter from my sister in Paris.

Espero una carta de mi hermana que está en París.

These letters are not dated.

Estas cartas no tienen fecha.

What is the date ?	¿ A cuántos estamos hoy ?
The first, second, third, *etc.*	A primero, á dos, á tres, *etc.*
Will you take this letter to the post ?	¿ Quiere Vd. llevar esta carta al correo ?
We are going to send them the answer to-morrow.	Vamos á enviarles la respuesta mañana.
How much do you ask for this?	¿ Cuánto pide Vd. por esto ?
How do you sell these ?	¿ A cómo vende Vd. estos ?
At the price which you see marked.	Al precio que ve Vd. marcado.
Is this the lowest price ?	¿ Es este el precio más bajo ?
Yes ; we mark our prices as low as possible, and we cannot reduce them.	Sí ; marcamos nuestros precios lo más bajo posible, y no podemos reducirlos.
These goods are sold at three shillings each.	Estos géneros se venden á tres chelines cada uno.
This is a very cheap article.	Este es un artículo muy barato.
It appears to me too much.	Me parece demasiado.
How much will you take ?	¿ Cuánto tomará Vd. ?
Do you think it will be enough ?	¿ Cree Vd. que será bastante ?
I was not satisfied with the material I bought here the other day.	No estaba satisfecho con el material que compré aquí el otro día.
I was inclined to send it back to you.	Estaba dispuesto á devolvérselo (á Vd.).
We are very sorry that you did not do so.	Sentimos mucho que Vd. no lo haya hecho.
We always do all we possibly can to satisfy our customers.	Hacemos siempre todo lo que podemos para satisfacer á nuestros parroquianos.
Can I show you anything else ?	¿ Puedo mostrarle á Vd. alguna otra cosa ?
I will take those ; please send them to my house.	Tomaré esos ; sírvase mandarlos á mi casa.
Where do you wish them to be sent ?	¿ Adónde quiere Vd. que se manden ?
To No. 17, Prince's Street.	A la calle del Príncipe, No. 17.

Is there a letter for me ?

¿ Hay carta para mí ?

They were obliged to go away.

Tuvieron que irse.

We shall go out to-night, if it is not too cold.

Saldremos esta noche, si no hace demasiado frío.

He asked us why we had come, but we did not answer him.

Nos preguntó por qué habíamos venido, pero no le contestamos.

Open the door, and shut all the windows.

Abra Vd. la puerta, y cierre todas las ventanas.

Is the door locked ?

¿ Está cerrada con llave la puerta ?

Do not come too late.

No venga Vd. demasiado tarde.

I beg your pardon.

Dispénseme Vd. *or* Perdone Vd.

There is no occasion for it.

No hay de qué.

There was no occasion for it.

No había de qué.

There would not be any need for it.

No habría de qué.

It is better not to say anything, than to speak too much.

Vale más no decir nada, que hablar demasiado.

It would be better not to say anything more.

Más valdría no decir nada más.

When we have finished our work, we shall go out.

Cuando hayamos acabado nuestro trabajo, saldremos.

Where are you going ?

¿ Adónde irán Vds. ?

We are going to hear a very celebrated speaker.

Vamos á oir á un orador muy célebre.

Did you enjoy yourselves at the theatre yesterday ?

¿ Se divirtieron Vds. ayer en el teatro ?

Thank you ; we enjoyed ourselves very much.

Gracias ; nos divertimos mucho.

Follow me ; I have something for you.   [me ?

Sígame ; tengo algo para Vd.
                             [me ?

Have you anything to show

¿ Tiene Vd. algo que mostrar-

Can you stay here for a little while ?

¿ Puede Vd. quedarse aquí un poco ?

I must go away at once.

Debo irme al instante.

I shall be here at a quarter to eight exactly.

Estaré aquí á las ocho menos cuarto en punto.

We are very glad that our father has come home again.

Nos alegramos mucho de que nuestro padre haya vuelto á casa.

Do you want an umbrella or a stick ?

¿ Quiere Vd. un paraguas ó un bastón ?

I do not want either.

No quiero ni uno ni otro.

Do you want anything else ?

¿ Quiere Vd. otra cosa ?

You must tell him as soon as he arrives.

Vd. debe decírselo en cuanto llegue.

As you please.

Como Vd. guste.

When you go downstairs, take this with you.

Cuando Vd. baje, llévese esto.

A week ago he was in the country, but he came back last night.

Hace una semana estaba en el campo, pero volvió anoche.

How many days have you been here ?

¿ Cuántos días hace que está Vd. aquí ?   [aquí ?

Have you been here long ?

¿ Hace mucho que está Vd.

We have been here ten minutes.

Hace diez minutos que estamos aquí.

I have been learning Spanish for a year.

Hace un año que aprendo español.

Let us talk a little.

Conversemos un poco.

What have you to tell me ?

¿ Qué tiene Vd. que decirme ?

We must not catch cold.

No debemos resfriarnos.

The children will catch cold.

Los niños se resfriarán.

I have a cold.

Estoy resfriado.

She has not got a cold.

No está resfriada.

They all had colds.

Estaban todos resfriados.

I am afraid he will catch cold.

Temo que se resfríe.

This bread is new (=fresh) ; it is not cold yet.   [hot.

Este pan está fresco ; no está frío todavía.   [lientes.

The coffee and the tea are not

El café y el té no están ca-

The iron was too hot.

El hierro estaba demasiado caliente.

At what time do you dine ?

¿ A qué hora comen Vds. ?

It is already five o'clock.

Ya son las cinco.

We shall dine at half past six. — Comeremos á las seis y media.

I saw the people coming out of church. — Ví á la gente salir de la iglesia.

I thought I should receive more money for my horses. — Creí que recibiría más dinero por mis caballos.

With your permission, I will read this letter. — Con permiso de Vd., leeré esta carta.

You are greatly mistaken. — Está Vd. muy equivocado.

I have come by coach, not by train. — He venido en coche, no en el tren.

Send him the answer by post. — Envíele Vd. la respuesta por correo.

The town consists of five hundred houses. — La ciudad se compone de quinientas casas.

This lady appears to be taller than her mother. — Esta señorita parece ser más alta que su madre.

Do you know that lady? — ¿ Conoce Vd. á esa señora ?

We have known her for some time. — Hace algún tiempo que la conocemos.

I have seen her, but I do not know her. — La he visto, pero no la conozco.

I know her by sight. — La conozco de vista.

We know her by name. — La conocemos de nombre.

What is this called? — ¿ Cómo se llama esto ?

I do not remember what it is called. — No me acuerdo como se llama.

What are these things called? — ¿ Cómo se llaman estas cosas ?

We do not know what they are called. — No sabemos como se llaman.

What is your friend's name? — ¿ Cómo se llama su amigo ?

My name is George. — Me llamo Jorge.

We shall come back at the end of the month. — Volveremos á fines del mes.

Knock at that door. — Llame Vd. á esa puerta.

Somebody is knocking at the door. — Alguien llama á la puerta.

It is a gentleman, but I do not know his name. — Es un caballero, pero no sé su nombre.

Go and see who it is.	Vaya Vd. á ver quien es.
Whom did he ask for ?	¿ Por quién ha preguntado ?
I am ashamed.	Tengo vergüenza.
Are you not ashamed ?	¿ No tienen Vds. vergüenza ?
He ought to be ashamed to say that.	Debía tener vergüenza de decir eso.
I am afraid he cannot wait any longer.	Temo que no pueda aguardar más.
Were you not very much afraid ?	¿ No tenía Vd. mucho miedo?
He will be afraid to go out this evening.	Tendrá miedo de salir esta noche.
I did not hear the question.	No oí la pregunta.
Ask whether they have printed the books yet.	Pregunte Vd. si han impreso los libros ya.
They brought a message to say she had died last week.	Trajeron un parte diciendo que había muerto la semana pasada.
I do not always hear all the words.	No oigo siempre todas las palabras.
I am very hot.	Tengo mucho calor.
Are you not warm ?	¿ No tiene Vd. calor ? [calor.
We shall be too hot here.	Tendremos aquí demasiado
We are not cold.	No tenemos frío.
Are you cold ?	¿ Tienen Vds. frío ?
She was very cold.	Ella tenía mucho frío.
You would be too cold in this room.	Vd. tendría demasiado frío en este cuarto.
These rooms are very cold.	Estos cuartos son muy fríos.
The water was not cold.	El agua no estaba fría.
We have not found what we were looking for.	No hemos hallado lo que buscábamos.
I shall not go out to-day, or to-morrow either.	No saldré hoy, ni mañana tampoco.
They arrived in time, but unfortunately he was not there.	Llegaron á tiempo, pero por desgracia él no estaba allí.
Those who are idle are seldom happy.	Los que son holgazanes son raramente felices.

Is this house for sale ?	¿ Se vende esta casa ?
No, madam ; it is to be let.	No, señora ; se alquila.
Have you any rooms to let ?	¿ Tiene Vd. cuartos para alquilar ?
I want to take lodgings near my friend's house.	Deseo alquilar un alojamiento junto á la casa de mi amigo.
How many rooms do you want?	¿ Cuántos cuartos desea Vd. ?
I should like three rooms on the second or third floor.	Quisiera tres cuartos en el segundo ó tercer piso.
For how long do you want them ?	¿ Por cuánto tiempo los quiere Vd. ?
For three or four months.	Por tres ó cuatro meses.
How much have I to pay a week ?	¿ Cuánto tengo que pagar por semana ?
The price is eight dollars a month.	El precio es ocho duros al mes (or por mes).
I think it is too much.	Creo que es demasiado.
These boots do not suit me.	Estas botas no me vienen bien.
They are too narrow.	Son demasiado estrechas.
They are not broad enough.	No son bastante anchas.
Did not the gloves fit him well ?	¿ No le vinieron bien los guantes ?
Your hat does not suit you.	Su sombrero no le viene bien.
It is too tight.	Es demasiado estrecho.
This ring fits me better.	Esta sortija me ajusta mejor.
His coats suit him very well.	Sus levitas le vienen muy bien.
This coat is very uncomfortable.	Esta levita me incomoda mucho.
He called me by my name, but I don't know who he was.	Me llamó por mi nombre, pero no sé quien era.
They appear to be a long way from here, but they are not.	Parecen estar muy lejos de aquí, pero no lo están.
I shall finish the list this very day.	Acabaré la lista hoy mismo.
It is not necessary that we should keep them waiting.	No es preciso que les hagamos esperar.
I shall see him next Sunday.	Le veré el Domingo que viene.

Do not keep us waiting any longer.

No nos haga Vd. esperar más.

Send for a cab.

Mande Vd. por un coche.

I have merely come to ask when you can finish it.

Solo he venido para preguntarle cuando puede acabarlo Vd.

Who has taken away my cup ?

¿ Quién se ha llevado mi taza ?

Take this umbrella with you.

Lleve Vd. este paraguas consigo.

Will you take the children home ?

¿ Quiere Vd. llevar los niños á casa ?

Are you wearing boots or shoes?

¿ Lleva Vd. botas ó zapatos ?

In summer I generally wear shoes, and in winter boots.

En verano uso (or llevo) generalmente zapatos, y botas en invierno.

Do you generally wear a jacket or a morning coat ?

¿ Usa Vd. generalmente casaca ó levita ?

My friend used to wear his clothes too tight.

Mi amigo usaba (or llevaba) su vestido demasiado estrecho.

This phrase is not correct ; it is better to write it in this way.

Esta frase no es correcta ; vale más escribirla de este modo.

They went away without speaking to anybody.

Se fueron sin hablar á nadie.

He always forgets the promises he makes.

Olvida siempre las promesas que hace.

This wine is all that we could wish.

Este vino es tal cual lo podíamos desear.

The provisions were not all that we could have wished.

Los víveres no eran tales cuales los podíamos desear.

I try as much as I can.

Procuro cuanto puedo.

We are doing what we can.

Hacemos cuanto podemos.

We will do all we can.

Haremos cuanto podamos.

It is the least they can do for her.

Es lo menos que pueden hacer por ella.

Will you do it for me ?

¿ Quiere Vd. hacerlo por mí ?

There are many men who can neither read nor write.

Hay muchos hombres que no saben ni leer ni escribir.

English	Spanish
Sit down.	Siéntese Vd.
Thank you ; I cannot stay.	Gracias ; no puedo quedarme.
I took advantage of his silence to explain what you had told me.	Me aproveché de su silencio para explicar lo que Vd. me había dicho.
We shall take advantage of their absence.	Nos aprovecharemos de su ausencia.
He has gone away without waiting for the answer.	Se ha ido sin aguardar la respuesta.
Both these books are ours.	Ambos libros son nuestros.
Both the shops are that merchant's.	Ambas tiendas son de aquel comerciante.
Which of the two do you prefer ?	¿ Cuál de los dos prefiere Vd. ?
They detained me nearly two hours.	Me han detenido casi dos horas.
He slept for more than ten hours.	Ha dormido más de diez horas.
There are more than fifty ships in the harbour.	Hay más de cincuenta buques en el puerto.
I receive more than twenty letters a day by post.	Recibo más de veinte cartas por correo cada día.
I cannot approve of his conduct.	No puedo aprobar su conducta.
Nobody likes to be deceived.	Nadie quiere ser engañado.
I thought you wanted to mislead me.	Creí que Vd. deseaba engañarme.
We have hardly had time to read the answer.	Apenas hemos tenido tiempo para leer la contestación.
I went to see his school yesterday.	Ayer fuí á ver su escuela.
Have you been to see your bed-room ?	¿ Ha ido Vd. á ver su alcoba ?
Yes ; it is convenient, but it is not very big.	Sí ; es cómoda, pero no es muy grande.
It is on the ground floor.	Está en el cuarto bajo.
Mine is on the third fioor.	La mía está en el tercer piso.
I prefer the first floor.	Prefiero el primer piso.

When you take the letters to the post, do not forget to pay the postage.

Cuando lleve Vd. las cartas al correo, no olvide de pagar el porte.

Have you dated them ?

¿ Les ha puesto Vd. la fecha ?

Yes, but I have not signed them.

Sí, pero no las he firmado.

I am very fond of music (=music pleases me).

Me gusta la música.

We do not like dancing.

No nos gusta bailar.

Does she like this picture ?

¿ Le gusta este cuadro ?

Do you like the pictures in the exhibition ?

¿ Le gustan á Vd. los cuadros de la exposición ?

I do not like them much.

No me gustan mucho.

I do not like this.

Esto no me gusta.

They all like country life.

A todos ellos les gusta la vida campestre.

Used they to like this wine ?

¿ Les gustaba este vino ?

We like the other better.

Nos gusta más el otro.

Which of the three do you like best ?

¿ Cuál de los tres les gusta á Vds. más ?

I am very fond of apples.

Me gustan mucho las manzanas.

I prefer pears.

Prefiero las peras.

We like oranges best.

Nos gustan más las naranjas.

So do I. So do we.

Yo también. Nosotros también.

Everybody knows it.

Todo el mundo lo sabe.

It is not yet known where they have gone.

Aún no se sabe adonde han ido.

I assure you that I did not do it.

Le aseguro que yo no lo hice.

While he was speaking, I wrote the letter.

Mientras él hablaba, yo escribía la carta.

While they were waiting, he went out.

Mientras aguardaban, salió.

Indeed !

¡ De veras !

When was that done ?

¿ Cuándo se hizo eso ?

Is this fruit good to eat ?

¿ Es esta fruta buena para comer ?

We do not think it is ripe yet.

No creemos que esté madura todavía.

They bought it the day before yesterday.	Lo compraron anteayer.
I will send it to them the day after to-morrow.	Se lo enviaré pasado mañana.
He does not generally come before seven o'clock.	Generalmente no viene antes de las siete.
They will come back at the end of a month.	Volverán al cabo de un mes.
It is not true.	No es verdad.
No such thing.	No hay tal cosa.
Not at all.	De ningún modo.
How long have you been living here?	¿Cuánto tiempo hace que vive Vd. aquí?
Since last month.	Desde el mes pasado.
If I pay you now, will you give me a receipt?	Si le pago ahora, ¿me dará Vd. recibo?
He would not pay the account without getting a receipt.	No quería pagar la cuenta sin tomar recibo.
How far is it from here to London?	¿Qué distancia hay de aquí á Londres?
About two hundred miles.	Cerca de doscientas millas.
How many miles is it from Madrid to Paris?	¿Cuántas millas hay desde Madrid á París?
I did not think it was so far.	No creía que fuese tan lejos.
He was not showing much dexterity.	No mostraba mucha destreza.
I live in the west of the town, but formerly I lived in the east.	Vivo en el oeste de la ciudad, pero antes vivía en el este.
We shall live in the south, and our relatives in the north.	Nosotros viviremos en el sud, y nuestros parientes en el norte.
They used to live opposite the market.	Vivían frente al mercado.
Can you walk more quickly?	¿Puede Vd. andar más aprisa?
Do not walk so quickly.	No anden Vds. tan aprisa.
He always used to walk too quickly.	Andaba siempre demasiado aprisa.

Let me copy it for you.	Déjeme copiarlo por Vd.
He began to run, but I easily caught him.	Empezó á correr, pero le alcancé fácilmente.
It is not so late as I thought.	No es tan tarde como yo creía.
It is much later than they thought.	Es mucho más tarde de lo que creían.
They are stronger than we expected.	Son más fuertes de lo que esperábamos.
You are walking more slowly than I like.	Vd. anda más despacio de lo que quiero.
Is the station far from here ?	¿ Está lejos de aquí la estación ?
Take the second street on the right.	Tome Vd. la segunda calle á la derecha.
Can you tell me where the ... Hotel is ?	¿ Puede Vd. decirme donde está el hotel ... ?
You must take the third turning on the left.	Vd. debe tomar la tercera calle á la izquierda.
The house you passed by this morning is my grandfather's.	La casa por la cual Vd. ha pasado esta mañana es de mi abuelo.
I want you to repair this lock.	Deseo que Vd. repare esta cerradura.
You ought to have a new key.	Vd. debiera tener una llave nueva.
At what time do you breakfast?	¿ A qué hora almuerza Vd. ?
They breakfasted with me yesterday morning.	Almorzaron conmigo ayer (por la) mañana.
I often breakfast with him.	Almuerzo amenudo con él.
We shall breakfast with them to-morrow at half past seven.	Almorzaremos con ellos mañana á las siete y media.
It is rather early for us.	Es algo temprano para nosotros.
They were informed of it.	Tenían noticia de ello.
I shall not be informed of that.	No tendré noticia de eso.
Where does this letter come from ?	¿ De dónde viene esta carta ?

She owes her life to him.	Le debe la vida.
We shall soon know whether it can be done.	Pronto sabremos si puede hacerse.
Why do you not get up ?	¿ Por qué no se levanta Vd. ?
I am going to get up now, but I went to bed rather late last night.	Voy á levantarme ahora, pero anoche me acosté un poco tarde.
I shall go to see them to-day, even if the weather is bad.	Iré á verlos hoy, aunque haga mal tiempo.
Breakfast is ready.	El almuerzo está servido.
Supper is not ready.	La cena no está servida.
Will you stop to supper ?	¿Quieren Vds. quedarse á cenar?
We are going to take tea.	Vamos á tomar el té.
Why do you not begin ?	¿ Por qué no empieza Vd. ?
You have not told us what we ought to do.	Vd. no nos ha dicho lo que debíamos hacer.
We remember this street very well.	Nos acordamos de esta calle muy bien.
Don't you remember that song ?	¿ No se acuerda Vd. de aquella canción ?
I remember this song, but not that one.	Me acuerdo de esta canción, pero no de esa.
Do not be angry ; it is not my fault.	No se enoje Vd. ; no es culpa mía.
He often gets angry without cause.	Se enoja amenudo sin causa.
Will you come for a walk with me ?	¿ Quiere Vd. dar un paseo conmigo ?
I will come for a walk with you with much pleasure.	Con mucho gusto daré un paseo con Vd.
I cannot go any farther ; I am very tired.	No puedo andar más ; estoy muy cansado.
At what time do your children get up ?	¿ A qué hora se levantan sus hijos (de Vd.) ?
Generally about seven o'clock.	Generalmente cerca de las siete.
Mine does not get up before eight.	El mío no se levanta antes de las ocho.
They never take enough care.	Nunca tienen bastante cuidado.

I have just written him a letter.	Acabo de escribirle una carta.
I have not sent it to the post yet.	No la he mandado al correo todavía.
My sister had just gone out.	Mi hermana acababa de salir.
They had just told him when you arrived.	Acababan de decírselo cuando Vd. llegó.
Do you not remember it ?	¿ No lo recuerda Vd. ?
There is nothing better than a good memory.	No hay nada mejor que una buena memoria.
What is your opinion ?	¿ Cuál es su parecer ?
Our opinion is that it is not true.	Nos parece que no es verdad.
Whom is that child like ?	¿ A quién se parece aquel niño ?
I'm sure I don't know.	Estoy seguro de que no lo sé.
I do not know whom he is like.	No sé á quien se parece.
I am very like my mother.	Me parezco mucho á mi madre.
It seems to me that we have enough.	Me parece que tenemos bastante.
Did you not tell us that nothing was the matter with her ?	¿ No nos dijeron Vds. que (ella) no tenía nada ?
On the contrary, she has got a very bad cold.	Al contrario, está muy resfriada.
His answer made me laugh.	Su respuesta me hizo reir.
If you say that, you will make your teacher laugh.	Si dice Vd. eso, hará reir á su profesor.
While he is out, I will read the newspaper.	Mientras está fuera, leeré el diario.
I am going to Paris this year, to see the exhibition.	Voy á París este año, para ver la exposición.
So am I. So is my brother.	Yo también. Mi hermano también.
It is necessary that you should go with him.	Es menester que Vd. vaya con él.
So must you. So must she.	Vd. también. Ella también.
He has never been in France.	Nunca ha estado en Francia.
I cannot believe him.	No puedo creerle.
Neither can we.	Nosotros tampoco.
Neither can his master.	Su amo tampoco.

Have you seen the key of my grammar?	¿Ha visto Vd. la clave de mi gramática?
It is better always to work without a key.	Es mejor trabajar siempre sin clave.
Do you remember the name of this flower?	¿Se acuerda Vd. del nombre de esta flor?
I should very much like a watch like yours.　[left.	De buena gana quisiera un reloj como el de Vd.
We shall have enough meat	Nos quedará bastante carne.
I have only one shilling left.	Solo me queda un chelín.
They only had ten shillings left.	Solo les quedaban diez chelines.
What is your income?	¿Cuánto tiene Vd. de renta?
My income is two hundred pounds.	Tengo doscientas libras de renta.
He asked your permission before taking the knife.	Le pidió permiso antes de tomar el cuchillo.
I cannot promise to bring the things to-night.	No puedo prometer que traeré las cosas esta noche.
I will try to persuade him to come.	Procuraré persuadirle de que venga.
Is there anything on this page which you cannot understand?	¿Hay algo en esta página que Vd. no pueda comprender?
What is the name of the bridge we are going over?	¿Cómo se llama el puente que cruzamos?
It is dangerous to cross the street.	Es peligroso cruzar la calle.
What are you going to do this afternoon?	¿Qué va Vd. á hacer esta tarde?
I must first finish my work, and then I shall see how much time I have left.	Debo acabar mi trabajo primero, y entonces veré cuanto tiempo me queda.
I do not agree with you.	No convengo con Vd.
When is this newspaper published?	¿Cuándo se publica este periódico?
It comes out twice a week.	Sale dos veces por semana.
They are published once a month.	Salen una vez por mes.

What did you do during your holidays ?	¿ Qué hizo Vd. durante sus vacaciones ?
Everyone denies having broken it.	Todo el mundo niega haberlo roto.
Have you any change about you ?	¿ Tiene Vd. cambio encima ?
The man who served me forgot to give me the change.	El tendero que me ha servido ha olvidado darme el cambio.
You should not have come away without it.	Vd. no debía (or debiera) haber salido sin él (or sin recibirlo).
Do you like Madrid ?	¿ Le gusta á Vd. Madrid ?
He is now employed in a foreign firm.	Está ahora colocado en una casa extranjera.
Please answer me when I ask you.	Sírvase contestarme cuando le pregunto.
At what time do you leave your office ?	¿ A qué hora sale Vd. de su oficina ?
How long ago did that happen ?	¿ Cuánto tiempo hace que sucedió eso ?
Do you find Spanish difficult?	¿ Encuentra Vd. difícil el español ?
No, I think it is a very easy language, but it wants practice, like everything else.	No, creo que es un idioma muy fácil, pero se necesita práctica, como en todo lo demás.
He cannot prove what he said just now.	No puede probar lo que acaba de decir
Will you translate this sentence for me ?	¿ Quiere Vd. traducir esta frase por mí ?
I do not know how this word is pronounced.	No sé como se pronuncia esta palabra.
We are going to begin ; are you ready ?	Vamos á empezar ; ¿ están Vds. listos ?
I shall be ready in half an hour.	Estaré listo en media hora.
Do you know the number of his house ?	¿ Sabe Vd. el número de su casa ?
What is the news ?	¿ Qué hay de nuevo ?
I do not know any news.	No sé nada de nuevo.

I cannot agree with you.	No puedo convenir con Vd.
We shall come back soon.	Volveremos pronto.
I do not want them to accompany me this time.	No quiero que me acompañen esta vez.
They were talking among themselves.	Hablaban entre sí.
Do it again.	Vuelva Vd. á hacerlo.
He does not want to copy the letters again.	No quiere volver á copiar las cartas.
Look for it carefully.	Búsquelo cuidadosamente.
I tried to find it, but I could not see it anywhere.	Procuré hallarlo, pero no pude verlo en ninguna parte.
He has gone to dress himself.	Ha ido á vestirse.
They cannot be long in arriving.	No pueden tardar en llegar.
Do not be long before coming back.	No tarde Vd. en volver.
Do not believe it.	No lo crea Vd.
I have let him keep all the documents.	Le he dejado guardar todos los documentos.
Will you allow me to read his answer ?	¿ Quiere Vd. dejarme leer su respuesta ?
This house is the one I like best.	Esta casa es la que me gusta más.
Tell me what they are going to do.	Dígame lo que van á hacer.
We shall not be able to take all these parcels with us.	No podremos llevar todos estos paquetes con nosotros.
Which paragraph do you mean ?	¿ Cuál párrafo quiere Vd. decir ?
How difficult this is !	¡ Qué difícil es esto !
How carefully he is doing the work !	¡ Qué cuidadosamente está haciendo el trabajo !
How lovely these flowers are !	¡ Qué hermosas son estas flores !
They are a present from my cousin.	Son regalo de mi primo.
We shall have a fine day to-day.	Tendremos hoy un buen día.
The country needs fine weather.	El campo necesita buen tiempo.

Is it going to rain ?

¿ Está para llover ?

I think not.

Creo que no.

We are sure it is.

Estamos seguros de que sí.

They are never punctual.

Nunca son puntuales.

Be as punctual as you possibly can.

Sea Vd. tan puntual como le sea posible.

Such a beautiful thing is not made for nothing.

Una cosa tan hermosa no se hace de balde (*or* por nada).

He would not dare to deny that.

No se atrevería á negar eso.

How do you dare to speak so ?

¿ Cómo se atreve Vd. á hablar así ?

He asked my permission before going out.

Me pidió permiso antes de salir.

They arrived an hour later.

Llegaron una hora después.

Why did you call us for such a trifling thing ?

¿ Por qué nos llamó Vd. para una cosa tan frívola ?

We have never seen this kind of machine.

No hemos visto nunca esta clase de máquina.

He let us do what we liked.

Nos dejó hacer lo que quisimos.

Why do you not take off your hat ?

¿ Por qué no se quita Vd. el sombrero ?

When I saw the others had gone away, I went too.

Cuando ví que los otros se habían ido, yo me fuí también.

We shall be there within half an hour.

Estaremos allí dentro de media hora.

At first sight, it seemed to be impossible.

A primera vista, parecía ser imposible.

We must not show it to them yet.

No debemos mostrárselo todavía.

Is it true that you have bought another bicycle?

¿ Es verdad que ha comprado Vd. otra bicicleta ?

They wanted more money to buy the jewels.

Necesitaban más dinero para comprar las joyas.

He spoke in a whisper, but I heard all that he said.

Habló en voz baja, pero oí todo lo que dijo.

Sit down by my side.

Siéntese Vd. á mi lado.

There will not be much difficulty in finding out his address.	No habrá mucha dificultad en hallar sus señas.
To tell the truth, I forgot to ask for the bill.	En verdad, olvidé pedir la cuenta.
Which of these books have you read? This one, or that one?	¿ Cuál de estos libros ha leído Vd. ? ¿ este ó ese ?
Take care what you are doing.	Tenga cuidado con lo que hace.
Take care, or you will fall.	Tenga cuidado, ó se caerá.
I would do it for you with pleasure, if I had time.	Lo haría por Vd. con gusto, si tuviera tiempo.
We want to ask you something.	Deseamos preguntarle algo.
Did you see what they were doing ?	¿ Ha visto Vd. lo que hacían ?
Did you not say I was to copy and send off the letters ?	¿ No dijo Vd. que yo debía copiar y mandar las cartas ?
It is neither good for you, nor for me.	No es bueno para Vd., ni para mí.
He acted under my advice.	El obró bajo mi consejo.
She died the next morning.	Murió á la mañana siguiente.
Look on the next page.	Mire Vd. la página siguiente.
He refused to help me, although I asked him to.	Rehusó ayudarme, aunque se lo pedí.
Did you not tell me that you were satisfied ?	¿ No me han dicho Vds. que estaban satisfechos ?
I advise you not to say anything about it.	Le aconsejo á Vd. que no diga nada de ello.
The house is too small for us.	La casa es demasiado pequeña para nosotros.
The greater part of the houses in this town are built of wood.	La mayor parte de las casas de esta ciudad son de madera.
I shall not wait, as they did not say when they would be back.	No esperaré, pues no dijeron cuando volverían.
I shall come, unless the weather is very bad.	Vendré, á menos que haga muy mal tiempo.

Do not go away until it leaves off raining.

No se vaya Vd. hasta que cese de llover.

See whether my umbrella is behind the door.

Mire Vd. si mi paraguas está detrás de la puerta.

Put the wine and the fruit on the table.

Ponga Vd. el vino y la fruta encima de la mesa.

The child has thrown its toys under the table.

El niño ha tirado sus juguetes debajo de la mesa.

Throw it out of window.

Tírelo Vd. por la ventana.

Go on with your work ; there is still a great deal to be done.

Siga Vd. con su trabajo ; todavía hay mucho que hacer.

It rained a great deal here yesterday.

Ayer llovió mucho aquí.

The weather will soon get warmer.

Pronto hará más calor.

That is not the way to do it.

Ese no es el modo de hacerlo.

We shall come as soon as we have put our papers straight.

Vendremos luego que hayamos arreglado nuestros papeles.

The servant has disarranged them.

La criada los ha desarreglado.

He has hardly done anything.

Apenas ha hecho algo.

It is not worth my while to buy another one.

No vale la pena de que compre otro.

I hope to see you again to-morrow morning.

Espero volverle á ver mañana por la mañana.

You do not look well.

Vd. no tiene buena cara.

Are you in a hurry ?

¿ Tiene Vd. prisa ?

I am not very busy to-day.

No estoy muy ocupado hoy.

We gave him all that we had.

Le dimos todo lo que teníamos.

We did what we could to persuade them.

Hicimos cuanto pudimos para persuadirles.

Nothing we could say to him convinced him.

Nada de lo que podíamos decirle le convencía.

This room is twenty feet long, and ten broad.

Este cuarto tiene veinte piés de largo, y diez de ancho.

How high is this house?	¿ Qué altura tiene esta casa ?
I am tired of listening to him.	Estoy cansado de escucharle.
How do you generally go to your office ?	¿ Cómo va Vd. generalmente á su oficina ?
Sometimes by rail, and sometimes by omnibus.	A veces por el ferro-carril, y á veces por el ómnibus.
Which is the quickest way ?	¿ Cuál es el camino más corto ?
There is not much difference.	No hay mucha diferencia.
He does not know how the word is spelt.	No sabe como se deletrea la palabra.
When are you going to take your holidays ?	¿ Cuándo tendrá Vd. sus vacaciones ?
I shall leave England in a few days.	Dentro de algunos días saldré de Inglaterra.
What do you think of the weather we have had during the last fortnight ?	¿ Qué piensa Vd. del tiempo que tenemos desde hace quince días ?
I cannot promise to lend you both songs.	No puedo prometer prestarle ambas canciones.
The gentleman who called here wanted to know why you had not sent the things he ordered.	El caballero que vino aquí quería saber por qué no había Vd. enviado los artículos que pidió.
They used to live here some years ago.	Vivían aquí hace algunos años.
Let us go on the other side of the street.	Vamos por el otro lado de la calle.
Which is the nearest way (to go) to the river ?	¿ Cuál es el camino más corto para ir al río ?
They would not be satisfied, if we did what they ask.	No estarían satisfechos, si hiciéramos lo que piden.
What are the four seasons of the year called in Spanish ?	¿ Cómo se llaman en español las cuatro estaciones del año?
They are as follow : Spring, Summer, Autumn, and Winter.	Son las siguientes : Primavera, Verano, Otoño, é Invierno.
He could not do it, even if he wanted to.	No podría hacerlo, aunque quisiera.

I have not had much opportunity of speaking Spanish since I came back to England.

No he tenido mucha oportunidad de hablar español desde que volví á Inglaterra.

How long were you in South America?

¿ Cuánto tiempo estuvo Vd. en Sud América ?

I was there nearly six months.

Estuve allí casi seis meses.

You ought to speak Spanish fairly well.

Vd. debe hablar español bastante bien.

Excuse me for keeping you waiting so long.

Dispénseme Vd. que le haya hecho aguardar tanto tiempo.

They went home without asking leave.

Se fueron á casa sin pedir licencia.

Have you heard what happened last night?

¿ Ha oído Vd. lo que pasó anoche ?

As you were not there, we went away at once.

Como Vd. no estaba allí, nos fuimos al instante.

Would you advise me to accept the money?

¿ Me aconsejaría Vd. que acepte el dinero ?

Write and tell them not to come.

Escríbales para decirles que no vengan.

He came after I had started.

Vino después que yo había partido.

I am glad you are better.

Me alegro de que Vd. se halle mejor.

I wonder (=who knows) what they will bring.

¿ Quién sabe lo que traerán ?

Did anybody call to see me while I was out?

¿ Vino alguien á verme mientras estaba fuera ?

A gentleman enquired for you, but he would not tell me his name.

Un caballero preguntó por Vd., pero no quiso decirme su nombre.

Tell me what you want, and I will give it to you if I can.

Dígame lo que necesita Vd., y se lo daré si puedo.

I was very much surprised when you told me that.

Me sorprendí mucho cuando Vd. me dijo eso.

He never pays what he owes.

Nunca paga lo que debe.

Give me some more apples, if there are any.

Déme Vd. más manzanas, si las hay.

I slept nearly all day.	Dormí casi todo el día.
You must have been very tired.	Vd. debe haber estado muy cansado.
Do not go out at the same time as the other clerk.	No salga Vd. á la misma hora que el otro dependiente.
Do not sell it for less than twelve shillings and six-pence.	No lo venda Vd. por menos de doce chelines y seis peniques.
I very much doubt whether they will give me so much for this ring.	Dudo mucho que me den tanto por esta sortija.
	[todavía.
The fire has not gone out yet.	El fuego no se ha apagado
This word is not spelt cor-rectly.	Esta palabra no está bien deletreada.
Whose turn is it ?	¿ A quién le toca ?
It was not my turn.	No me tocaba á mí.
They have just reached home.	Acaban de llegar á casa.
Whom has he married ?	¿ Con quién se ha casado ?
She is going to marry her cousin.	Ella se va á casar con su primo.
It is not worth more than five pesetas.	No vale más de cinco pesetas.
How much have you paid for this ?	¿ Cuánto ha pagado Vd. por esto ?
I will pay you as soon as I possibly can.	Le pagaré á Vd. tan pronto como me sea posible.
Take it upstairs at once.	Llévelo arriba al instante.
Did you go there on horseback?	¿ Fué Vd. allí á caballo ?
No ; we all went on foot.	No ; todos fuimos á pié.
They have gone by coach.	Han ido en coche.
Everyone said at the time that it was impossible.	Todo el mundo dijo entonces que era imposible.
Now it appears to be easy enough.	Ahora parece ser bastante fácil.
When will the performance take place ?	¿ Cuándo se celebrará la fun-ción ?
You should try to speak Spanish oftener.	Vd. debía procurar hablar español más amenudo.

They could not agree among themselves.	No podían convenir entre sí.
How long has your brother been in Spain ?	¿ Cuánto tiempo hace que su hermano está en España ?
Where is he going to next ?	¿ Adónde va luego ?
He is going to Italy, but he will not stay there long.	Va á Italia, pero no se quedará allí mucho tiempo.
Read the letter to me again.	Vuelva Vd. á leerme la carta.
We were very sorry not to find them at home.	Sentimos mucho no hallarlos en casa.
It may be so, but I very much doubt it.	Puede ser que sí, pero lo dudo mucho.
It was raining very hard when we went out.	Llovía muy fuerte cuando salimos.
It thundered a great deal last night.	Anoche tronó mucho.
Did it lighten yesterday ?	¿ Relampagueó ayer ?
Perhaps it will snow to-morrow.	Quizás nevará mañana.
Did it hail much this morning ?	¿ Ha granizado mucho esta mañana ?
It is freezing hard.	Está helando muchísimo.
I think it will thaw to-morrow.	Creo que deshelará mañana.
We do not believe what she has just told us.	No creemos lo que acaba de decirnos.
I have not enough paper to finish my lesson.	No tengo bastante papel para acabar mi lección.
Unfortunately, you did not know it in time.	Por desgracia, Vd. no lo supo á tiempo.
It is not very long since it happened.	No hace mucho tiempo que sucedió.
How long did you stay in Paris ?	¿ Cuánto tiempo se quedó Vd. en París ?
This bridge is very old ; it is hardly safe.	Este puente es muy viejo ; apenas está seguro.
There will not be any difficulty in finding another one.	No habrá ninguna dificultad en hallar otro.
Tell me if I may keep it.	Dígame si puedo guardarlo.

Do not trouble yourself about that.	No se moleste Vd. por eso.
How soon shall we arrive at the house ?	¿ En cuánto tiempo llegaremos á la casa ?
I would not pay so much for that picture.	No quería pagar tanto por ese cuadro.
I called on you yesterday, but you were out.	Fuí á verle ayer, pero Vd. estaba fuera.
Drink out of this cup ; there is no other.	Beba de esta taza ; no hay otra.
Whose umbrella did you borrow ?	¿ A quién ha pedido Vd. prestado el paraguas ?
Is this dog yours, or your brother's ?	¿ Es este perro suyo, ó de su hermano ?
Did you go to town on foot ?	¿ Fué Vd. á pié á la ciudad ?
No, we went by rail.	No ; fuimos por el ferrocarril.
My train is nearly always late.	Mi tren está casi siempre retrasado.
I thought the weather would change.	Creí que cambiaría el tiempo.
How cold it is to-day !	¡ Qué frío hace hoy !
She has got a head-ache.	Ella tiene dolor de cabeza.
This child had the tooth-ache last week.	Este niño tenía dolor de muelas la semana pasada.
Do not fail to come by half past seven.	No deje Vd. de venir á eso de las siete y media.
I have sent for a porter.	He enviado por un mozo.
Go and fetch me a cab.	Vaya á buscarme un coche.
I shall leave here to-morrow morning.	Saldré de aquí mañana por la mañana.
It is very dusty.	Hay mucho polvo.
There was not much mud.	No había mucho barro.
Can you speak any foreign language ?	¿ Sabe Vd. hablar algún idioma extranjero ?
This word is not pronounced as it is spelt.	Esta palabra no se pronuncia como se deletrea.
How much does the account come to ?	¿ A cuánto llega la cuenta ?

I have not seen him for six months.

Hace seis meses que no le he visto.

He is going to call on his lawyer.

Va á ver á su abogado.

You do not visit us very frequently.

Vd. no nos visita muy frecuentemente.

There isn't room for so many people in this room.

No cabe tanta gente en este cuarto.

Why did you let him go away before having done all the work ?

¿ Por qué le ha dejado Vd. irse antes de haber hecho todo el trabajo ?

He was carrying the box on his head.

Llevaba la caja sobre la cabeza.

Where does this road lead to ?

¿ Adónde va (or conduce) este camino ?

You ought to take more care.

Vd. debiera tener más cuidado.

Is this all the wine there is left ?

¿ Es este todo el vino que queda ?

I hope you are not making a mistake.

Espero que Vd. no se equivoca.

[casas ?

When were these houses built?

¿ Cuándo se edificaron estas

Show the man your ticket as you go in.

Muestre Vd. al hombre su billete al entrar.

We lost our train, although it was ten minutes late.

Perdimos nuestro tren, aunque iba diez minutos retrasado.

The weather was very fine when the children went out.

Hacía muy buen tiempo cuando salieron los niños.

Afterwards it rained a great deal.

Después llovió mucho.

I should like to speak to you before I go away.

Quisiera hablarle á Vd. antes de irme.

I never feel well in cold weather.

Nunca me siento bien en tiempo frío.

Why do you not sit down ?

¿ Por qué no se sientan Vds. ?

We are in a great hurry.

Estamos muy deprisa.

It is impossible for me to leave business earlier.

Me es imposible salir de los negocios más temprano.

My father's business compels him to travel a great deal.

Las ocupaciones de mi padre le obligan á viajar muchísimo.

He was in London at the end of last month.

Estuvo en Londres á fines del mes pasado.

When you came back, it was very late.

Cuando Vd. volvió, era muy tarde.

How is this phrase translated into Spanish ?

¿ Cómo se traduce esta frase en español ?

I am afraid it will rain during the day.

Temo que llueva durante el día.

Have you at last been able to find his address ?

¿ Ha podido Vd. al fin hallar su dirección (or sus señas) ?

I thought you knew French and German.

Creí que Vd. sabía francés y alemán.

I can read books written in Spanish and Italian.

Puedo leer libros escritos en español é italiano.

He cannot speak either of the languages.

No sabe hablar ninguna de ambas lenguas.

We do not know whether they will take our advice.

No sabemos si tomarán nuestro consejo.

I cannot understand why it is not here.

No puedo comprender por qué no está aquí.

It is a pity you cannot stay any longer.

Es una lástima que Vd. no pueda quedarse más tiempo.

What is the reason of that ?

¿ Cuál es el motivo de eso ?

This rule has several exceptions.

Esta regla tiene varias excepciones.

In my opinion, this chain is the cheapest.

En mi opinión, esta cadena es la más barata.

They will pay me the balance next month.

Me pagarán el saldo el mes que viene.

The boys would not be quiet, although I told them to.

Los niños no querían callarse, aunque se lo mandé.

Tell them again, and we will see whether they obey you.

Vuelva Vd. á mandárselo, y veremos si le obedecen.

What is the price of a return ticket ?   [to travel ?

¿ Cuál es el precio del billete de ida y vuelta ?

By what class are you going

¿ En qué clase va Vd. á viajar ?

I generally travel third class.

Por lo general, viajo en tercera clase.

It is cheaper, and the carriages are very comfortable. — Es más barato, y los coches son muy cómodos.

We should like you to wait for us. — Quisiéramos que Vd. nos esperase.

Be careful, or else you will hurt yourself. — Tenga Vd. cuidado, ó se lastimará.

He seemed very much surprised at seeing you here. — Pareció sorprenderse mucho al verle aquí.

Let me carry it for you. — Déjeme que lo lleve por Vd.

If you move a little this way, there will be room for everybody. — Si Vd. se corre un poco hacia aquí, habrá lugar para todos.

The servant stole this money from his master. — El criado robó este dinero á su amo. [vino.

Those bottles are full of wine. — Esas botellas están llenas de

Put the glass here, near this one. — Ponga Vd. el vaso aquí, cerca de este.

Are there any friends of yours here this evening? — ¿ Hay aquí esta noche algunos amigos de Vd. ?

What do you think of the climate of this country? — ¿ Qué piensa Vd. del clima de este país ? [fuego.

Sit round the fire. — Siéntense Vds. al rededor del

Have you ever been in Spain? — ¿ Ha estado Vd. alguna vez en España ?

I should very much like to spend a few weeks there. — Me gustaría mucho pasar algunas semanas allí.

Tell the man to come in. — Diga Vd. al hombre que entre.

That is the house we used to live in. — Esa es la casa en que vivíamos.

What is it they are making? — ¿ Qué es lo que están haciendo ?

This is the smallest watch I have seen. — Este es el reloj más pequeño que he visto.

Show me the clock you bought a few days ago. — Muéstreme el reloj que compró Vd. hace algunos días.

It only cost me thirty shillings. — Solo me costó treinta chelines.

Do not tell them so on any account. — No se lo diga Vd. de ningún modo.

He knew nothing about it. — No sabía nada de ello.

She has gone to the shop her-self, on account of the mistake in the bill.

Ella misma ha ido á la tienda, á causa del error en la cuenta.

Come nearer the table; I should like to show you something.

Acérquense Vds. más á la mesa; quisiera mostrarles algo.

I usually work an hour a day at home.   [price.

Acostumbro á trabajar una hora en casa cada día.   [cio.

They have gone to enquire the

Han ido á informarse del pre-

This way.—That way.

Por aquí.—Por allí.

Which way?

¿ Por dónde?   [cansados.

You all seem very tired.

Vds. parecen estar todos muy

My companion is tired too.   [tea?

Mi compañero también está cansado.   [de té?

Will you take another cup of

¿ Quiere Vd. tomar otra taza

If you lose this piece of paper, we will give you another.

Si pierde Vd. este pedazo de papel, le daremos otro.

My brother has obtained a good situation.   [to?

Mi hermano ha logrado una buena colocación.

Where is the coachman going

¿ Adónde va el cochero?

Where do you come from?

¿ De dónde viene Vd.?

We saw him last Sunday morning.   [week.

Le vimos el Domingo pasado por la mañana.

She will come next Tuesday

Vendrá del martes en ocho días.

I do not suppose they will be back until next month.

No supongo que vuelvan hasta el mes que viene.

The concert will take place to-morrow evening.

El concierto se celebrará mañana por la noche.

Did you hear from your father yesterday morning?

¿Recibió Vd. noticias de su padre ayer por la mañana?

He will go home again early next week.

Volverá á casa á primeros de la semana que viene.

Where were your cousins last week?

¿ Dónde estaban sus primos de Vd. la semana pasada?

He never comes before the end of the month.

Nunca viene hasta fines del mes.

Who is there?   It is I.

¿ Quién está ahí?   Soy yo.

It is not he.   Is it they?

No es él.   ¿ Son ellos?

It is you. Is it not your uncle?

Es Vd.   ¿ No es su tío de Vd.?

Do not put on your gloves.

No se ponga Vd. los guantes.

Ask what the messenger wants.

Pregunte Vd. lo que quiere el mensajero.

Ask whether you may keep it.

Pregunte si lo puede Vd. guardar.

It is not time to leave off yet.

No es tiempo de cesar aún.

Tell the boy to make haste.

Diga Vd. al chico que se apresure.

He would not make haste.

No quería apresurarse.

It hardly ever snows here, even in the severest winters.

Apenas nieva aquí, aún en los inviernos más crudos.

Are you sleepy?

¿ Tiene Vd. sueño ?

I am very sleepy.

Tengo mucho sueño.

The sun is not shining.

No hace sol.

The moon was shining last night.

Hacía luna anoche.

It is not daylight. It is night.

No es de día. Es de noche.

The sun is setting Is the moon rising? [drawer.

El sol se pone. ¿ Sale la luna ?

Nothing is missing from this

Nada falta de este cajón.

How much a yard is this silk? [walk ?

¿ Cuánto vale una yarda de esta seda ? [paseo ?

Are you disposed to go for a

¿ Tiene Vd. ganas de dar un

They have gone to dress themselves.

Han ido á vestirse.

He will change his opinion when he hears that.

Al saber eso, cambiará de opinión.

I am very much obliged to you.

Le estoy muy agradecido.

On returning home, I found the letter. [certain.

Al volver á casa, encontré la carta.

He told me he knew it for

Me dijo que lo sabía de cierto.

Do not pay any attention to that.

No haga Vd. caso de eso.

It is necessary to pay attention to what the teacher says.

Es necesario prestar atención á lo que dice el maestro.

The children would not dare to go into the garden without permission.

Los niños no se atreverían á entrar en el jardín sin permiso.

I beg you will show it to us at once.	Le ruego que nos lo muestre al instante.
I cannot pronounce very well yet. [takes.	No puedo pronunciar muy bien todavía.
I am afraid of making mis-	Temo equivocarme.
He will probably reply by return of post.	Probablemente contestará á vuelta de correo.
He is in the habit of coming once a week.	Acostumbra á venir una vez por semana.
I used to be in the habit of meeting him every day.	Acostumbraba á encontrarle cada día.
Come upstairs.— Come down-stairs.	Suba Vd.—Baje Vd.
Please walk upstairs.	Sírvase Vd. subir. [del lado.
Mr. N— lives next door.	El Señor N— vive en la casa
Do not fail to be there at noon.	No falte Vd. allí al mediodía.
I seldom used to go to bed before midnight.	Rara vez me acostaba antes de media noche.
Ask this man where the en-trance is.	Pregunte Vd. á este hombre donde está la entrada.
We could not find the way out for some time.	No pudimos hallar la salida por algún tiempo.
To-morrow is a holiday.	Mañana es fiesta.
Did you enjoy yourself during your holidays ?	¿ Se divirtió Vd. durante sus vacaciones ?
You must not stay where you are. [umbrella ?	Vd. no debe quedarse donde está. [raguas ?
Don't you know your own	¿ No conoce Vd. su propio pa-
I am not quite sure whether it is mine, or not.	No estoy bien seguro si es mío, ó no.
Have you given anything to the waiter ?	¿ Ha dado Vd. algo al mozo ?
I suppose that the concert will soon be over.	Supongo que pronto acabará el concierto.
I suppose so too.	También lo supongo yo.
Whose turn is it to pay to-day?	¿ A quién le toca pagar hoy ?
It is yours.—Mine, I think.	Le toca á Vd.—A mí, me parece.

It is not your brother's turn.	No le toca á su hermano.
We are greatly obliged to you for this visit.	Le agradecemos á Vd. mucho esta visita.
Let me know as soon as you can. [trouble.	Hágamelo Vd. saber tan pronto como pueda.
It caused us a great deal of	Nos molestó mucho.
I assure you it is impossible.	Le aseguro á Vd. que es imposible.
I shall fall asleep directly I lie down.	Me dormiré en cuanto me acueste.
You had better go to bed soon.	Es mejor que se vaya Vd. á la cama pronto.
Tell the children not to go away yet. [the river.	Diga Vd. á los niños que no se vayan aún.
We walked along the bank of	Andábamos á lo largo del río.
Your coat is hanging behind the door.	Su levita está colgada detrás de la puerta.
Go on with your work.	Siga Vd. con su trabajo (or Continue Vd. su trabajo).
It is not a question of money, but of time.	No es cuestión de dinero, sino de tiempo.
There must be some better way of arranging it.	Debe haber algún otro modo mejor de arreglarlo.
There is no doubt about that.	No hay duda alguna sobre eso.
Repeat these words after the teacher. [vice.	Repita Vd. estas palabras después del maestro.
He would not follow my ad-	No quería seguir mi consejo.
Everybody was asking after you.	Todo el mundo preguntaba por Vd.
The child has fallen asleep, in spite of the noise.	El niño se ha dormido, á pesar del ruido.
Have you cut your finger ?	¿ Se ha cortado Vd. el dedo ?
He only writes to us once a month.	Solo nos escribe una vez al mes.
What did she say about that when she last wrote ?	¿Qué dijo ella sobre eso cuando escribió la última vez ?
Please pass me a clean plate.	Sírvase Vd. pasarme un plato limpio.

It is no use to say that.

No sirve de nada decir eso.

See whether you can borrow another copy of the book.

Vea Vd. si puede tomar prestado otro ejemplar del libro.

We have sent him to borrow a dictionary.

Le hemos mandado á pedir prestado un diccionario.

There is no need to make so much haste.

No hay razón para darse tanta prisa.

I was very much surprised that you did not come.

Extrañé mucho que Vd. no viniese.

They were looking attentively at each other.

Se miraban atentamente unos á otros.

After all, it does not matter.

Al fin y al cabo, no importa.

I cannot see the necessity for doing it again.

No puedo ver la necesidad de hacerlo de nuevo.

Will you change this cheque for me ?

¿ Quiere Vd. cambiarme este cheque ?

I will take half in gold, and the other half in silver.

Tomaré la mitad en oro, y la otra mitad en plata.

Thank you.—Don't mention it.

Gracias.—No hay de qué.

It is some time since he wrote to me.

Hace algún tiempo que me escribió.   [tiempo.

We saw them not long ago.

Los vimos no hace mucho

What is there to eat ?

¿ Qué hay para comer ?

There is nothing ready now.

No hay nada listo ahora.

We are in a great hurry.

Estamos muy de prisa.

We shall arrive about 2 o'clock.

Llegaremos á eso de la dos.

He is the same age as his cousin.   [house.

Tiene la misma edad que su primo.

I saw him as he passed by the

Lo ví cuando pasó por la casa.

However difficult it may seem, you must try to do it.

Por difícil que parezca, Vd. debe probar á hacerlo.

The more I give him, the more he wants.

Cuanto más le doy, más quiere.

The English, as well as the foreign letters, have been posted.

Tanto las cartas inglesas como las extranjeras se han echado al correo.

How much is the postage of a letter from here to Spain ?

¿ Cuánto vale el franqueo de una carta de aquí á España ?

With regard to the assertion he made, we must see whether it can be proved.

Respecto á la aserción que hizo, hemos de ver si puede probarse.

I tied the parcel tightly, so that the things should not come out.

Até el paquete fuertemente, para que las cosas no se saliesen.

Notwithstanding this, the string broke. [gave him.

A pesar de esto, el bramante se rompió. [dábamos.

He always spent what we

Siempre gastaba lo que le

You shall be served in five minutes. [ing so fast.

Serán Vds. servidos dentro de cinco minutos. [deprisa.

There is no pleasure in walk-

No hay placer en andar tan

The table is almost in the middle of the room.

La mesa está casi en el centro del cuarto. [mio.

The boy deserves a prize.

El muchacho merece un pre-

There are many reasons which would take a long time to explain.

Hay muchas razones que serían muy largas de explicar.

They explained everything to me, so that I might know what I had to say.

Me lo explicaron todo, á fin de que pudiese saber lo que tenía que decir.

Perhaps they will start during the week. • [accident.

Tal vez partirán durante la semana.

According to him, it was an

Según él, fué una desgracia.

Can I do anything else for you?

¿ Puedo hacer algo más por Vd. ?

He did it for [instead of] you.

Lo hizo por Vd.

My business will prevent me from coming very often.

Mis negocios me impedirán venir muy amenudo.

The result is not generally known yet. [soon.

El resultado no se conoce bien todavía.

I hope you will come again

Espero que volverá Vd. pronto.

The numbers in this street from twenty upwards are on the opposite side.

Los números de esta calle del veinte para arriba están en el otro lado.

We expect her every moment.

La esperamos de un momento á otro.

They must be somewhere.

Deben estar en alguna parte.

There is a great deal of difference between the meanings of the words.

Hay mucha diferencia entre los significados de las palabras.

They are very polite to everybody.   [he went out.

Son muy corteses con todo el mundo.   [salió.

It is not five minutes since

No hace cinco minutos que

These cups and saucers are partly clean, and partly dirty.

Estas tazas y platillos están medio limpios y medio sucios.   [mala.

It is a very bad habit of mine.

Es una costumbre mía muy

You ought to learn this list of words by heart.

Debería Vd. aprender de memoria esta lista de palabras.

I generally see him on Saturdays.   [Sundays.

Generalmente le veo los Sábados.   [Domingos.

He only wears this coat on

Solo lleva esta chaqueta los

Can you count from one to a hundred without looking at the book?

¿ Puede Vd. contar de uno á ciento sin mirar el libro ?

Put it somewhere else.

Póngalo Vd. en otra parte.

The mistake is really very serious.

El error es en verdad muy serio.   [tiempo.

He was here not long ago.

Estuvo aquí no hace mucho

It often happens that no one comes the whole day.

Sucede amenudo que nadie viene en todo el día.

Did you stay long in South America?

¿ Estuvo Vd. mucho tiempo en la América del Sur ?

I was there for three years.

Estuve allí durante tres años.

It is good practice to read aloud every day.

Es buena práctica leer en alta voz todos los días.

I do not understand Spanish well enough to do it.

No comprendo el español bastante bien para hacerlo.

Try to express your thoughts in the simplest way.   [phrases.

Trate Vd. de expresar sus pensamientos de la manera más sencilla. [complicadas.

Avoid long and complicated

Evite Vd. las frases largas y

Choose sentences which can be translated into Spanish word for word.

Escoja Vd. sentencias que puedan traducirse al español palabra por palabra.

SPANISH COMMERCIAL CORRESPONDENCE.

The **Date** at the head of letters is written thus :

Londres, 12 (de) Abril de 1912.   Madrid, 1º (de) Agosto de 1911, etc.

(See ' SPANISH SIMPLIFIED," paragraph 90.)

The date is followed by the name of the person or firm to whom the letter is addressed.

In the full address on the envelope, the number of the house is put **after** the name of the street, thus :—*Calle de Quevedo, (núm.) 15.*

The following are the ordinary methods of **commencing letters :—**

SIR, DEAR SIR	*Muy señor mio*
GENTLEMEN, DEAR SIRS	*Muy señores mios*
MADAM, DEAR MADAM	*Muy señora mia*

[The three foregoing are the ordinary business forms of address.]

Sir (writing to a person of title or distinction)	*Excelentisimo señor* (abbreviated to *Exmo. Sr.*)
Sir (to a superior holding a high official position)	*Ilustrisimo señor*(abbrevd. to *Illmo. Señor*) ; or *Muy ilustre señor*
Madam, Dear Madam (to a friend)	*Apreciable señor(it)a*
Dear Henry, Peter, etc.	*Querido Enrique, Pedro,* etc.
My Dear Sister	*Querida hermana mia*
My Dear Friends	*Queridos amigos mios*

There are various forms for **concluding letters,** all of them effusively polite, and so long and cumbrous that the initial letter only of many of the words is employed. The following ending, which is equivalent to " YOURS TRULY " or " YOURS FAITHFULLY," is the best to employ in ordinary business correspondence.

Soy de Vd. atto S. S.

Q. B. S. M.

(This is an abbreviation of *Soy de Vd. atento seguro servidor, que besa sus manos* : literally, " I am your attentive faithful servant, who kisses your hands." *Soy* and *atto.* must be changed to **somos** and **attos.,** and *Vd.* to **Vds.,** when necessary.

If **affmo.** (abbreviation of *afectisimo,* most loving) is substituted for *atento,* or *y afectisimo* inserted after *atento,* in the preceding phrase, it becomes somewhat less formal, and corresponds to " YOURS SINCERELY."

The equivalent to " YOURS RESPECTFULLY " is :

Su respetuoso servidor (written in full) *Q. B. S. M.*

In writing to a superior, when in English " YOUR OBEDIENT SERVANT " would commonly be employed, the usual ending (written in full) is *Dios guarde á Vd. muchos años* : literally, God preserve your worship many years. In writing to a friend, the usual ending is *S. S. y amigo* (your servant—*su servidor*—and friend). For an ordinary letter, not strictly a formal business one, to a person with whom the writer has a slight acquaintance only, *su atento servidor* is sufficient.

COMMERCIAL PHRASES.

I am in receipt of your letter of the 14th inst. ;—of the 1st ult.

Obra en mi poder su carta del 14 del corriente ;—del 1° del próximo pasado (p.p^{do}).

Referring to your favor of the 9th ult. ...

Respecto á su apreciable (apble.) del 9 del mes pasado.

In reply, I have the pleasure to inform you ...

En contestación tengo el gusto de manifestarle ...

Some of the things were rather damaged.

Algunos de los artículos estaban algo deteriorados.

Nearly all the goods suffered serious damage in transit. [return of post.

Casi todos los géneros sufrieron gran avería en su transporte. [de correo.

Send it to me without fail by

Envíemelo Vd. sin falta á vuelta

I hope to receive it by the 7th of next month, at the latest.

Espero recibirlo para el 7 del mes que viene, á más tardar.

I am greatly in want of the first three items on the list.

Me hacen mucha falta los tres primeros artículos de la lista.

The delay in sending off the goods causes me considerable inconvenience.

El retraso en el despacho de las mercancías me perjudica mucho.

In your last letter, you promised to allow us a discount of 5 per cent.

En su última, prometió Vd. concedernos un descuento de 5 por ciento.

You have only taken off 2½ per cent.

Solo nos ha descontado Vd. un dos y medio por ciento.

Our prices are in all cases strictly nett.

Nuestros precios se entienden siempre estrictamente netos.

Your consignment arrived safely yesterday.

Su consignación llegó ayer sin novedad.

I will send you a cheque as soon as I receive the goods.

Le remitiré á Vd. un cheque en cuanto reciba los géneros.

We shall be obliged by your remitting the balance.

Le agradeceremos nos remita el importe del saldo.

Kindly send us your price list, conditions, etc.

Sírvase Vd. mandarnos su lista de precios, condiciones, etc.

Please let me know your lowest terms for cash on delivery;—on receipt of the goods.

Sírvase Vd. indicarme sus condiciones más favorables para pago al contado;—al recibo de los géneros.

How much will the packing, carriage, and customs duty amount to?

¿A cuánto subirán los gastos de embalaje, transporte, y derechos de aduana?

Do your best to see that the cost of carriage is as low as possible.

Haga Vd. lo posible para que los gastos de transporte sean lo más reducido posible.

By book post—by parcel post—in a registered letter.

Como impresos—en paquete postal—en carta certificada.

You may draw on us at three months.

Puede Vd. girar á nuestro cargo á tres meses.

The bill is payable at sight.

La letra es pagadera á la vista.

Kindly send us a cheque at your earliest convenience for the amount due.

Tengan Vds. la bondad de remitirnos lo antes posible un cheque por la cantidad vencida.   [meses.

                    [overdue.
This account is six months

Esta cuenta venció hace seis

We cannot wait any longer; be good enough therefore to forward the amount without further delay.

No podemos esperar más; por lo tanto le suplicamos que nos remita el importe cuanto antes.

We shall be greatly obliged by your sending us a remittance by an early post.

Le agradeceremos infinito nos remita el importe por uno de los primeros correos.

I have several large accounts to meet next week.

Tengo que satisfacer algunas cuentas de consideración la semana próxima.   [acogida.

                    [dishonored.
The bill has been returned

La letra ha sido devuelta mal

I have already applied to you several times for a settlement.

Ya me he dirigido á Vd. en diferentes ocasiones para la liquidación.

I shall have to take legal proceedings to recover the amount due.

Tendré que recurrir á la ley para la satisfacción de la deuda.

We think it right to inform you at once.

Creemos conveniente comunicárselo á Vd. al momento.

Herewith we send you samples of both qualities.

Con la presente le enviamos muestras de ambas calidades.

Your esteemed order is duly to hand.

Su estimado pedido ha llegado debidamente á nuestro poder.

Your instructions shall receive our best attention.

Sus instrucciones serán objeto de nuestra mayor atención.

No invoice was enclosed with the goods.

No acompañaba á los géneros factura alguna.

The boxes were nearly all broken, and their contents much damaged by water.

Casi todas las cajas estaban rotas, y sus contenidos muy averiados por el agua.

The goods were very carelessly packed.

Las mercancías se embalaron con muy poco cuidado.

We charge two per cent. to cover the cost of packing.

Cargamos dos por ciento para cubrir los gastos de embalaje.

There is always great delay in the execution of these orders. [prompt reply...

Siempre hay gran retraso en la ejecución de estos pedidos. [pronta contestación.

Awaiting the favor of a

Esperando verme honrado con

Relying on your promise, I undertook to deliver the goods by Monday next. [should pay the duty.

Confiando en su promesa, me comprometí á entregar los géneros para el lunes próximo. [los derechos.

It was arranged that you

Se convino que Vd. pagaría

You promised to send off the first part of the order a week ago.

Hace una semana, prometió Vd. despachar la primera parte del pedido.

Let me know at once when I may depend on receiving the remainder of the order.

Indíqueme Vd. al momento cuando puedo contar con el resto del pedido.

Mr. ...., of Cadiz, has kindly favored me with your address.

El Sr. ..., de Cádiz, ha tenido la bondad de favorecerme con sus señas de Vd.

For references you can apply to the firm of ...

Para informes pueden Vds. dirigirse á la casa de ...

If you take a gross at a time we will allow you an extra $2\frac{1}{2}$ per cent. discount.

Si toma Vd. una gruesa de una vez, le concederemos un descuento extra de $2\frac{1}{2}$ por ciento.

The terms quoted do not include carriage.

En las condiciones indicadas no se incluye el transporte.

Our agent informs us that the firm has been established many years.

Nuestro agente nos informa que la casa cuenta ya muchos años de existencia.

It is reported that the bank has suspended payment.

Se dice que el banco ha suspendido pagos.

If the tea finds a ready sale, I shall give you larger orders afterwards.

Si el té halla buena salida, en lo futuro les haré pedidos de mayor consideración.

There is no demand for such articles in this market.

No hay salida para tales artículos en este mercado.

We have recently opened a branch in Barcelona.

Acabamos de abrir una sucursal en Barcelona.　　[ensayo.

This is only a trial order.

Este pedido no es más que un

I have been appointed sole agent for the sale of this machine in Spain.

He sido nombrado agente exclusivo para la venta de esta máquina en España.

You had better carry it forward to the new account.

Sería más conveniente que lo pasara Vd. á cuenta nueva.

We are quite willing to open a monthly or quarterly account, if you prefer it.
　　　　　　　[last invoice.

Estamos dispuestos á abrir una cuenta mensual ó trimestral, si así lo prefiere Vd.　　　　[factura.

There was a mistake in the

Hubo un error en la última

The bill of lading has not yet come to hand.

El conocimiento no se ha recibido todavía.

The cheque was payable to bearer, not to order.

El cheque era pagadero al portador, no á la orden.

I cannot make any reduction in the quoted prices, except the usual discount for cash at a month.

No puedo conceder ninguna reducción en los precios cotizados, excepto el descuento corriente por pago mensual.

I unfortunately have none of the common sorts in stock at the present time.

Por desgracia, hoy no tengo en depósito ninguna de las calidades comunes.

We only supply the trade, and do no retail business.

Solo surtimos al comercio, y no efectuamos ninguna transacción al por menor.

We have debited you with the balance.	Le hemos adeudado en cuenta el saldo.
Kindly credit me with the value of the returned goods.	Sírvase Vd. abonarme en cta. el valor de los géneros devueltos.
We send you a draft payable one month after date, in settlement of last month's account.	Le remitimos una letra pagadera á treinta días fecha, para liquidar la cuenta del mes pasado.
Please endorse it, and honor it on maturity.	Sírvase Vd. endosarla, y acogerla á su vencimiento.
Ship the bales by the next steamer.	Embarque Vd. las balas por el próximo vapor.
Do not send the boxes by rail, but by steamer ; the latter means of transit comes cheaper.	No mande Vd. las cajas por ferro-carril, sino por vapor ; este medio de transporte resulta más barato.
In accordance with your request, I enclose a duplicate invoice.	De conformidad con su deseo, adjunto una factura duplicada.
I trust you will excuse the delay.	Espero se servirá Vd. dispensar el retraso.
Do you deliver free on board in London ?	¿ Hace Vd. la entrega franco á bordo en Londres ?
We are thinking of chartering an entire steamer, and must calculate how much cheaper the expenses of freight would be than if we shipped in small consignments.	Estamos pensando en fletar un vapor completo y hemos de calcular cuanto más económico nos resultaría el precio del flete que cuando embarcamos por pequeñas partidas.
The shares of this company are not to be recommended just now.	Las acciones de esta compañía no son muy recomendables ahora.
It would be wise to wait until the publication of the yearly balance sheet.	Sería prudente aguardar hasta que publiquen el balance anual.
Our commission is 5 per cent., if you put the necessary sums at our disposal.	Nuestra comisión es de 5 % si Vds. ponená nuestra disposición las sumas necesarias.

KEY

TO THE

"STANDARD" EDITION

OF

SPANISH

GRAMMAR

SIMPLIFIED.

PUBLISHED BY

Hugo's Institute for Teaching Foreign Languages,

33 GRACECHURCH STREET, LONDON, E.C. ; and Branches.

To

HUGO'S LANGUAGE SCHOOLS,
33 GRACECHURCH STREET,
LONDON, E.C.

Please send to the undermentioned address a
copy of Hugo's " Spanish Verbs Simplified," for
which a crossed postal order* for 1/- is enclosed.

Name in full :

M..

Address..

....

....

* Stamps cannot be accepted in payment.

SPECIAL NOTICE.

To simplify the Irregular Verbs, we have omitted from the Grammar the Tenses which need not be learnt if our rules (pars. 52 and 117) on the formation of Tenses have been mastered. These rules, which are original and copyright, enable the Student to form any other Tense correctly.

For purposes of Reference only, not for study,

EVERY TENSE OF EVERY IRREGULAR VERB

is given in Hugo's " Spanish Verbs Simplified," (96 pages, bound in limp cloth, price 1s. 6d.).

Purchasers of Hugo's Spanish Grammar and Key can obtain a copy of "Spanish Verbs Simplified" at two-thirds of the published price, by filling up, and sending direct to 33 Gracechurch Street, the form on the previous page, with remittance for 1s.

Key to Lesson I.

EXERCISE I.—1. they (MASC.) have ; 2. have I ? 3. have I not ? 4. she has not ; 5. have we (MASC.) ? 6. you (SING.) have not ; 7. have they (FEM.) not ? 8. have you (PLUR.) ? 9. we (MASC.) have not.

10. ella tiene ; 11. ¿ no tienen ellos ? 12. ¿ tiene Vd. ? 13. yo no tengo ; 14. Vds. no tienen ; 15. ¿ no tengo yo ? 16. nosotros tenemos ; 17. ¿ no tienen Vds. ? 18. ella no tiene.

EXERCISE II.—1. padres ; 2. libros ; 3. nueces ; 4. señores ; 5. lápices ; 6. plumas ; 7. ciudades ; 8. hombres ; 9. luces ; 10. tías ; 11. iglesias ; 12. leyes ; 13. sombreros.

EXERCISE III.—1. un hermano ; 2. una hermana ; 3. unos hermanos ; 4. unas hermanas ; 5. el hermano ; 6. los hermanos ; 7. la hermana ; 8. las hermanas ; 9. las casas ; 10. el agua ; 11. un ala ; 12. lo hermoso ; 13. un padre ; 14. los libros ; 15. una pluma ; 16. el lápiz ; 17. la tinta ; 18. unos lápices ; 19. una aldea.

EXERCISE IV.—1. I have not a book. 2. Has he the pens ? 3. We have a house. 4. You (PLUR.) have some pens ; we have some books.

5. Vd. tiene un hermano. 6. El pájaro tiene dos alas. 7. Vds. no tienen los libros. 8. ¿ No tiene él la tinta ? 9. La madre tiene dos casas. 10. Yo no tengo una pluma, pero mi amigo tiene unas plumas. 11. ¿ Tiene él la carta ?

Key to Lesson II.

EXERCISE I.—1. del hombre ; 2. á un hombre ; 3. de la iglesia ; 4. del agua del pantano ; 5. á un libro ; 6. de las madres ; 7. á las piedras ; 8. de unas cartas ; 9. de las alas de un pájaro ; 10. á unos libros ; 11. de unos pájaros ; 12. á una casa ; 13. al libro ; 14. de la tinta ; 15. de los hermanos ; 16. de las alas de los pájaros ; 17. el libro del muchacho ; 18. el caballo de un soldado ; 19. los caballos del soldado.

COLLECTIVE EXERCISE.—1. (Nosotros) hemos escrito unas cartas. 2. Vd. no ha visto las casas. 3 ¿ No tenemos (nosotros) los sombreros ? 4. ¿ Tiene la iglesia un altar ? 5. (Yo) he visto el altar de la iglesia. 6. Los reyes tienen los caballos. 7. ¿ Quién ha tomado la tinta ? 8. El hombre tiene un hacha. 9. El buque tiene un ancla. 10. ¿ Ha dado el criado una silla al caballero ? 11. Yo* no tengo un sobre, pero mi hermano tiene unos sobres. 12. ¿ Qué han hecho Vds. ? 13. ¿ Ha visto Vd. los jardines del rey ? 14. Los hombres tienen unos caballos. 15. ¿ Por qué no ha escrito Vd. las cartas ? 16. Un hombre ha hablado con el criado. 17. ¿ No tenemos (nosotros) un libro para la mujer ? 18. Sí, tenemos un libro y dos plumas. 19. (Nosotros) no hemos visto la casa del hombre. 20. Las muchachas no han tomado las plumas. 21. Vd. tiene unas cartas. 22. Vd. no tiene los libros. 23. El hermano de la muchacha no ha escrito una carta al caballero.

* This yo, being emphasized, cannot be omitted.

Key to Lesson III.

EXERCISE I.—1. mi jardín ; 2. su tinta ; 3. su tinta ; 4. su tinta ; 5. nuestro vaso ; 6. nuestra aldea ; 7. mi tía ; 8. mis tías ; 9. su gato ; 10. sus gatos ; 11. nuestros guantes ; 12. sus zapatos ; 13. sus hermanas ; 14. sus hermanas ; 15. su dinero ; 16. mi criado ; 17. nuestras manos ; 18. sus ojos ; 19. su deseo ; 20. su deseo ; 21. sus nombres ; 22. su pluma (de Vd.†) ; 23. su libro (de Vd.) ; 24. su casa (de Vds.) ; 25. sus manos (de Vd.) ; 26. sus manos (de Vds.) ; 27. No ha roto su pipa. 28. ¿ Han tomado los niños los guantes de Vd. ? 29. ¿ Ha tomado Vd. su dinero ?

EXERCISE II.—1. we are ; 2. they are not ; 3. am I ? 4. she is not ; 5. are we not ? 6. I am not ; 7. are you ? 8. you (PLUR.) are not.

9. ¿ es ella ? 10. él no es ; 11. ¿ no son ellas ? 12. Vds. son ; 13. ¿ no es Vd. ? 14. ¿ somos nosotros ? 15. ¿ no soy yo ? 16. (yo) soy ; 17. ella no es ; 18. (yo) no soy.

† In a complete sentence, the de Vd., de Vds., is seldom required.

EXERCISE III.—1. I am not ; 2. is he ? 3. are we not ? 4. you are not ; 5. are they ? 6. are you ? 7. you (PLUR.) are. 8. estamos ; 9. ¿ no está Vd. ? 10. ellas no están ; 11. ¿ estoy yo ? 12. Vds. están ; 13. ¿ no está él ? 14. ella no está ; 15. ¿ estamos nosotros ? 16. Vd. no está ; 17. no estoy ; 18. ¿ está Vd. ?

EXERCISE IV.—1. No somos obreros. 2. ¿ Está Vd. listo ? 3. (Ellas) están aquí. 4. ¿ Es Vd. soldado ? 5. No estoy escuchando. 6. ¿ Quién está en la calle ? 7. Es muy laborioso. 8. Soy inglesa. 9. No soy italiano. 10. Estamos hablando con su primo. 11.¿No son (ellos) príncipes ? 12. Somos marineros. 13. (El) no está escribiendo. 14. Es cartero. 15. No estamos fumando. 16. ¿ Es Vd. español ? 17. Son mis tíos. 18. Mi tía no está aquí. 19. (Ella) no está en casa. 20. Estamos aguardando. 21. Es profesor.

COLLECTIVE EXERCISE.—1. Nuestros amigos están en el jardín, buscando sus perros. 2. ¿ Es Vd. el tío de mi amigo ? 3. No, señor, no soy su tío, soy su padre. 4. Mi amigo está en la calle, fumando un cigarro. 5. ¿ Quién está allí ? 6. ¿ Qué están Vds. buscando ? 7. Estoy escribiendo una carta á su padre (de Vd.). 8. Sus hijos (de Vd.) están creciendo mucho. 9. El hermano de mi amigo no es laborioso. 10. ¿ Tiene Vd. un criado ? 11. Nuestra hermana es hábil. 12. Su madre (de Vd.) está en el jardín. 13. Mis zapatos están en el suelo, cerca de la silla. 14. Vds. no son soldados. 15. Mi libro está en el cajón. 16. ¿ Está fumando su hermano de Vd. ? 17. ¿ A quién ha escrito Vd. una carta ? 18. No estamos estudiando nuestras lecciones.

Key to Lesson IV.

EXERCISE I.—1. bueno (MASC. SING.), buena (FEM. SING.), buenos (MASC. PLUR.), buenas (FEM. PLUR.) ; 2. caro (M. S.), cara (F. S.), caros (M. P.), caras (F. P.) ; 3. capaz, capaz, capaces, capaces ; 4. aplicado, aplicada, aplicados, aplicadas ; or laborioso, laboriosa, laboriosos, laboriosas ;

5. francés, francesa, franceses, francesas ; 6. fácil, fácil, fáciles. fáciles ; 7. barato, barata, baratos, baratas ; 8. seco, seca, secos, secas ; 9. valiente, valiente, valientes, valientes ; 10. frío, fría, fríos, frías ; 11. cálido, cálida, cálidos, cálidas ; 12. alemán, alemana, alemanes, alemanas ; 13. difícil, difícil, difíciles, difíciles ; 14. inglés, inglesa, ingleses, inglesas ; 15. pesado, pesada, pesados, pesadas ; 16. persa, persa, persas, persas ; 17. un buen caballo ; 18. buenos caballos ; 19. una mala pluma ; 20. malas plumas ; 21. una lección difícil ; 22. lecciones difíciles.

COLLECTIVE EXERCISE.—1. Sus amigos no son valientes. 2. La modista francesa ha vendido un sombrero barato. 3. Nuestras lecciones son muy fáciles. 4. ¿ Tiene Vd. un buen criado ? 5. No, señor, mis criados no son buenos. 6. He visto á un soldado valiente. 7. Tengo carne fría. 8. Somos marineros ingleses. 9. ¿ Por qué no están Vds. estudiando sus lecciones ? 10. Las muchachas alemanas son felices. 11. ¿ A quién ha dado Vd. sus libros ? 12. He dado mis libros españoles al primo de mi amigo. 13. Nuestra lección es muy difícil. 14. ¿ Cómo está Vd. ? 15. Muy bien, gracias ; pero he estado enfermo. 16. Su (or la) hermana de Vd. no está enferma. 17. Sus tías (de Vds.) son muy hábiles. 18. Sus hermanos están enfermos. 19. Su amiga (de Vd.) es italiana. 20. No es italiana, es española. 21. ¿ Qué ha hecho Vd. con mi libro ? 22. Está sobre la mesa.

Key to Lesson V.

EXERCISE I.—1. compro ; 2. Vd. compra ; 3. (él) compra ; 4. compramos ; 5. Vds. compran ; 6. (ellos) compran ; 7. (él) toma ; 8. hallamos ; 9. hallo ; 10. (ellas) toman ; 11. Vd. halla ; 12. Vds. toman ; 13. fuma ; 14. fuman ; 15. Vd. lleva ; 16. llevo ; 17. enviamos ; 18. Vds. envian.

EXERCISE II.—1. bebo ; 2. Vd. bebe ; 3. (él) bebe ; 4. bebemos ; 5. Vds. beben ; 6. (ellos) beben ; 7. cree ;

8. creemos ; 9. comen ; 10. como ; 11. Vd. aprende ; 12. Vds. creen ; 13. aprende ; 14. poseo ; 15. poseen.

EXERCISE III.—1. recibo ; 2. Vd. recibe ; 3. (él) recibe ; 4. recibimos ; 5. Vds. reciben ; 6. (ellos) reciben ; 7. escribe ; 8. escribimos ; 9. Vd. surte ; 10. surto ; 11. divide ; 12. dividimos ; 13. Vds. escriben ; 14. surtimos.

EXERCISE IV.—1. Vd. halla, Vd. no halla ; 2. ¿ halla Vd. ? ¿ no halla Vd. ? 3. los hombres beben, los hombres no beben ; 4. ¿ beben los hombres ? ¿ no beben los hombres ? 5. descubrimos, no descubrimos ; 6. ¿ descubrimos (nosotros)? ¿ no descubrimos (nosotros) ? 7. recibo, no recibo ; 8. ¿ recibo (yo) ? ¿ no recibo (yo) ? 9. la muchacha debe, la muchacha no debe ; 10. ¿ debe la muchacha ? ¿ no debe la muchacha ?

COLLECTIVE EXERCISE.—1. ¿ Debe Vd. dinero á mi amigo ? 2. No debo dinero á su amigo. 3. El criado español llama á su perro. 4. No fumamos cigarros. 5. El discípulo aplicado aprende fácilmente sus lecciones. 6. ¿ Qué desea su madre (de Vd.) ? 7. ¿ No trabajan (ellas) bien ? 8. ¿Quién vive en la casa de su tía ? 9. Mis primos viven allí, pero mi tío está en Madrid. 10. El oficial bebe un vino delicioso. 11. Recibimos cartas de los tíos de Vd. (or sus tíos) cada día (better, 'todos los días '='all the days.') 12. No deseo un bastón, porque tengo un paraguas. 13. Creemos que sus muestras están en la tienda. 14. ¿ Cuánto dinero debemos ? 15. Creo que debemos cuatro chelines al tendero, y tres (chelines) al criado. 16. Tal vez no fuma. 17. ¿ Quién presta dinero á mi amigo ? 18. Yo presto amenudo dinero á su amigo. 19. ¿ A qué hora sale el tren para Londres ? 20. Mi tren no sale todavía. 21. No temo el castigo ; no es muy grande. 22. Los muchachos no tiran piedras. 23. Vd. no bebe cerveza. 24. ¿ No comprende Vd. la lección ? 25. Comprendo las lecciones muy bien. 26. ¿ Comprenden (ellos) su explicación ? 27. ¿ Dónde viven sus primos (de Vd.) ? 28. Mi prima vive en Madrid, y yo (vivo) en Londres.

8

Key to Lesson VI.

EXERCISE I.—1. ese *or* aquel muchacho ; 2. estas mujeres ; 3. esos *or* aquellos sobres ; 4. esta mesa ; 5. esa *or* aquella iglesia ; 6. esas *or* aquellas calles ; 7. estos caballos ; 8. esta tinta ; 9. este gato ; 10. esos *or* aquellos cuadros ; 11. ese *or* aquel pan ; 12. esta ciudad ; 13. estos números ; 14. esa señora ; 15. no estamos seguros de eso ; 16. no creo esto.

EXERCISE II.—1. fumando, fumado ; 2. debiendo, debido ; 3. viviendo, vivido ; 4. preguntando, preguntado ; 5. leyendo, leído ; 6. ¿ no ha tenido Vd. ? 7. no estoy teniendo ; 8. siendo soldados ; 9. estando en el cuarto (*or* la habitación) ; 10. no habiendo escrito la carta ; 11. ¿ Ha estado Vd. en España ? 12. No hemos sido marineros. 13. (Ella) no está leyendo. 14. ¿ Qué está (él) bebiendo ? 15. ¿ Dónde ha estado el hombre ? 16. ¿ No son valientes los soldados ingleses ? 17. ¿ No está hablando esta señora (*or* no está esta señora hablando*) ? 18. Mi tío no ha llegado.

COLLECTIVE EXERCISE.—1. ¿ No ha leído Vd. esa carta ? 2. ¿ Por qué no está ese muchacho estudiando sus lecciones ?* 3. Esos criados han bebido una botella de buen vino, y cinco (botellas) de cerveza alemana. 4. ¿ Están fumando cigarros ? 5. Habiendo leído el libro, lo enviaré á mi hermano. 6. ¿ Cuándo sale el buque ? 7. ¿ Cuánto dinero ha enviado el comerciante á su banquero ? 8. ¿ No han aprendido los discípulos estas lecciones ? 9. Estos sobres blancos son de mi tío. 10. Esas señoras son mis sobrinas. 11. El profesor español está hablando ahora. 12. Estoy leyendo un periódico francés. 13. Hemos estado en el campo. 14. Estas botellas no están llenas. 15. He sido carpintero. 16. ¿ Ha tenido Vd. tiempo para leer esta carta ? 17. ¿ Ha olvidado Vd. esto ? 18.

* As pointed out in par. 32 of the Grammar, the construction in such sentences is usually optional, and is merely a question of taste and euphony. To avoid needless repetition, only one way is given in this Key ; but such constructions as ¿ Por qué no está estudiando sus lecciones ese muchacho ? are quite permissible.

¿ Están esas señoras buscando un coche ? 19. ¿ Cree Vd.
eso ? 20. No comprendo esto. 21. No estando satisfecho
con el libro, lo venderé. 22. No es feo aquel perro ?

Key to Lesson VII.

EXERCISE I.—1. ¿ cuál caballero ? 2. ¿ cuáles caballeros ? 3. ¿ cuál silla ? 4. ¿ cuáles calles ? 5. ¿ qué
nombre ? 6. ¿ cuál zapato ? 7. ¿ qué hombres ? 8. ¡ qué
ruido ! 9. ¿ cuál tren ? 10. ¡ qué niebla ! 11. ¡ qué lástima !
12. ¿ cuál mujer ? 13. ¿ cuáles días ? 14. ¿ cuáles lámparas ?
15. ¿cuál taza ? 16. ¡ qué sombreros ! 17. ¿ De quién es este
cuchillo ? 18. ¿ De quién es esta tinta ? 19. ¿ De quién son
amigas estas señoras ? 20. ¿ De quién es esto ? 21. ¡ Qué
muchachos tan holgazanes ! 22. ¡ Qué error tan grande ! 23.
¿ Cuál es el precio de esto ? 24. ¿ Cuál es el número ?

EXERCISE II.—1. ha comprado ; 2. ¿ han comprado
(ellos) ? 3. no he comprado ; 4. ¿ no ha comprado Vd. ? 5.
¿ han hablado (ellas) ? 6. la muchacha ha hablado ; 7. ¿ ha
escrito el médico ? 8. el comerciante no ha vendido ; 9. ¿ no
han llegado los buques ? 10. no he comido ; 11. ¿ no ha
enviado el tendero ? 12. Vd. ha escrito ; 13. Vds. han visto ;
14. ¿ no han hallado (ellos) ?

EXERCISE III.—1. Hemos visto á un general muy
célebre. 2. ¿ Han hallado Vds. á sus amigos ? 3. ¿ Tiene él
hermanos ? 4. He visto á aquel señor en Madrid. 5. ¿ Espera
Vd. á sus sobrinas hoy ? 6. No esperamos cartas. 7. Estamos
buscando nuestras llaves. 8. ¿ Está Vd. buscando á su
sobrino ? 9. No he visto hoy al rey.

COLLECTIVE EXERCISE.—1. ¿ Ha hallado Vd. á mi
hermano en el jardín ? 2. ¿ Cuál libro ha tenido Vd. ? 3.
¿ De quién es ese caballo ? 4. ¿ Qué hombre no ama á su
madre ? 5. ¿ De quién es este paraguas ? 6. ¿ Han visto
Vds. á los viajeros ingleses ? 7. ¡ Qué reloj tan barato ha
comprado Vd. esta mañana ? 8. El dependiente ha recibido

ese dinero. 9. ¿ Quién está fumando en este cuarto ? 10. No ha enviado los géneros á tiempo. 11. ¡ Qué lecciones tan fáciles tiene Vd. ! 12. ¿ Para quién son estas cartas ? 13. ¿ A quién ha prestado Vd. su cuchillo ? 14. ¿ Quiénes son estos hombres ? 15. Qué gente hay en la casa ? 16. ¿ No ha llamado Vd. á la criada ? 17. ¿ Cuáles tazas ha roto (ella) ? 18. ¿ En cuál cuarto ha hallado Vd. la tinta roja ? 19. ¡ Qué pluma tan mala es esta ! 20. ¿ Cuáles desea Vd. ? 21. Cuál es el camino á la estación ? 22. ¿ Cuál es la causa de su silencio ? 23. ¿ Cuáles son sus planes ? 24. ¿ Qué es eso ?

Key to Lesson VIII.

EXERCISE I.—1. Este bastón no es mío. 2. ¿ Es esa casa de* él* ? 3. Estas cartas son nuestras. 4. Sus discípulos (de Vd.) son aplicados, y los míos son holgazanes. 5. Estos lápices son de* ella*. 6. Nuestra amiga está aquí, pero la de* ella* no ha llegado todavía. 7. Esa llave es mía. 8. Nuestras lecciones son difíciles, pero las de* ellos* son muy fáciles.

EXERCISE II.—1. mis mesas de roble y (las de) caoba ; 2. querida madre mía (*simpler*, mi querida madre) ; 3. una tía suya (*clearer*, una tía de él) ; 4. mis deseos, los suyos, y los de ellos ; 5. Este es un trabajo suyo. 6. Es un dependiente mío. 7. ¿ Es de Vds. este jardín ? 8. Esas llaves no son de Vd., son mías. 9. ¿ Es de Vd. este periódico ? 10. Son amigos nuestros (*or* nuestros amigos). 11. Ese no es error mío ; es de ella. 12. Ni su tienda ni la de su vecino están abiertas.

EXERCISE III.—1. we shall be ; 2. will he not have ? 3. will you (PLUR.) speak ? 4. I shall not receive ; 5. you will not drink ; 6. will she find ? 7. they will write.

8. ¿ tomaré (yo) ? 9. Vd. no tendrá ; 10. ¿ serán (ellos) ? 11. no estaremos ; 12. dividirá ; 13. Vd. no habrá vendido ; 14. fumarán 15. ¿ habremos enviado ? 16. ¿ tendré (yo) ?

---

* Better than suya, suyos, suya, suyas. Such constructions as ¿ es suya esa casa ? are correct grammatically ; but the meaning is clearer if de él, de Vd., de ellos, etc., are employed.

COLLECTIVE EXERCISE.—1. El profesor ha corregido mis temas, pero no los de Vd. 2. ¿ Dónde estará Vd. mañana ? 3. Mi amigo será médico. 4. No tendré bastante dinero. 5. Hablaremos á su padre de Vd. 6. ¿ Cuánto recibirá Vd. ? 7. Mi amigo ha vendido su casa, y la de su hijo ; vivirá ahora en la mía. 8. Compraré una mesa y seis sillas. 9. Ese error será muy grave. 10. Romperán aquella ventana. 11. No compraré esta casa. 12. Habré enviado sus pedidos y los de sus vecinos. 13. Su hermana ha hallado sus sortijas de oro y (las de) plata. 14. Aquí está mi bastón ; dónde está el de Vd. ? 15. Hemos visto á nuestra madre, y á la suya, pero no á la de ella. 16. Será falta de él, no de Vd. 17. ¿ Por qué ha traído Vd. su paraguas, y no el mío ? 18. Guardaremos este reloj, y venderemos el otro.

Key to Lesson IX.

EXERCISE I.—1. El café está más frío que el té. 2. Ese hombre es más fuerte que Vd. 3. Las manzanas no están más maduras que las peras. 4. Esta agua no está (*or* es, *according to meaning*) más fría que la otra. 5. Londres es más grande que París. 6. ¿ No es la ciudad de Madrid más pequeña que París ? 7. Esta cerveza es muy buena, pero el vino es mejor. 8. No recibiré menos de cinco chelines. 9. Esta casa es más barata de lo que Vd. cree.

EXERCISE II.—1. ¿ Es el más holgazán de sus criados de Vd. 2. Es muy difícil. 3. Ese cuadro es el más hermoso de la colección. 4. Esta agua es la más clara. 5. Estas ventanas son las mas pequeñas. 6. El error más pequeño tiene á veces consecuencias muy graves. 7. Nuestra casa es la más conveniente.

EXERCISE III.—1. ¿ Ha recibido Vd. tanto dinero hoy como ayer ? 2. Su hijo de Vd. es tan hábil como laborioso. 3. Estas sillas son tan baratas como esas. 4. ¿ Tiene Vd. tantas plumas como yo ? 5. Esta señora no es tan alta como Vd.

6. Ha traído tantos regalos como ella. 7. No hemos comprado tantos muebles como Vd.

EXERCISE IV.—1. vendí; 2. ¿ compraron (ellos)? 3. Vds. recibieron; 4. ¿ no llegó (ella)? 5. no tuvieron; 6. ¿ estuvo (él)? 7. ¿ temimos (nosotros)? 8. fumé; 9. no hallamos; 10. Vd. no fué; 11. ¿ envió Vd.? 12. ¿ no hube (yo)? 13. escribimos; 14. Vds. no hubieron aprendido; 15. ¿ No estuvieron (ellos) en el cuarto?

Key to Lesson X.

EXERCISE I.—1. La casa que Vds. han comprado es más conveniente que la mía. 2. ¿ Es este el capitán cuyo buque Vd. ha visto? 3. El señor que habló con los niños es su tío. 4. No estamos seguros cuáles guardará. 5. El muchacho á quien hemos visto está enfermo. 6. Ha olvidado Vd. el nombre del caballero (or señor) con quien vivo? 7. Ha leído la carta que recibí, lo que es una lástima. 8. El caballo que he comprado no es muy fuerte. 9. He traído seis libros, los cuales prestaré esta tarde al hermano de Vd. 10. No, no es este señor quien está fumando.

EXERCISE II.—1. Let us drink [some] water. 2. Sell your horse. 3. Do not let us wait. 4. Do not buy these cigars. 5. Do not let us keep these samples. 6. Do not smoke (PLUR.) yet. 7. Be in time. 8. Have pity! 9. Take this chair.

10. Preste (Vd.)* su paraguas á mi primo. 11. Deje (Vd.)* hablar al muchacho. 12. Comamos ahora. 13. Que esperen (ellos). 14. Que compre el vestido. 15. Esté (Vd.)* allí esta tarde. 16. Envíe (or mande) Vd. los paquetes á mi casa. 17. Tenga Vd. la bondad de aguardar un poco.

COLLECTIVE EXERCISE.—1. Tome Vd. el paraguas que está en el rincón. 2. No rompa Vd. los platos que compré ayer. 3. No olviden Vds. de comprar té, café, y azúcar. 4. No preste Vd. dinero á ese hombre. 5. Comamos esta fruta.

* Optional always in Imperative, but better inserted.

6. Mire Vd. esas tiendas.   7. No rompa Vd. ese vaso.   8. No hablemos á ese hombre.   9. La persona para quien trabaja está aquí.   10. Los oficiales á quienes ha hallado Vd. abajo estarán aquí mañana.   11. El pan que Vd. comió es tan bueno como este.   12. No han recibido los periódicos que envié, lo que es muy estraño.   13. Adivine Vd. cuál de las muchachas es la mejor.   14. He hallado varios documentos importantes, los cuales enviaré á nuestro abogado.   15. No conteste Vd. á esa pregunta.   16. ¿ Son ellos quienes están trabajando ? 17. No sea Vd. tan descortés.

Key to Lesson XI.

EXERCISE I.—1. Vd. tenía ;   2. ¿ no estaban fumando ? or ¿ no fumaban ?   3. no dividía ;   4. ¿ estaba comiendo ? or ¿ comía ?   5. era ;   6. no estábamos ;   7. ¿ no habían Vds. tomado ?   8. ¿ no fumaba Vd. ?   9. no éramos ;   10. ¿ había comido ?   11. estaba escuchando, or escuchaba ;   12. ¿ leía Vd. ?   13. estábamos trabajando, or trabajábamos ;   14. ¿ no estaban llamando ?   15. Eran amigos míos.   16. No tenía tiempo.   17. Habíamos olvidado su nombre.

EXERCISE II.—1. recibirían ;   2. no hallaría ;   3. ¿ creería Vd. ?   4. tendríamos ;   5. no habría vendido ;   6. ¿ sería ? 7. Vd. no estaría : 8. ¿ no habrían hablado Vds. ? 9. romperíamos ;   10. no escribiría ;   11. enviaríamos ;   12. ¿ aprendería Vd. ?

EXERCISE III.—1. para ella ;   2. hacia nosotros ;   3. por él ; 4. de Vd. ;   5. sin ellas ;   6. con Vds. ;   7. en él ; 8. á mí ; 9. á ella ;   10. de ellos ;   11. conmigo ;   12. por nosotras ; 13. sin él ; 14. contra Vd. ;   15. entre sí ;   16. para ellos ;   17. con ella ; 18. para sí.

COLLECTIVE EXERCISE.—1. Estábamos trabajando con él.   2. Estudiaríamos español.   3. La leche estaba en el jarro. 4. ¿ Hablaría Vd. al comerciante ?   5. El papel no era bueno, pero las plumas eran muy buenas.   6. Han estado siempre conmigo.   7. ¿ Quién era el capitán de este buque ?   8. ¿ No teníamos siete sillas en este cuarto ?   9. ¿ No fué Vd. quien ha traído este regalo para mí ?   10. Las cucharas no eran nuestras.   11. Fueron estos soldados quienes ganaron la batalla.   12. ¿ No era temprano cuando llegó ?   13. ¿ Compraría Vd. estos cuchillos y tenedores ?   14. No guardaría ese vestido.   15. Hablaba siempre de sí.   16. No viajábamos sin él.   17. ¿ A qué hora comía Vd. ?   18. Lleve Vd. á sus niños consigo.

Key to Lesson XII.

EXERCISE I.—1. La tenemos   2. Los ha tomado.   3. ¿ Me comprende Vd. ?   4. Lo compraré mañana.   5. El tendero no nos cree.   6. ¿ Le ha pagado Vd. la cuenta ? 7. Los hemos visto en la calle.   8. No los aguardaría.   9. Lo habría Vd. vendido ?   10. Mi amigo las guardará.   11. Su tío (de Vd.) nos había olvidado.   12. Le hablaré esta tarde.

EXERCISE II.—1. Me lo enviaban cada día.   2. ¿ Nos los ha enviado ?   3. Le ha escrito á ella y á su madre.   4. Su tía me ha hablado á mí, pero no á Vd.   5. ¿ Se lo leyó ayer ? 6. El banquero se lo prestará á ellos, pero no á su abogado. 7 ¿ Se lo ha explicado Vd. (á ellos) ?   8. No se lo he explicado todavía, pero se lo explicaré esta noche.   9. Les vendemos á Vds., no á ellos.   10. Nos la venderá mañana. 11. El dependiente no me las ha explicado.

EXERCISE III.—1. Léamelo Vd.   2. Léame Vd. la carta. 3. Léanos Vd. esa carta.   4. No nos las lea Vd.   5. Véndales Vd. su reloj.   6. No le envíe Vd. la carta.   7. Cómprenlo Vds.   8. ¿ Estaba hablándole (or Le estaba hablando) á Vd. ó á su padre ?   9. Présteselo Vd.   10. No le preste Vd. dinero.   11. No es fácil comprenderle.   12. Enséñenselo Vds. 13. No se lo enseñen Vds.   14. Que me escuche.

COLLECTIVE EXERCISE.—1. Mírele Vd. á él, no á mí. 2. Déjeme Vd. tenerlo.   3. ¿ Por qué le ha vendido Vd. su

sortija ? 4. No los olvidará. 5. ¿ Nos lo deben ? 6. No le
escuche Vd. 7. No nos las ha traído. 8. Le prestaba
dinero á Vd., pero no á mí. 9. ¿ Cuándo lo comprarán Vds. ?
10. ¿ Quién lo ha hecho ? 11. ¿ Cuánto dinero le debemos ?
12. Se los he prestado á ella. 13. Los tendrá mañana. 14.
Véndanselos Vds. 15. No me lo envíe Vd. 16. ¿ Nos lo
debe ? 17. ¿ Guardémoslo. 18. ¿ Le espera Vd. hoy ?

Key to Lesson XIII.

EXERCISE I.—1. seguramente ; 2. baratamente ; 3.
pesadamente ; 4. fríamente ; 5. hábilmente ; 6. valiente-
mente ; 7. alegremente ; 8. doblemente ; 9. puramente.

EXERCISE II.—1. Copie Vd. cuidadosamente los nombres. 2. Están escuchando aún ? 3. Ayer compré un reloj,
y mañana lo venderé. 4. Este hombre no trabaja siempre
bien. 5. Apenas había acabado mi trabajo, cuando mis
amigos llegaron. 6. Bebemos siempre té y café. 7. Mañana
recibiremos ocho libras.

EXERCISE III.—1. No tendré ninguna dificultad. 2. Ni
mi esposo ni mi hijo están arriba. 3. El criado no ha traído
ni café ni té. 4. Nadie está abajo. 5. No encontré á nadie
en el jardín. 6. Ninguna casa sería bastante grande. 7.
Nada es más seguro. 8. Este muchacho no comprende nada.

COLLECTIVE EXERCISE.—1. Tengo aquí un vestido azul.
2. Apenas aguardó un minuto. 3. Tal vez recibiré mañana
unos regalos. 4. Ese parroquiano ya ha comprado la lámpara.
5. Les hablaré de seguro esta noche. 6. ¿ No halló Vd. aquí mi
paraguas ? 7. Nadie está escuchando. 8. Rehusó firmemente
continuar. 9. A veces bebo cerveza, pero nunca bebo vino.
10. Deseo principalmente hablarle á él, no á su socio. 11.
Habló clara y enérgicamente. 12. ¿ Espera Vd. hoy una carta ?
13. No es de ninguna consecuencia. 14. No cree nada. 15. No
hallaron á nadie en casa. 16. Nunca he leído libro mejor

Key to Lesson XIV.

EXERCISE I.—1. treinticinco (*or* treinta y cinco) niños ;
2. diecinueve días ; 3. seis semanas ; 4. doce meses·; 5.
ochentiocho años ; 6. un minuto ; 7. una semana ; 8.
noventisiete libras ; 9. veintitres chelines ; 10. dieciocho
peniques ; 11. cuarentidos duros ; 12. ciento siete libros ;
13. quinientos setentitres chelines ; 14. mil trescientas
cincuentiuna casas ; 15. cinco mil doce horas ; 16. dieciseis
mil setecientas sesenticuatro millas ; 17. cien millones de
libras ; 18. cien escuelas ; 19. cinco millones doscientos
ochentiseis mil cuatrocientos quince habitantes.

EXERCISE II.—1. las once ; 2. las ocho menos veinticinco ; 3. las diez y media ; 4. las once menos cuarto ; 5. la
una y cinco ; 6. las ocho menos diez ; 7. Son las nueve y
cuarto. 8. ¿ Es la una ? 9. No son las doce todavía. 10. Son
las tres menos diecinueve.

COLLECTIVE EXERCISE.—1. ¿ Qué hora es ? 2. No sé
qué hora es. 3. Son las doce y media. 4. El tren sale á las
ocho y veintitres. 5. Ha viajado doscientas ochentiuna
millas. 6. Tenemos en el banco mil novecientas cincuenti-
cuatro libras diecisiete chelines y seis peniques. 7. Este país
tiene cien millones de habitantes. 8. Les he prestado mil
ochocientas cincuenta libras. 9. No hay cien buenos soldados
en el regimiento. 10. Estará aquí á la una menos diez. 11.
Son las doce menos cuarto. 12. Ese comerciante tiene
quinientas mil libras. 13. Catorce mil ochocientos cincuenta
soldados pelearon en esa batalla. 14. No son las tres y cuarto
todavía. 15. Han enviado noventidos paquetes ; ¿ no es
verdad ? 16. ¿ Cuántos días hay en una semana ? 17. Hay
siete días, ciento sesentiocho horas, ó diez mil ochenta
minutos en una semana. 18. ¿ Cuáles son los nombres de los
días ? 19. Domingo, Lunes, Martes, Miércoles, Jueves,
Viernes, Sábado. 20. Hay doce meses, ó trescientos
sesenticinco días en un año. 21. Los meses son : Enero
Febrero, Marzo, Abril, Mayo, Junio, Julio, Agosto, Sep-
tiembre, Octubre, Noviembre, Diciembre.

Key to Lesson XV.

EXERCISE I.—1. los primeros habitantes; 2. la octava parte; 3. el décimo error; 4. la quinta tienda; 5. las segundas clases; 6. la séptima calle á la derecha; 7. la tercera ventana á la izquierda; 8. el quince (15) de Octubre; 9. el primero (1º) de Mayo; 10. el veinticinco (25) de Agosto; 11. Pío nono; 12. Isabel segunda; 13. Carlos doce; 14. París, 18 de Junio 1907, *or* Junio 18 de 1907.

EXERCISE II.—1. No he hallado nada. 2. Un hombre rico tiene siempre muchos amigos. 3. Lo miraban cada diez minutos. 4. ¿ Cuántas libras le debo á Vd. ? 5. No beba Vd. toda el agua. 6. ¿ Ha comprado Vd. hoy algunos libros? 7. ¿ Hay alguien arriba? 8. Se lo vendimos (á ellos) el otro día. 9. Vd. tiene demasiados perros.

EXERCISE III.—1. un mal viaje; 2. un gran ruido; 3. una chimenea grande; 4. un gran favor; 5. San Pablo; 6. el tercer muchacho en la primera clase; 7. Hay un poco de café, pero no tengo ni azúcar ni leche. 8. Nunca gasta dinero aquí. 9. Tengo una mala pluma, pero buen papel.

COLLECTIVE EXERCISE.—1. Alejandro primero murió el primero de Diciembre de 1825. 2. ¿ Cuánta tinta hay en los tinteros? 3. Este es un buen muchacho, pero los otros no han hecho ningun trabajo. 4. Es el primero de la clase, la cual es muy grande. 5. Mis primas son casi siempre las primeras en la lista, y mi hermana es la última. 6. ¿ Quién fué el primer rey de España? 7. Copie Vd. cada cuarto renglón. 8. ¿ Cuántas palabras han escrito Vds. ? 9. Catalina segunda nació el dos de Mayo de 1729, y murió el diecisiete de Noviembre de 1796. 10. Esta es la primera vez que he hallado á alguien en casa. 11. La segunda lección es la más difícil. 12. Al contrario, creo que las primeras lecciones son muy fáciles, y que la octava es la más difícil. 13. ¿ No cree Vd. que los últimos capítulos de este libro son muy divertidos? 14. Fué una gran reina. 15. Este es el primer

error que he hecho hoy.   16. He llenado este tintero, y mi
hermano ha llenado todos los otros. 17. ¿ Cuántos hermanos
tiene Vd. ? Tengo solamente uno.

Key to Lesson XVI.

EXERCISE I.—1. Préstele Vd. algunas herramientas. 2.
Tenemos (un poco de) sal, pero no tenemos ni mostaza ni
pimienta. 3. ¿ No ha encontrado Vd. á nadie ? 4. ¿ Ha traído
el mozo pan y queso ? 5. Mi esposa (or señora) ha comprado algunos muebles. 6. ¿ No ha visto Vd. hoy unas
muestras ?   7. Este discípulo no tiene tinta.   8. Esa criada
ha roto algunos platos, pero no ha roto ningun vaso.   9. Me
ha dado algunos regalos para mi hija.

EXERCISE II.—1. me lavaré ; 2. no nos estamos lavando ;
3. ¿ no se han lavado ?   4. Vd. se cansará ;   5. se felicitaría ;
6. no se cansen Vds. ;   7. ¿ se ha lastimado ?   8. ¿ no se han
lastimado Vds. ?   9. se felicitan ;   10. lávense Vds. ;   11. los
obreros se cansaban ; 12. nos felicitaremos.

EXERCISE III.—1. no se queje Vd. ;   2. mi amigo se ha
equivocado ; 3. ¿ por qué se mete Vd. ? 4. me meteré ; 5. no
se metían ; 6. ¿ se ha escapado el hombre ? 7. ¡ levántese Vd.
inmediatamente !   8. me estoy cansando ;   9. ¿ no se ha
apeado todavía ?   10. nos levantaríamos ;   11. alegrémonos ;
12. apéese (or bajese) Vd. aquí ; 13. se han casado.

COLLECTIVE EXERCISE.—1. Ese dependiente es muy
descuidado, pero cree que nunca se equivoca. 2. Se apearon
á la puerta de la iglesia. 3. No me quejo de esto, sino
de eso.   4. ¿ Por qué no se lava ese muchacho ?   5.
No me he equivocado esta vez.   6. Nos levantamos cada día
(BETTER, todos los días) á las seis y media. 7. No nos
meteremos en eso. 8. Los niños se han comportado muy
bien. 9. Su amigo de Vd. se felicitó demasiado pronto.
10. No se cansen Vds. 11. No deseamos cansarnos. 12.
Apeémonos en esta estación. 13. Me vendieron (á mí) un poco

de buen tabaco, y á él algunos cigarros muy buenos. 14. Este es un buen discípulo ; raramente se equivoca. 15. ¿ A qué hora se levantan ? 16. Nos apearemos á la puerta del hotel. 17. Se levanta siempre demasiado tarde. 18. No se meta Vd. en estos asuntos. 19. ¿ Cuándo se casarán ? 20. Ya se han casado. 21. ¿ Por qué no se levanta Vd. ?

Key to Lesson XVII.

EXERCISE I.—1. no son creídos ; 2. ¿ no es Vd. temida ? 3. fuimos llamados ; 4. ¿ es amada ? 5. los vasos serán rotos ; 6. la ventana fué rota por el criado ; 7. la reina es amada ; 8. ¿ no soy creído ? 9. no son amados.

EXERCISE II.—1. Se cambia dinero extranjero en esa tienda. 2. ¿ Se prestan estos libros para leer ? 3. Se cree que la reina está muy enferma. 4. Se venden estas naranjas á seis peniques la docena. 5. Esos amos son respetados de sus criados. 6. Aquí se vende leche. 7. Aquí se venden cigarros. 8. La caja fué hecha por este carpintero. 9. Se teme que el accidente será grave. 10. Se presta dinero. 11. Las cartas serán escritas por el dependiente. 12. Se espera que llegará mañana.

EXERCISE III.—1. creyeron ; 2. paguemos ; 3. no lo recojamos ; 4. alcancé ; 5. toquemos ; 6. que lo recoja ; 7. ¿ venzo ? 8. leyó ; 9. no leí ; 10. gocé ; 11. tóquelos Vd. ; 12. no los toquen Vds. ; 13. no llegue Vd. demasiado tarde ; 14. págueme Vd. ; 15. que pague ; 16. toqué ; 17. Venzamos esta dificultad. 18. Recoja Vd. esa manzana. 19. Busquemos un coche. 20. Dirija Vd. las cartas. 21. No toque Vd. esos libros.

COLLECTIVE EXERCISE.—1. Aquí se venden periódicos. 2. Pague Vd. al carpintero. 3. Esta ventana no fué rota ayer.* 4. Llegué el diez de Diciembre. 5. Luego que le alcancé, le

---

* =nobody broke it yesterday. **Esta ventana no estaba rota** etc. ⟹ the window was not broken (when I saw it).

hablé. 6. Recoja Vd. esa piedra ; deseo examinarla. 7. Creyeron que me había equivocado. 8. Sin duda los paquetes serán hallados por el muchacho. 9. El parte fué enviado á los capitanes. 10. Cojamos esta barandilla ; la escalera no está muy segura. 11. No toquemos los papeles, porque los desarreglaremos. 12. Se dirijió á su amigo, pero no recibió ninguna contestación. 13. Se cree que ha naufragado un buque. 14. Una buena madre es amada de sus hijos. 15. Fueron heridos por los soldados. 16. Se duda si tendrá bastante paciencia. 17. Avancé cuidadosamente hacia la cabeza del caballo. 18. Se creía que el parte había llegado. 19. No se reciben equipajes aquí.

Key to Lesson XVIII.

EXERCISE I.—1. cerremos ; 2. no cierre Vd. ; 3. cuesta ; 4. costarán ; 5. no muevo ; 6. ¿ movemos ? 7. pierden ; 8. no perdemos ; 9. llueve ; 10. ¿ no está lloviendo ? 11. volveré ; 12. ¿ no contaba Vd. ? 13. ¿ muestra el niño ? 14. no nos muestre Vd. ; 15. pensaríamos ; 16. ¿ piensa Vd. ? 17. no lo niego ; 18. muéstreme Vd. ; 19. sentémonos ; 20. ¿ Por qué no se sienta Vd. ? 21. ¿ Cree Vd. que helará mañana ? 22. Volvamos á casa ; pronto lloverá. 23. Si le encuentro, le hablaré. 24. Volverían á las nueve y media. 25. Ahora no truena. 26. ¿ Por qué no vuelve su criado ? 27. Si lo niegan, nc les creeré. 28. ¿ No ha encendido el fuego todavía ?

EXERCISE II.—1. en trabajar ; 2. después de haber aguardado ; 3. plata ú oro ; 4. hijos é hijas ; 5. hijos ó hijas ; 6. antes de salir ; 7. sin beber ; 8. antes de prestarlo ; 9. hermanos y hermanas ; 10. después de haberme mostrado su música é instrumentos ; 11. en mostrárselos ; 12. diez ú once chelines ; 13. Cambie Vd. esta taza por la otra. 14. No es culpa mía, sino de él. 15. El buque no ha llegado hoy, pero tal vez llegará mañana.

COLLECTIVE EXERCISE.—1. Su amo no aprueba su conducta. 2. Antes de recomendar el libro, lo examinaré.

3. Lo compraron sin examinarlo.   4. Creí que llovería.   5. Después de haberme sentado, conté los hechos é incidentes de mi viaje.   6. ¿ Es su cuarto de Vd. claro ú obscuro ?   7. No me mostró á mí su billete, sino á Vd.   8. ¿ Niega Vd. que los descubrimientos é invenciones de este siglo han sido muy útiles ?   9. Empecemos ahora.   10. No empiece Vd. todavía ; no estoy listo.   11. No encienda Vd. el fuego en mi cuarto, pero cierre las ventanas.   12. Si vuelvo á tiempo, explicaré todas mis opiniones é ideas.   13. Muéstreme Vd. lo que tiene en la mano.   14. Tengo siete ú ocho chelines en mi bolsillo.   15. Me vendió su sortija por sesenta duros.   16. Volvió la semana pasada.   17. No vuelva Vd. sin hablarle.   18. Caliéntese Vd. antes de salir.   19. ¿ Cuánto recibió Vd. por su reloj ?   20. Después de haber hecho su trabajo, volverán.   21. Nos recomendó una gramática, pero hemos olvidado el título.   22. Mi almuerzo me cuesta aproximadamente dos chelines cada día.   23. El mío me cuesta más.

Key to Lesson XIX.

EXERCISE I.—1. dí ;   2. no daré ;   3. ¿ sabe Vd. ?   4. no fué ;   5. ¿ sabrán ?   6. no doy ;   7. supieron ;   8. vamos ;   9. no sé ;   10. yendo ;   11. voy ;   12. Vd. no daba ;   13. ¿ sabían ?   14. ¡ váyase Vd. !   15. ¿ se va Vd. ?   16. no damos ;   17. no den Vds. ;   18. ¡ sepa Vd. !   19. ¡ váyanse Vds. !   20. Démosle esta gramática.   21. El profesor está dando una lección.   22. Vayan Vds. á su casa pasado mañana.   23. Dénoslo Vd. pronto.   24. Se lo dimos á Vd. la semana pasada.   25. ¿ No irá su primo de Vd. esta noche ?   26. ¿ Lo sabe Vd. ?   27. No sé quién ha ido á comprarlos.

EXERCISE II.—1. veamos ;   2. dijeron ;   3. no veo ;   4. ¿ no diremos ?   5. dicen ;   6. veía ;   7. no vemos ;   8. ¿ qué está diciendo ?   9. Vd. vió ;   10. hemos dicho ;   11. no diga Vd.   12. viendo ;   13. ¿ dijimos ?   14. no vea Vd. ;   15. no digo ;   16. Vaya á ver quién está en el jardín.   17. Dígame si está Vd. cansada.   18. No me ha dicho nada.

COLLECTIVE EXERCISE.—1. El capitán no dió nada á los marineros. 2. Me dijeron que su dependiente no tenía ninguna experiencia. 3. Digámosles lo que pensamos. 4. No sé si van todos los días (*better than* cada día) por ferrocarril. 5. Cuando voy al campo, los veo. 6. Veamos quién ha ido á casa. 7. No comprende lo que están diciendo. 8. Voy á explicárselo. 9. Vamos á ver á nuestro tío. 10. Vaya Vd. á ver quién está á la puerta. 11. Sabía varios idiomas, pero los ha olvidado. 12. Dígame Vd. cuándo volverá. 13. ¿ Por qué no nos dicen la verdad ? 14. Vaya Vd. á casa ; su padre desea verle. 15. Si veo al hombre, le diré lo que Vd. desea. 16. Fuimos á Londres el año pasado. 17. Iban amenudo al teatro. 18. Nunca vemos á nuestros amigos hasta la noche. 19. ¿ Por qué no le da Vd. una silla ? 20. ¿ Quién le ha dicho eso ? 21. Le digo que es verdad. 22. Cuando le ví, iba á casa. 23. Lo sabré pronto. 24. Nunca se lo doy. 25. Iré mañana á la estación. 26. No se lo dé Vd. á él, sino á mí.

Key to Lesson XX.

EXERCISE I.—1. pondría ; 2. no hago ; 3. hagamos ; 4. no pongan Vds. ; 5. ¿ valgo ? 6. no valen ; 7. Vd. ha puesto ; 8. haremos ; 9. ¿ valdrá ? 10. poniendo ; 11. no hicieron ; 12. hacemos ; 13. ¿ puso Vd. ? 14. no pongo ; 15. valgamos ; 16. ¿ no valdría ? 17. ¿ Dónde los pondremos ? 18. No lo haga Vd. todavía. 19. Póngalos Vd. en el rincón. 20. ¿ Pone aquí sus cartas ? 21. No los hacía. 22. ¿ Qué ha hecho Vd. esta mañana ? 23. No estoy haciendo nada.

EXERCISE II.—1. hace veinte años ; 2. valdría más ; 3. no hay ninguna dificultad ; 4. allí está su sombrero ; 5. ¿ hacía calor ? 6. No había ninguna silla ; 7. ¿ había un tren ? 8. ¿ no valdrá ? 9. hace una hora ; 10. allí están nuestros primos ; 11. ¿ no es seguro ? 12. ¿ hará viento ? 13. no habrá bastante pan ; 14. no hace calor hoy ; 15. no había ningun error ; 16. ¿ hace frío ? 17. ¿ no valía más ? 18. ¿ hay agua? **19.** allí está la estación ; **20.** hace seis meses ; **21.** Necesitaba dinero, pero no lo tenía.

EXERCISE III.—1. son muy estimados ; 2. ¿ está Vd. fatigada ? no mucho ; 3. un mal muchacho ; 4. un muchacho muy malo ; 5. ¿ hace tanto viento como ayer ? 6. no estoy tan satisfecho como Vd. ; 7. un pintor muy célebre ; 8. Hará mucho frío. 9. ¿ No hacía mucho calor ? 10. No fué muy aplaudido. 11. ¿ Es muy amada la reina ? 12. No tengo tanto dinero. 13. Fué tan odiado como su padre.

COLLECTIVE EXERCISE.—1. Hága(me) Vd. el favor de esperar un poco. 2. ¿ Vale este cuadro tanto como el otro ? 3. Había varios niños que estaban haciendo ruido. 4. Ponga Vd. vino sobre la mesa. 5. Espero que no hará tanto viento. 6. Lo haré mañana, si tengo tiempo. 7. Estos hermosos muebles se hicieron cien años há. 8. Pondrá flores en la ventana. 9. El rey no es tan estimado como la reina. 10. Creo que mañana hará mucho calor. 11. Los puse en la caja hace una semana. 12. No hay sitio para poner nuestros sombreros. 13. ¿ Lo ha puesto Vd. aquí ? 14. Allí está el bastón ; déselo Vd. 15. No habrá bastante tiempo para hacerlo. 16. Nunca lo hago. 17. Había un cuadro que fué muy admirado. 18. Esos son los cuadros que fueron tan admirados. 19. Los viajeros estaban cansados, pero no mucho. 20. No he puesto nada en las cajas. 21. ¿ Qué está poniendo dentro del cajón ? 22. ¿ Por qué no hace su trabajo ? 23. Lo pongo allí ahora.

Key to Lesson XXI.

EXERCISE I.—1. queriendo ; 2. no quiero ; 3. ¿ pudo ? 4. no querremos ; 5. ¿ puede ? 6. ¿ no querrán ? 7. ¿ quiso Vd. ? 8. pudimos ; 9. podríamos ; 10. pudiendo ; 11. ¿ no quieren Vds. ? 12. podía ; 13. no queremos ; 14. no podrá ; 15. ¿ querría ? 16. ¿ podemos ? 17. Vd. no puede ; 18. querían ; 19. ¿ quiere Vd. ? 20. ¿ no podría ? 21. no podemos ;

22. Vd. no puede dudarlo.   23. No pude llegar á (or en) tiempo. . 24. No sabía hablar español.   25. ¿ No sabe leer el niño ?

EXERCISE II.—1. Los hemos convidado á comer con nosotros.   2. Empezó á llover.   3. No puedo contestar.   4. ¿ Quiere Vd. darme su tarjeta ?   5. Le escribí ayer, para decirle que Vd. había llegado.   6. Fuimos á ver á su tío (de Vd.) ayer.   7. Parece ser imposible.   8. No intentó mirarlos. 9. Ha traído la carta á casa para leerla.   10. Enseñaba á nadar á mis niños.   11. Hágame Vd. el favor de darme un vaso de agua.   12. Cesen Vds. de hablar.

EXERCISE III.—1. Debemos ir á casa.   2. Vd. no debiera hacer eso.   3. Vd. tendrá que aguardar hasta la tarde.   4. ¿ Cuánto trabajo tiene Vd. que hacer (or ha de hacer Vd.) ? 5. Tenían (or Tuvieron) que salir sin comprar sus billetes. 6. ¿ Debe Vd. copiarlo ?   7. Tiene varias cosas que hacer. 8. No tendríamos que pagar tanto dinero como Vd.   9. No debieran fumar tanto.

COLLECTIVE EXERCISE.—1. Los soldados debieran obe- decer al oficial, pero no lo hacen siempre.   2. ¿ Por qué no quiere Vd. mostrarme el cuadro ?   3. No quiero ponerlo aquí. 4. ¿ Quiere Vd. decirle su nombre ?   5. No puedo prestarle este libro ; no es mío.   6. No tenía nada que hacer.   7. Debo enseñarle á hablar más correctamente.   8. Pudimos acabarlo ayer.   9. Podríamos acabarlo mañana.   10. No han podido hallarlos todavía.   11. Lo hemos dicho para per- suadirle.   12. Quisieron aprender á hablar español.   13. Corra Vd. á ver quién está á la puerta.   14. No podíamos (or pudimos) aguardar para verle ; teníamos que irnos.   15. Quería guardar todo el dinero para sí.   16. No querrá volver sin recibir una respuesta. 17. Vd. debiera darme más tiempo. 18. ¿ Pudo el abogado comprender ?   19. Esperamos recibir una respuesta mañana.   20. Me escribió para decir(me) que se había equivocado.   21. ¿ Podría Vd. enviarnos los géneros hoy ?   22. Debemos preguntar ahora á nuestro amo.   23.

Voy á dárselos, para demostrarle que no estoy ofendido. 24.
Vd. no debe cantar tan alto. 25. ¿ No sabe hablar alemán
su amigo (de Vd.)? 26. ¿ No debería Vd. convidarlos á
comer? 27. ¿ Cuándo sabré dibujar tan bien como Vd.?
28. No sé tocar el piano.

Key to Lesson XXII.

EXERCISE I.—1. oigo ; 2. no venga Vd.; 3. ¿anduvieron?
4. Vd. no saldrá ; 5. vendrán ; 6. vine ; 7. andábamos ;
8. salido ; 9. viniendo ; 10. ¿ oímos ? 11. no salgamos ;
12. andando ; 13. no vengo ; 14. ¿ vienen Vds. ? 15. no
oyeron ; 16. Vd. oirá ; 17. oyendo ; 18. veníamos ; 19.
oigamos ; 20. ¿ no sale ? 21. ¿ venimos ? 22. vendría ; 23. no
salgan Vds. ahora. 24. He venido á verle (á Vd.). 25. Me ha
oído hablar. 26. Anduvo muy deprisa. 27. Salgo á ver la
ciudad. 28. Vendremos la semana que viene. 29. Me oyó
perfectamente, porque hablé despacio. 30. Vengo á explicárselo á Vd. 31. Trate Vd. de oir lo que se dice. 32. No se
oye amenudo el ruido desde aquí.

EXERCISE II.—1. jugamos ; 2. ¿ no juega Vd. ? 3. escribía ; 4. ¿ han abierto ? 5. no traemos ; 6. no traigan Vds. ;
7. cabe ; 8. no cabían (or cupieron) ; 9. no hemos impreso ;
10. no caiga Vd. ; 11. Vd. no ha traído ; 12. está cubierto ;
13. ¿ no ha vuelto todavía ? 14. imprimámoslo ; 15. no los
abro ; 16. no cabrá ; 17. he traído ; 18. no traigo ; 19. Vd.
caerá ; 20. no juegue Vd. ; 21. cúbralos Vd. ; 22. caigo ; 23.
Todo el dinero cabe en esta caja. 24. Tráigamelo Vd. ahora.
25. Espero que caerán. 26. ¿ Quiere Vd. abrir la ventana ?
Ya está abierta. 27. No quepo en este coche. 28. Aquí se
imprimen toda clase de libros extranjeros. 29. Tráiganos
Vd. la contestación lo antes posible. 30. ¿ Por qué no se
cubre Vd. ?

EXERCISE III.—1. segurísimamente ; 2. felicísimo ;
3. felicísimamente ; 4. rarísimos ; 5. bonísimas ; 6. muy
honorables ; 7. con muchísimo gusto ; 8. Mis perros son

fidelísimos. 9. Estos niños son bonísimos. 10. Su contestación es utilísima. 11. Es un trabajo facilísimo.

COLLECTIVE EXERCISE.—1. Tráigamelos Vd. lo antes posible. 2. Nunca viene muy temprano. 3. Debiéramos dárselo. 4. Vd. debiera esperar un poco. 5. No volverá antes de las seis. 6. Volvieron el mes pasado. 7. Volveremos mañana por la mañana. 8. Tendremos que abrir todas las ventanas enseguida. 9. Abra Vd. los cajones. 10. Las cosas cabrán en esta caja. 11. Espero que volverán pronto. 12. Deberá (or Tendrá que) traérmelo mañana por la mañana. 13. A qué horá volverá el coche ? 14. Tengo que salir á comprar varias cosas. 15. ¿ Por qué anda Vd. tan despacio ? 16. Espero que vendrán á vernos la semana que viene. 17. Es casi imposible oir el ruido. 18. Los niños están jugando abajo. 19. El tren sale siempre á las ocho y media. 20. Nunca los trae bastante temprano.

Key to Lesson XXIII.

EXERCISE I.—1. Vd. pidió ; 2. no repetimos ; 3. ¿ reirá ? 4. no elijan Vds. ; 5. sonriendo ; 6. Vd. reía ; 7. ¿ no rige Vd. ? 8. seguimos ; 9. No se sabe si puede impedirlo. 10. ¿ Por qué está Vd. riendo ? 11. No ría Vd. 12. Síganos Vd.

EXERCISE II.—1. ¿ consintió ? 2. no sugerí ; 3. ¿ qué sugirió Vd. ? 4. no herimos ; 5. consentirán también ; 6. No lo difiera Vd. ; 7. ¿ Cuál de los dos prefiere Vd. ? 8. ¿ No mentía ? 9. Ahora se arrepiente (or se está arrepintiendo). 10. ¿ No sintió Vd. el golpe ? 11. Arrepintámonos. 12. Lo sentimos mucho. 13. Siento mucho molestarle.

EXERCISE III.—1. contradecirá ; 2. no se duerma Vd. ; 3. dormimos ; 4. murieron ; 5. no convinieron ; 6. muriendo ; 7. dormí ; 8. Vd. moriría ; 9. ¿ no dormían Vds. ? 10. ¿ había supuesto ? 11. no contrahagamos ; 12. Murió algo joven. 13. ¿ Duerme Vd. alguna vez por la tarde ? 14. ¿ No están durmiendo los niños ? 15. Supongo que sí.

EXERCISE IV.—1. compra ; 2. temed ; 3. hallas ; 4.
¿ debéis ? 5. no temes ; 6. enviabais ; 7. romperás ; 8. no
harías ; 9. habéis venido ; 10. ¿ estás lista ? 11. ¿ no has puesto ?
12. ¿ qué tienes ? 13. fuisteis ; 14. escribid ; 15. ¿ estáis
escuchando ? 16. ¿ queréis venir ? 17. no tendréis ; 18. no
tuviste ; 19. ¿ habíais esperado ? 20. muéstramelo ; 21.
hacedlo ; 22. ¿ no eres inglés ? 23. no sois obreros.

EXERCISE V.—1. tomad ; 2. no toméis ; 3. escribe ; 4. no
escribas ; 5. véte ; 6. idos ; 7. háblame ; 8. no nos hables ;
9. no te canses ; 10. no os canséis ; 11. aprended ; 12. no
aprendáis. 13. Compra este reloj. 14. No vendas este reloj.
15. Prestadme vuestro paraguas. 16. No leas la carta. 17. Léela.

COLLECTIVE EXERCISE.—1. Me pidió cinco chelines. 2.
Se los daré esta tarde. 3. Muéstreme lo que Vd. ha elegido.
4. Sírvase Vd. tomar asiento. 5. Cuando llegué, los niños
estaban durmiendo (or dormidos). 6. Le pediré algo. 7.
Repítalo Vd. 8. ¿ Quiere Vd. seguirme ? 9. Nunca nos
corrige, cuando nos equivocamos. 10. Sírvanse Vds. esperar un
poco. 11. Uno de los dos ha mentido, pero no sé cuál. 12.
Lo encuentro dificilísimo. 13. Siente mucho que no podrá
venir esta noche. 14. ¿ Cuándo murió ? 15. Sírvase (Vd.)
decirme la hora exacta. 16. No puedo decírselo (or decír-
sela) ; mi reloj no anda. 17. Siento mucho ese accidente.
18. No haga (Vd.) ningún ruido ; ambos están dormidos
(or durmiendo). 19. Supongo que llegarán pronto. 20. Repita
lo que Vd. ha dicho. 21. Consintió enseguida. 22. Se rieron
cuando les dijimos eso. 23. Nos impidió de verlo.

Key to Lesson XXIV.

EXERCISE I.—1. crezco ; 2. no crece ? 3. no lució ;
4. ¿ cuecen ? 5. no conozco ; 6. no reconozca Vd. ; 7.
nacieron ; 8. produjimos ; 9. traduzcamos ; 10. ¿ no cuezo ?
11. ¡ luzca Vd. ! 12. dedujeron ; 13. ¿ cocía Vd. ? 14. ¿ Cuándo
nació Vd. ? 15. ¿ Parezco estar cansado ? 16. Traducirán esta

carta en media hora. 17. No conozco el precio. 18.¿ Conoce Vd. á este señor ? 19. No le reconozco.

EXERCISE II.—1. ¿ distribuye Vd. ? 2. huyeron ; 3. siguiendo ; 4. no atribuyo ; 5. sigo ; 6. no seguimos ; 7. Vd. destruirá ; 8. ¿ no distinguirían Vds. ? 9. arguyo ; 10. Vd. no distribuía ; 11. Sírvase Vd. seguirlos (or seguirlas). 12. No destruya Vd. estos documentos.

EXERCISE III.—1. PRES. SUBJ. tenga, tengas, tenga ; tengamos, tengáis, tengan. IMPF. SUBJ. tuviese, tuvieses, tuviese ; tuviésemos, tuvieseis, tuviesen. FUT. SUBJ. tuviere, tuvieres, tuviere ; tuviéremos, tuviereis, tuvieren. COND. SUBJ. tuviera, tuvieras, tuviera ; tuviéramos, tuvierais, tuvieran.

2. PRES. haya, hayas, haya ; hayamos, hayáis, hayan. IMPF. hubiese, hubieses, hubiese ; hubiésemos, hubieseis, hubiesen. FUT. hubiere, hubieres, hubiere ; hubiéremos, hubiereis, hubieren. COND. hubiera, hubieras, hubiera ; hubiéramos, hubierais, hubieran.

3. PRES. sea, seas, sea ; seamos, seáis, sean. IMPF. fuese, fueses, fuese ; fuésemos, fueseis, fuesen. FUT. fuere, fueres, fuere ; fuéremos, fuereis, fueren. COND. fuera, fueras, fuera ; fuéramos, fuerais, fueran.

4. PRES. esté, estés, esté ; estemos, estéis, estén. IMPF.: estuviese, estuvieses, estuviese ; estuviésemos, estuvieseis, estuviesen. FUT. estuviere, estuvieres, estuviere ; estuviéremos, estuviereis, estuvieren. COND. estuviera, estuvieras, estuviera ; estuviéramos, estuvierais, estuvieran.

5. PRES. tome, tomes, tome ; tomemos, toméis, tomen. IMPF. tomase, tomases, tomase ; tomásemos, tomaseis, tomasen. FUT. tomare, tomares, tomare ; tomáremos, tomareis, tomaren. COND. tomara, tomaras, tomara ; tomáramos, tomarais, tomaran.

6. PRES. beba, bebas, beba; bebamos, bebáis, beban. IMPF. bebiese, bebieses, bebiese; bebiésemos, bebieseis, bebiesen. FUT. bebiere, bebieres, bebiere; bebiéremos, bebiereis, bebieren. COND. bebiera, bebieras, bebiera; bebiéramos, bebierais, bebieran.

7. PRES. dé, des, dé; demos, déis, den. IMPF. diese, dieses, diese; diésemos, dieseis, diesen. FUT. diere, dieres, diere; diéremos, diereis, dieren. COND. diera, dieras, diera; diéramos, dierais, dieran.

PRESENT.	IMPERFECT.	FUTURE.	CONDIT.
8. escriba, etc.	escribiese, etc.	escribiere, etc.	escribiera, etc.
9. vea, etc.	viese, etc.	viere, etc.	viera, etc.
10. venga, etc.	viniese, etc.	viniere, etc.	viniera, etc.
11. pueda, etc.	pudiese, etc.	pudiere, etc.	pudiera, etc.
12. vaya, etc.	fuese, etc.	fuere, etc.	fuera, etc.
13. diga, etc.	dijese, etc.	dijere, etc.	dijera, etc.
14. muera, etc.	muriese, etc.	muriere, etc.	muriera, etc.

Key to Lesson XXV.

EXERCISE I.—1. ¿Desea que (ella) lo lea? 2. Desean que Vd. acepte esto. 3. No desearán que lo guardemos. 4. Desea que nos quedemos allí. 5. No deseamos que nos oigan. 6. ¿Desea Vd. que cierre la puerta? 7. ¿Qué desea (él) que haga? 8. Desean que paguemos la cuenta enseguida.

EXERCISE II.—1. No es necesario que nos pague mucho. 2. Es necesario que salga al instante. 3. Es posible que el dinero sea suyo. 4. Sentimos que no nos haya hallado. 5. Teme que venga. 6. ¿Es necesario que les escribamos? 7. ¿Quiere Vd. que abra las ventanas? 8. ¿Quiere (él) que lo pongamos aquí?

EXERCISE III.—1. después que venga á vernos; 2. para que no cueste demasiado; 3. antes que hagan el trabajo. 4. Cuando reciba su contestación, se la enseñaré (or mostraré).

5. Le esperaré (á **Vd.**), á menos que llueva. 6. Cuando llegue, le hablaré. 7. Les enviaremos los géneros cuando tengamos tiempo. 8. Avíseme cuando esté Vd. desocupado. 9. Espere Vd. hasta que estén listos. 10. Les pagaremos antes que lo hayan terminado (*or* antes que lo terminen). 11. Pagarán su cuenta cuando tengan más dinero. 12. Cuando viene á verme, nunca permanece (*or* se queda) mucho tiempo. 13. Cuando vuelvan, se lo explicaré. 14. Siempre me habla cuando me ve.

EXERCISE IV.—1. No creo que desee salir. 2. No dijo si podría hacerlo. 3. No creemos que reciba ningún premio. 4. ¿ No es probable que puedan verlo ? 5. ¿ No espera Vd. que su primo venga pasado mañana ? 6. No esperamos que lo traigan. 7. No es necesario que copiemos las direcciones que nos dió.

Key to Lesson XXVI.

EXERCISE I.—1. No creí que hubiese venido. 2. Desearíamos que no hubiesen empezado (*or* comenzado). 3. Desearía que no estuviese aquí. 4. ¿ Deseaba (él) que lo hiciese ? 5. No fué necesario que hablasen. 6. Hubiera negado que su hermano estuviese allí. 7. Quisiera tener más dinero.

EXERCISE II.—1. Le ayudaría, si estuviese menos ocupado. 2. Lo copiaría, si tuviese más tiempo. 3. Les pagaríamos enseguida, si tuviésemos bastante dinero. 4. Si estuviese aquí, se los daría. 5. Trabajaría mejor, si tuviese mejores herramientas. 6. Pregúnteles Vd. si estarán en la estación esta noche. 7. ¿ Sabe Vd. si vive en Madrid ahora ?

HOW TO SPEAK FRENCH
IN 100 HOURS!

This can easily be done by anyone possessing only a slight knowledge of French, by the aid of

HUGO'S
French Conversation Simplified

272 pages,   strongly bound in cloth, 4s.
progressively arranged in three distinct sections.

I.—Simple Sentences, with PRONUNCIATION. II.—Easy Conversation,
with Explanatory Notes. III.—Conversation of Medium Difficulty.

COLLOQUIAL, PRACTICAL, AND UP-TO-DATE.

This work is indeed a ROYAL ROAD TO TALKING FRENCH.

No one who has mastered the first section can ever be at a loss to express
his meaning in good simple French. This can be accomplished in a few
weeks by anyone with a fair knowledge of French grammar who works an
hour or two a day, on the plan laid down in the preface.

In the First Section, the
PRONUNCIATION OF EVERY SENTENCE IS IMITATED,
an arrangement of inestimable advantage to self-taught students. It has
been abundantly proved that by Hugo's phonetically imitated pronunciation
a very near approach to the exact sounds can be obtained.

French Idioms Simplified.

96 pages, 1s. 6d. ; post free, 1s. 7d.

Practical Sentences, introducing all the Important Idioms and
peculiarities of French construction.

Hugo's Institute for Teaching Foreign Languages
83 GRACECHURCH STREET, LONDON, E.C. ; and Branches.

HUGO'S FRENCH
COMMERCIAL
CORRESPONDENT.

**Revised and Enlarged
Edition,
312 pp., 4s.**

A large and varied selection of good Mercantile Letters, such as are used in business circles at the present day, with full translation on same page, copious notes, explanation of difficulties and idioms, commercial phrases, conversation bearing on office routine, etc., etc.

To this valuable work has now been added (152 pages extra):

A COMPREHENSIVE DICTIONARY
OF COMMERCIAL PHRASES,

with copious examples, showing the various ways of translating the principal words employed in business letters.

This book is of a thoroughly up-to-date character, and will be found invaluable to all qualifying for a commercial career.

A Concise Dictionary of the
French & English Languages.

BY F. E. A. GASC.

950 pp., 3s. 6d.   post free, 3s. 11d.

This work has been compiled with the author's well known scrupulous care and attention to detail, and is thoroughly up-to-date in every respect. It is not merely a dictionary of words; it contains all the IMPORTANT IDIOMS AND COLLOQUIALISMS, A LIST OF ABBREVIATIONS commonly employed in French, a list of French and English geographical, Christian, and classical names, and a full explanation of the METRIC SYSTEM, with tables showing the exact French equivalent of the various British coins, weights, and measures.

A really dependable dictionary, printed in clear type and on good paper, is now for the first time issued at a price within the reach of all.

HUGO'S LANGUAGE INSTITUTE, 33 Gracechurch St., E.C.

HUGO'S COMPLETE GUIDE TO FRENCH PRONUNCIATION. -

One Shilling.

In addition to the Rules, this valuable little work contains an absolutely original and complete List of Exceptions to those Rules : Articles on the Long and Short Vowel Sounds, the Linking of Final Consonants, the Elision of the Unaccented E, the 'Tonic' Accent, etc. The clearest and most comprehensive treatise on French Pronunciation ever published.

FRENCH VERBS SIMPLIFIED.

limp cloth, 1s.6d

All the difficulties usually encountered in the study of French Verbs speedily disappear with the help of this handy little book. It gives clear *rules by which one tense can be formed from another,* and shows a natural and easy way of learning the full conjugation, instead of the arbitrary order usually adopted. It also groups the irregular Verbs in sections, and points out how the irregularities can best be mastered.

The book also deals fully with IMPERSONAL and REFLECTIVE VERBS, the PASSIVE VOICE, IDIOMATIC USES of Verbs, the Verbs which govern *à* or *de*, the agreement of the PAST PARTICIPLE, etc., etc. The whole forms a handy and comprehensive guide to every point connected with the study of the French Verb, invaluable to beginners as a text-book, and to advanced students as a book of reference.

FRENCH GENDERS SIMPLIFIED.

One Shilling.

A simple original rule which can be mastered in a few minutes, and readily applied, as it consists of TEN TERMINATIONS ONLY.

By its aid the Gender of forty-nine out of fifty French Nouns can be infallibly ascertained from their terminations. The book also contains

A COMPLETE LIST OF EXCEPTIONS TO THIS RULE,
and of the Nouns varying in Gender according to meaning.

Hugo's Language Institute,
33 GRACECHURCH STREET, LONDON, E.C.; and Branches.

HUGO'S SPANISH

COMMERCIAL CORRESPONDENT

256 pages - - 4s.

A collection of practical up-to-date letters and commercial phrases, with full translation and explanatory notes; to which is added a description of the Spanish coinage and the Metric System, with table of exact equivalents in English measurements; a full List of Abbreviations used in Spanish, etc., etc.

This book is of a thoroughly up-to-date character, and will be found invaluable to all qualifying for a commercial career.

HUGO'S SPANISH
VERBS SIMPLIFIED.

96 pages - -

limp cloth, 1s. 6d.

An exhaustive treatise, with ORIGINAL RULES on the
FORMATION OF TENSES,
showing the easiest and quickest way of learning all Spanish Verbs, REGULAR AND IRREGULAR.

This invaluable work also deals with the

**Defective, Impersonal, and Reflective Verbs,
the use of the various tenses, the Auxiliaries,
the Polite Form of address, etc., etc.**   -

COMPLETE LISTS & TABLES for REFERENCE.

This book is more convenient for reference than the Grammar, and may be used simultaneously with it.

HUGO'S LANGUAGE INSTITUTE. 33 Gracechurch St., E.O.

Hugo's Portuguese Simplified.

Complete, 224 pages ... 4s.

In this important work, the intricacies of Portuguese are made easy for the first time in the history of the language. Its varied contents comprise the following sections :

Rules of Pronunciation.

A Concise Grammar.

Practical Exercises.

The Irregular Verbs classified and simplified.

Amusing Anecdotes & Dialogues, with Vocabularies & Foot-notes.

Progressive Conversation.

Complete Conjugations of the Regular and Auxiliary Verbs.

WITH THE IMITATED PRONUNCIATION OF EVERY WORD.

The first two of the three parts of which the above work consists are also sold in packets, in paper covers, under the title of—

"Portuguese in Three Months Without a Master," 2s. 6d. -

HUGO'S GERMAN

COMMERCIAL CORRESPONDENT.

192 pages ... ... 3s.

This is a PRACTICAL work, arranged in a PRACTICAL way, with the German and its corresponding English on the same page. The selection of Mercantile Letters and Phrases is really representative of modern business correspondence.

This book is of a thoroughly up-to-date character, and will be found invaluable to all qualifying for a commercial carreer.

HUGO'S LANGUAGE INSTITUTE, 33 Gracechurch St., E.C.

TERMS for CLASS LESSONS FRENCH, GERMAN or SPANISH.

Special Classes (DAY OR EVENING)

of one hour, averaging three Students, and limited to five, meet at all hours from 9 a.m. to 9 p.m.

COMPLETE COURSE OF
24 WEEKLY LESSONS - - **36s.**

Half Course of 12 weekly Lessons - - **21s.**

RUSSIAN & ITALIAN CLASSES (at Oxford Street only)
(limited to five students) 24 Lessons ... RUSSIAN 42s. ; ITALIAN 36s.

Ordinary Classes (FRENCH and GERMAN only)

of one hour, averaging seven Students, meet every evening (except Saturday) at 6.30, 7.0, 7.15, 7.30, etc., up to 9.30.

COMPLETE COURSE OF
24 WEEKLY LESSONS - - **24s.**

Half Course of 12 weekly Lessons - - **15s.**

Private Lessons in FRENCH, GERMAN, SPANISH, ITALIAN, or ENGLISH.

12 Lessons of one hour each - - **£2. 8s.**

24 LESSONS of one hour each - **£4. 4s.**

48 Lessons of one hour each - - **£7. 4s.**

100 Lessons of one hour each - - **£14. 0s.**

Reduced terms for extended courses, and for two or more friends attending together for private lessons. Detailed prospectus on application.

RUSSIAN, PORTUGUESE, DUTCH, - -
- *SWEDISH, NORWEGIAN, DANISH or LATIN.*

12 Lessons - £3 | 24 Lessons - £5. 8s.

All the above fees include the necessary books, and are payable in advance.

HUGO'S LANGUAGE INSTITUTE, 33 Gracechurch St., E.C.,
64-66, Oxford St., W. ; 205, Earl's Court Road, S.W.
Established 1875.